THE MADNESS
OF AUSTRALIAN CHILD PROTECTION

Why Adoption Will Rescue
Australia's Underclass Children

The Madness
of Australian Child Protection

WHY ADOPTION WILL RESCUE AUSTRALIA'S UNDERCLASS CHILDREN

Jeremy Sammut

FOREWORD BY DEBORRA-LEE FURNESS

connorcourt
PUBLISHING

Connor Court Publishing Pty Ltd

Copyright © The Centre for Independent Studies Limited 2015

ALL RIGHTS RESERVED. This book contains material protected under International and Federal Copyright Laws and Treaties. Any unauthorised reprint or use of this material is prohibited. No part of this book may be reproduced or transmitted in any form or by any means, electronic or mechanical, including photocopying, recording, or by any information storage and retrieval system without express written permission from the publisher.

PO Box 224W
Ballarat VIC 3350
sales@connorcourt.com
www.connorcourt.com

ISBN: 9781925138832 (pbk)

Cover design by Ian James

Printed in Australia

I have been impressed by the work of Dr Jeremy Sammut of the Centre for Independent Studies in relation to the failures in Australian child protection systems and the low reliance in Australia on adoption as a permanent placement option for children in the child protection system.

—Inquest into the death of Chloe Lee Valentine, conducted by Mark Johns, state coroner of South Australia, 9 April 2015

Adoption has become almost taboo for 40 years as welfare agencies have became preoccupied with preserving biological families, however dysfunctional. Proportionately, only a fraction of the number of children adopted in the US and Britain are adopted in Australia. As Centre for Independent Studies research fellow Jeremy Sammut argues: "Too many children are being left in dangerous situations due to the misguided bias towards keeping abusive and neglectful families together, which has swung the pendulum too far in favour of protecting the 'rights' of dysfunctional biological parents at the expense of the best interests of children." In his report, Mr Johns agreed. So do we.

—*The Australian*, editorial, 16 April 2015

Labor senator Claire Moore cut to the chase. "Where do you go?" she asked. "One side talks about early intervention and the other side led by one of those fabulous think tanks talks about the need for adoption ... which I have to admit scares the hell out of me." She dug through her papers to find a quote from Dr Sammut championing more local adoptions. "It's a red flag question," confirmed the committee chair, Greens senator Rachel Siewert.

—Kate Legge, "Adoption: Why is it So Hard?" *The Weekend Australian Magazine*, 30 May 2015

Author's note

This book draws on a considerable number of figures (graphs) that are referred to in the appropriate places throughout the text. Instead of dotting the various chapters, and in order not to distract or deter readers, these figures have been collected together in a separate section. See the appendix, "Counting the cost of the crisis."

Contents

Foreword by Deborra-lee Furness — xi

1. Hiding in plain sight: Australia's child protection crisis — 1

2. Under-responding: the marginalisation of child rescue — 41

3. Advocacy: the political economy of child abuse — 77

4. System abuse: re-institutionalising out-of-home care — 109

5. Cultural correctness: the sorry tale of the social revolution — 138

6. Kinship conundrum: politicisation of the Stolen Generations — 173

7. Taboo no more: normalising "open" adoptions from care — 211

Author's acknowledgements — 240

Appendix: Counting the cost of the crisis — 243

Selected bibliography — 271

Endnotes — 285

Index — 317

THE SUPPORT FOR THIS BOOK OF
SOS CHILDREN'S VILLAGES AUSTRALIA
IS GRATEFULLY ACKNOWLEDGED.

Founded in 1949, SOS Children's Villages International is a private, non-political and non-denominational organisation dedicated to protecting and caring for children who have lost parental care. A global federation of 117 national associations, SOS Children's Villages currently operates in 132 countries with projects to support families, aid development, and protect children's rights.

The mission of SOS Children's Villages Australia is: "Protection, Security, and a Future for Every Child."

Foreword

By Deborra-lee Furness

I am thrilled that Jeremy is shining a light on the subtleties and complexities of adoption in Australia. He addresses the barriers that have been created over decades, in sustaining a system that is failing our most vulnerable citizens … our children.

Jeremy's astute observations help us to understand how and why we are struggling with the issue of vulnerable children at this moment in time. He gives us a clear road map on how to shift to a pro-adoption culture and provides answers as to how we can ADOPT CHANGE and ensure we, as Australians, can be proud of how we take care of the children that need our support, guidance and love.

Jeremy's comprehensive research will hopefully propel our policy makers to make vulnerable children's issues a priority.

Jeremy is one man who is taking a stand and speaking out about an injustice. His contribution in undertaking this research will play a part in ensuring that future generations of children who are unable to be raised within their birth families will have a chance of belonging to a permanent loving family. They will be afforded the opportunity to realise and reach their full potential. I applaud everyone and anyone who joins in and puts their hand up to say, "we need to do this better."

We need to speak up for so many children who don't have a voice.

They are depending on us to advocate for them.

1

HIDING IN PLAIN SIGHT: AUSTRALIA'S CHILD PROTECTION CRISIS

Fatally flawed

National attention was drawn to the crisis in the Australian child protection system by the shocking circumstances surrounding the death in November 2007 of "Ebony",[1] a seven-year-old autistic girl who died of starvation in her parents' Housing Commission home in the mid-North Coast NSW town of Hawks Nest. When police discovered her dead body in the faeces-strewn bedroom where she had been held prisoner behind a locked door, Ebony weighed just 9kg, less than three times the weight of an average newborn baby. Black vomit and bull ants ran from her mouth and nose. Ebony's parents were charged and prosecuted for her death. At trial, both were found criminally responsible and were jailed.[2] But this was just the start of the search for answers.

It was not only the horrific details of Ebony's starvation that caused widespread consternation. Also incomprehensible was how children such as Ebony could live and sometimes die in the custody of obviously inadequate and deeply troubled parents, even though these chaotic and dysfunctional families were already "known" to child protection authorities.

Ebony was a known child because she and her family had been the subject of many prior reports of suspected risk of child harm. As such, they had a long history of involvement with the NSW Department of Community Services (DoCS). DoCS (since rebranded Family and Community Services or FACS) is the NSW government agency responsible for administering child welfare laws. This includes investigating reports of child maltreatment and initiating "statutory interventions": court-approved removal of children from the custody of parents and the provision of alternatives such as state-funded foster care and other forms of "out-of-home" care. The department had received numerous reports of concerns for Ebony's safety, a younger sibling had been previously removed from the family, and Ebony's parents repeatedly refused entry to the home for caseworkers responsible for checking on her welfare. Despite all these warnings and chances to intervene, DoCS had taken no action that might have saved Ebony's life.[3]

The impact of Ebony's death was reinforced by the similar circumstances surrounding another notorious child death. In October 2007, two-year-old Dean Shillingsworth had been strangled by his mother, who shoved his body into a suitcase and disposed of it in a lake in Western Sydney. Dean and Ebony shared a history of long parental involvement with social services, involving numerous reports of suspected child harm combined with repeat failures by DoCS to carry out home visits to "sight" children (as the terminology goes) and verify their well-being.

In Dean's case, the department had received 34 reports about his family. In addition, a taxpayer-funded charitable organisation – contracted by the NSW government to deliver early intervention family support services – downplayed the level of assistance Dean's family required and tried to ensure the mother kept custody of her son. This was despite the mother telling the charity's social worker, eight days before his murder, that she "couldn't stand him" and "wanted him gone as soon as possible."[4]

No child protection system is perfect. It is impossible to predict child abuse and neglect with total accuracy, because some cases involve difficult-to-assess risks of harm. Mistakes, including failures to intervene, are inevitable. But the excuse that no child protection system can possibly save every child misses the point.[5] Speculating about a hypothetical "Everychild" glosses over the truth that Ebony and Dean were not marginal cases. Both children lived and died hiding in plain sight of the government department that was legally obliged to protect them.

If child protection authorities could get it so terribly and fatally wrong in these appalling cases, and if children could die despite a string of warning signs affording opportunities to remove them to safety, it seemed apparent that the child protection system could no longer be relied on to fulfil its core responsibility – to rescue vulnerable children from serious parental abuse and neglect. Ebony and Dean's cases were at the extreme end of the child maltreatment spectrum. But if child protection authorities missed these kinds of cases, there could be little confidence that less extreme but still severe cases of abuse and neglect were not also being missed.

Denial and minimisation: the orthodox account

In the wake of Ebony and Dean's deaths, renewed media interest in and heightened political scrutiny of the way the child protection system operates prompted influential child protection experts to step forward. They gave the orthodox explanation for these catastrophic failures to protect children in even the worst and most clear-cut cases of abuse and neglect.

That explanation was that the most serious cases of child maltreatment can fall through the cracks, and not receive a full and proper investigation, because departments like NSW DoCS and its counterparts in other jurisdictions are swamped by "over-reporting" of allegedly less-serious cases of suspected child maltreatment. Child protection authorities were reputedly so overwhelmed by the increasing number of reports received each year that finding an Ebony was like looking for the proverbial needle in the haystack. The sheer volume of reports, this account goes, made it logistically impossible for departmental caseworkers to follow up on and investigate all notifications of alleged child harm, to identify the most at-risk children and intervene to protect them.

The policy solution these experts proposed in response to the supposed overloading of the system was to divert less-serious reports that did not involve imminent risk of harm. These cases, it was advised, should be followed up by non-government organisations (NGOs) in the not-for-profit sector. Allowing charitable organisations to provide taxpayer-funded social-support services for these children and families, with a focus on early intervention and prevention of the family and parental problems that cause child maltreatment, would allow government agencies to concentrate on their core role of investigating higher-risk reports. This would reduce the likelihood of missing the most serious cases of abuse and neglect. Redesigning and unclogging the statutory intervention part of the child protection system in this way is known as creating a dual track or dual reporting pathway.

This book began as a series of research reports published between 2009–2014 in my role as a Research Fellow at the Sydney-based think tank The Centre for Independent Studies. When I first started researching the crisis in the Australian child protection system, I initially accepted the orthodox account of the problems and solutions at face value. Since the late 1990s, following the nationwide introduction of mandatory-reporting laws, there had been a substantial increase in the number of reports to state and territory child protection authorities. These laws require certain professions, including doctors, nurses, teachers, and police, to report their concerns when they suspect children are at risk of harm, under threat of legal penalties.

In 2007, the year Ebony and Dean died, NSW DoCS received over 300,000 reports of risk of child harm – a fourfold increase since the introduction of mandatory reporting in 2000. It seemed plausible that the administrative burden of assessing an overload of lower-risk cases was diverting resources and distracting attention. Critics of mandatory reporting argued this burden explained why only a fraction of reports to DoCS (around 13%) received an investigation that included a home visit. This, they said, was a major contributing factor to the most serious cases of child maltreatment being missed.

It appeared that mandatory reporting had clogged the reporting and investigation systems, and that raising the mandatory-reporting threshold was a sound idea. Allowing NGO family support services to provide the first response to less-serious cases would remove the bottlenecks that prevented child protection agencies from properly identifying and responding to cases involving the most significant risk of harm.

The (apparent) logic of this strategy seemed to offer a better way to protect the children who were most at risk of harm, and appeared to explain the policy traction the orthodox explanation had achieved. As a result, a consensus emerged among policy advisers and policymakers, in favour of establishing a dual-track reporting system. This explanation that over-reporting is the problem and a dual-track system is the solution to the child protection crisis is the standard account advanced today by virtually all academic specialists in the field. The overwhelming majority of government and non-government stakeholders in the child and family welfare social services sector also adhere to it. Establishing a dual-track system is the approach to reform endorsed by *Protecting Children is Everyone's Business: National Framework for Protecting Australia's Children 2009–2020*, a report published by the Rudd government in 2009.[6]

As said, I initially accepted this account of the problems and the appropriate response. But as my research progressed, the weight of evidence against it led me to question not only these explanations, but also the notion that the key to better child protection outcomes is to provide more families with more family support services. I came to the conclusion that the orthodox view and accompanying policy recommendations in fact offered a flawed and ultimately misleading account of a failing system. They are the products of a closed policy world dominated by too much unquestioned, mutually reinforcing, and self-serving way of thinking.

The orthodox account therefore denies and minimises the real, systemic, and sometimes fatal flaws in the current approach to child protection, which compromise child welfare. Worse, it downplays the true nature and scale of the crisis, as measured by the long-term negative impact that failures in child protection policy and practice have on children unfortunate enough to be caught up in the system.

Too little, too late: the paradox of family preservation

There is a paradox at the heart of the child protection crisis. Authorities' failure to respond appropriately to the needs of abused and neglected children is due to family preservation–based child protection policies and practices. In theory, these are meant to prevent child maltreatment and lessen the need for statutory intervention and removal into care.

Since the 1970s, Australian child protection agencies' approach to dealing with child abuse and neglect has assumed that keeping children with their families should be the main goal. According to the Australian Institute of Health and Welfare (AIHW):

> The current emphasis in policy and practice is to keep children with their families wherever possible. Where children, for various reasons, need to be placed in out of home care, the practice is to attempt to reunite children with their families.[7]

The last 40 years have been marked by a revolution in child protection practice that has ongoing implications for what the system does and doesn't do to protect children. The embrace of family preservation as official policy in all Australian jurisdictions has supplanted the traditional approach to child protection, which focused on the investigation of child welfare reports by caseworkers trained to assess whether a child needed to be removed from the family home, into alternative care. The once-unquestioned idea that the core role of child protection authorities was to ensure the timely rescue of abused and neglected children via removal into care has been marginalised. The once radical idea that children should be kept with their families wherever possible is now widely accepted — and it has enfeebled the community response to child abuse and neglect.

Family preservation means taking action to remove children from unsafe homes (again in the words of the AIHW) is a "last resort". Removal tends only to occur following provision of extensive social-service interventions, the delivery of which is usually outsourced to NGOs. These family support services are designed to help struggling parents address the entrenched and often insoluble social and personal problems — such as welfare dependence, drug and alcohol abuse, family violence, mental illness, and sole parenthood — that destroy capacity to parent children properly.[8]

In practice, the overemphasis on family preservation means doing everything possible to keep even highly and demonstrably dysfunctional families together. This has created a situation of chronic under-responding to child maltreatment.[9] "On the Road with the DoCS Crisis Response Team", a feature article published in the *Daily Telegraph* in 2011, gives a chilling insight into exactly what the official terminology — "removal as a last resort" — entails when put into frontline practice:

> "Removing a child is a last resort," a caseworker says. "Quite often we try not to remove the child …" Another call comes in and this one is even more disturbing. A four-month-old baby's head has been slammed into a concrete pylon because the parents are intoxicated and unable to walk properly. The

parents are already known to welfare workers and three of the baby's siblings are in foster care.[10]

There are a number of ways to measure the impact of family preservation on children, as well on the functioning and performance of the child protection system. Perhaps the best measure of how much under-responding occurs is the high degree to which the same children are reported on time and time again. The same children, and the same families, end up being reported multiple times, mainly by mandatory reporters, because in the opinion of the reporter, no action or inadequate action has been taken in response to the initial report of child harm. Subsequent re-reports attempt to prompt child protection authorities into taking action on unresolved child safety and welfare concerns.

The amount of re-reporting that takes place due to family preservation exposes the major flaw in the orthodox account, which is that the children most at risk are not needles buried in a haystack of reports. On the contrary, of the 300,000 reports NSW DoCS received in the year Ebony and Dean died, nearly half concerned a relatively small "hard core" of 7,500 frequently re-reported families, who represented the worst cases of child harm and constitute an underclass of problem families.[11]

In the child protection context, the term *underclass* refers to the growing number of families that are long-term and increasingly intergenerationally welfare-dependent, and display a range of behavioural issues induced and exacerbated by that condition. The most common are serious drug- and alcohol-abuse problems.

The complex range of personal problems and social dysfunctions these families experience include serious concerns for child well-being due to a downwards behavioural spiral. The erosion of personal responsibility begins with the breakdown of social norms surrounding work and self-reliance. This deterioration then extends to norms concerning family life, severely impairing the ability to care adequately for children and socialise them properly.[12] This produces the situation where, for many members of the underclass, disadvantage is 'inherited' – an intergenerational problem passed on through ruinously poor child-rearing. The behavioural poverty of underclass parents perpetuates personal and social dysfunction by way of poor role-modelling and insecure child–parent attachment, which harms child welfare.[13]

The breakdown of social norms in underclass families often engenders a failure to meet basic needs in infancy, which are crucial for children's physical, social, emotional, and neurological development. Due to physical and intellectual impairments including low birthweight, fetal drug and alcohol effects, and poor nutrition, children from underclass families figure significantly in the estimated 11% of children in Australia who, according to the Australian Early Childhood Development Census, enter school behind in their development compared to their peers in at least two of five important areas – physical well-being, social competence, emotional maturity, language and cognitive skills, and communication skills and general knowledge.[14]

Perhaps the most telling failure of underclass families to meet the basic needs of older children is the frequent inability to ensure that their children attend school each day well-rested, fed, clean, and appropriately clothed. The daily routine of getting children to school in a condition that enables them to learn may not be the hardest part of proper parenting, but it is certainly one of the most important. Underclass parents are chronically incapable of fulfilling this fundamental obligation.

Two generations ago, in the 1960s, truancy was not a significant problem. Everyone's children went to school as a matter of course, and truancy officers appeared to be a 19th-century anachronism. Today, state and federal policy initiatives to address social disadvantage and social exclusion target increased levels of school non-attendance.[15] The re-emergence of truancy as a social problem is a significant measure of how the downward behavioural spiral associated with welfare dependence has underpinned the emergence of the underclass.[16]

The significance of NSW re-reporting data to the debate about child protection policy cannot be overstated. The extraordinary level of re-reporting showed that mandatory reporting had worked incredibly well, and was anything but the failure the orthodox account made it out to be. Because mandatory reporters made the bulk of all reports, it was safe to assume they were also making the bulk of re-reports. Hence, what the level of re-reporting showed was how thoroughly mandatory reporting had mass-screened the expanding underclass. Heightened surveillance of dysfunctional families had driven the growth in the number of reports, and the most at-risk children had been identified and re-identified.

How, then, could the orthodox account be valid? How could an excess of less-serious reports be the reason cases like Ebony and Dean were missed, when a relatively small number of easily identifiable underclass families – like Ebony's and Dean's – accounted for half of the DoCS workload?

The extent of re-reporting clarified the real, systemic problems with the child protection system. Re-reporting data put the small proportion of reports that received an investigation into context. The workload issues DoCS struggled with were a genuine problem, but one of its own making. Over half the agency's workload consisted of re-reports attributable to the flawed policies of family preservation, which meant that children and families were re-reported more than 20 and 30 times, in thousands of high-risk, potentially catastrophic cases.

The real problem with the system, it turned out, was in the insufficient quantity and quality of basic child protection work, and the lack of response to cases involving known, frequently reported children. The good, if misguided, intentions behind family preservation had run the system onto the rocks. By seeking to keep families intact at nearly all costs, DoCS ended up presiding over rather than eradicating family dysfunction and child mistreatment.

Keeping children with parents, and trying to prevent abuse and neglect by fixing parental problems, sounds like a humane and appropriate policy. Of course, depending on their circumstances, families that come to the attention of child protection authorities might benefit from being given initial help and support that gives them an opportunity to get their acts together and properly care for their children. But the flaw in the policy of family preservation is that efforts to fix families are inappropriately prolonged, with parents given virtually endless opportunities to address their problems despite family support often being a Sisyphean labour. The problems of highly dysfunctional parents prove virtually impossible to solve, as studies demonstrating the lack of success of child abuse prevention programs suggest. Prolonged efforts to fix these problem families and keep them intact means that damaged parents stay damaged ... and damage their children.

These insights into the flaws in the system are more than a hunch or hypothesis. The NSW re-reporting data starkly demonstrated that children remained in harm's way because nothing had been done to remove them from it.

The core problems identified in the NSW system were not confined exclusively to that jurisdiction. The same problems, which stemmed from an institutionalised culture of under-responding, plagued child protection systems in other states and territories. In other jurisdictions, too, mandatory reporters must report children multiple times in an often vain attempt to have children rescued from unsafe homes.[17] In Victoria, for example, recent inquiries have found over two-thirds of child safety notifications are re-reports of known children who had been reported in the same or previous year,[18] and only a quarter of all reports prompt a face-to-face investigation.[19]

Such is the reality of the Australian child protection system in the twenty-first century, and such is the extent of the crisis. The central truth of the crisis is that children suffer prolonged exposure to abuse and neglect by clearly unfit parents because of the policy and practices of family preservation, which seek to fix even the kinds of families that starve and strangle children.

The vicious treadmill: high-needs and highly unstable

Extended exposure to abuse and neglect is bad enough for child welfare. The long-term outcome of family preservation is even worse. Examining the parlous state of the out-of-home Care (OOHC) part of the child protection system in Australia further confirms the policy's failure to protect children.

In the last decade, the number of Australian children in out-of-home care has more than doubled, to over 43,000 children. This and other associated statistics need to be examined carefully to not be misled. The significant growth in the number of children living in care may foster doubt that family preservation is really the chief problem for child welfare, given that record numbers of children are removed each year. It might encourage the belief that child protection authorities are anything but reluctant to remove children from families and so rescue them from dysfunction. But this is not what the numbers signify.

The growing size, cost, and complexity of the OOHC system actually shows how badly child protection systems built around the principle of family preservation – keeping removal as a last resort – tragically fail children. When removal does finally occur, it is often too late, so a growing proportion of the increasing numbers of children in care – perhaps *virtually all* children in care – has some degree of "high needs". This means they suffer from some form of developmental, emotional, or behavioural problems stemming from abuse and neglect. Children in care are likely to have high needs because they are likely to have experienced chronic maltreatment before they eventually entered care.[20]

In other words, these children have been left with parents who abused and neglected them – an observation consistent with the re-reporting data. When finally taken into care as a last resort, they have already been damaged by maltreatment. This again contradicts the orthodox account, which makes these children's experiences a justification for family preservation, obscuring the actual causes of the disastrous outcomes for so many children in care.

The problem in the system is not that there is too little family support, as is routinely alleged. Nor is it that children are too quickly removed, as supporters of family preservation also claim.[21] The real problem is that family preservations are too prolonged and the results too damaging. Too little is done to remove children from a family before they are damaged, and if action is taken at all, it is only after a child has been damaged by parental abuse and neglect. By then, it is often too late: the damage cannot be undone.

The ill-effects of abuse and neglect are compounded by the instability of time spent in care. In the radical shift from child rescue to family preservation, the timely and permanent removal of abused and neglected children from their parents has been ruled unacceptable. Instead, the goal of family preservation dictates that when families can no longer remain together due to unresolved child safety issues, removal into care should be temporary, and children should be reunited with their families as quickly as possible.

Overzealous efforts to achieve family reunification see many children continually moving in and out of care while attempts to work with parents to achieve restoration drag on and on. When reunifications occur, they are prone to breaking down when parental problems and child maltreatment recur, forcing children to re-enter care. Foster care placements for damaged children are also likely to break down due to their high needs–related personal and behavioural problems. This adds another layer of damaging instability to children's lives, further denying them the emotional security, educational opportunities, and proper parenting that all children need to thrive.

The cycle of prolonged maltreatment at home, removal as a last resort, and the extended instability of "temporary" periods in care – involving multiple entries, exits, and placements – can consume entire childhoods. In practice, family preservation does not prevent child abuse and neglect, or keep families together. In reality, it puts children on a treadmill that destroys childhoods, perpetuates intergenerational dysfunction and disadvantage, and ultimately creates the next generation of abusive and neglectful parents.

The adoption taboo

The flaws in family preservation-based child protection policies and practices expose children to "system abuse", where they are actively harmed by the operation of the system that should rescue and protect them from abuse. The following chapters of this book examine different aspects of the existing child protection system, each adding to the picture of a failed system sketched in this introductory chapter. The account given here is radically different to the orthodox version, and so are the policy recommendations made to ensure the system properly protects children.

To break the cycle of abuse, neglect, instability, and disadvantage, child protection authorities need to intervene decisively in families where parental capacity is severely impaired. More timely statutory intervention is needed to permanently remove children from unsafe homes. Children who need to be removed – who cannot live safely with their parents – must be provided with safe, stable, and permanent alternative homes. This will mean taking legal action to terminate the parental rights of demonstrably unfit parents, to free children for adoption by suitable (properly screened and vetted) families. This is the (too-often) unspoken truth about the child protection crisis: many children's life chances would be vastly improved if the child protection system was committed to more rapidly rescuing them from their dysfunctional families via adoption.

Early child removal and adoption is the best way to protect children and promote their well-being and development when their parents are neglectful, abusive, and incapable of providing the physical, emotional, and developmental support that they have the right to receive. It is especially important that this strategy be used to protect very young children, as the most serious maltreatment is typically perpetrated on children under school age, during the crucial periods of early childhood development.

Many underclass families are not only broken; they are unfixable. Efforts to support these families instead of separating them produce worse outcomes for children. The priority given to family preservation, at the expense of protecting children, is inappropriate. The kind of child-centred, rather than family-centred, approach advocated by others who also dissent from the orthodoxy – including Monash University's Child Abuse Prevention Research Australia (CAPRA), the Australian Childhood Foundation (ACF), and Barnardos Australia – needs to be implemented in all jurisdictions. The key to unlocking better outcomes is to make greater use of adoption to provide good families for vulnerable children who need to be permanently removed from the custody of abusive and neglectful parents.[22]

This policy recommendation is controversial because adoption is taboo in contemporary Australia. This once common and accepted practice is no longer considered socially acceptable even for child protection when parents are incapable of properly caring for children.

In child protection circles, adoption – the legal process of extinguishing the parental rights of biological parents and transferring responsibility to new adoptive parents – is by its nature directly at odds with the principle of family preservation. However, adoption also has a bad reputation in the broader community, including among the media and political class, due to perceived associations with forced adoption practices involving unwed mothers in the 1950s and 1960s, and with the forced removal of members of the Stolen Generations of Indigenous children throughout the 20th century.

This partly explains why permanent removal through adoption from out-of-home care is officially taboo, regardless of whether parental consent is gained or has to be dispensed with by court order. The power of this taboo within the child protection world explains why child protection authorities almost never take legal action to free children for adoption, even where children languish in care with little prospect of ever safely being returned home.

Adoption was formerly thought to be a socially important way of finding permanent homes for children who needed new families. Today, for historical reasons, separation from birth parents, extended families, and ethnic communities is widely perceived as having negative psychological effects on the personal identity of "stolen" children. This view is based on the experiences of some adopted children in the past, who were denied knowledge of and contact with their biological and cultural heritages in the era when adoptions were "closed" and records were sealed.

Because of the harm that earlier child protection and adoption practices did to some parents, children, and families, adoption has been stigmatised as inherently harmful. A range of scholars, activists, and organisations coalesce as the Australian anti-adoption movement, which campaigns to have all adoptions banned in Australia, including international adoptions of foreign-born children by Australian parents. The anti-adoption movement uses, and arguably abuses, the memory of past practice to successfully promote its anti-adoption agenda.

It is to this movement that we owe the conventional but misguided, and largely unchallenged, wisdom that maltreated children are almost always better off being kept with their natural parents, and that all efforts should be made restore them to their family if they are separated from it, so that historical mistakes are not repeated. Due to the sensitivities and potential political problems associated with adoption, risk-averse policymakers usually prefer to profess support for preserving families, lest they be accused of stealing children and separating families all over again. Hence, according to Greens senator Rachel Siewert, chair of the 2012 Senate inquiry into past forced adoption practices in Australia, calls for greater use of adoption for child protection purposes are "a red flag question".[23]

However, the taboo on adoption is more than an effort to learn from past mistakes. It is also a product of radical shifts in the field of child protection over the last 40 years, and of the commitment to the principle of family preservation at nearly all costs, which has swung the pendulum too far towards preserving the presumed parental rights of disadvantaged people at too great an expense of intervention to protect the rights and best interests of children.

The commitment to family preservation is ingrained within the child and family welfare services sector to the point that it borders on an ideological obsession. The determination to reject traditional child rescue practices, except as a last resort, reluctantly employed, is based on the conviction that removing children victimises the poor, punishing disadvantaged parents. This presents a problem when deciding on the appropriate response to child abuse and neglect, because these principles are impervious to the realities of parental dysfunction and child harm, and those who hold them can be oblivious how the current, malfunctioning system is delivering more and more damaged children into long stays in care.

The result of the obsession with family preservation is that there were only 203 local adoptions in Australia during 2013–14.[24] During the same period, more than two-thirds (almost 30,000) of the 43,000 children in government-funded out-of-home care placements throughout Australia had been in care continuously for more than two years.[25]

Australia's low rate of adoption persists even though contemporary adoption practices have been revised in light of past mistakes. Modern adoptions are "open", meaning adopted children can know of and maintain contact with birth parents and extended family members, maintaining their heritage and identity. Today's practices recognise past wrongs in the era of closed adoptions, which undoubtedly harmed some children and families, and are designed not to repeat them.

The anti-adoption movement argues that keeping children even with "flawed" parents is best because closed adoptions caused some children to "suffer seriously with mental health problems caused by wrenching them away from their origins."[26] But what is done today in the name of family preservation and not repeating past mistakes is also harmful and damaging for many children.

The "importance of stable, attuned care-giving adults cannot be overstated", argues the Australian and New Zealand College of Psychiatrists, because children "who experience extremes of abuse or neglect are at risk of failure to thrive, reduced brain size, [and] impaired development that can lead to ongoing mental health issues."[27] Other countries, including the United States and Britain, also have flawed child protection histories marked by mistreatment of children, parents, and families. Yet the benefits of open adoption, compared to the well-known, highly damaging experiences of many children in care, are recognised in these countries today.

Australia's rejection of adoption makes it an international outlier. In the United States, for example, more than 50,000 children are adopted from care each year. If Australian children in care were adopted at the same rate as in the United States, there would be more than 5,000 adoptions each year around the country.[28]

Cultural and political obstacles to change

Almost all the evidence cited in this book is in the public domain. This includes the crucial evidence of the scale of re-reporting, which highlights the serious problem of under-responding that follows from the doctrinaire commitment to family preservation. It also includes the finding that family preservation harms the many thousands of high-needs children in care, which is drawn from the standard literature on the challenges facing the care system in all Australian states and territories.

The systemic failures of the child protection system can also be seen in the fact that Australian governments are being forced to re-institutionalise the care system to cater to the needs of those children who are most damaged and disturbed by family preservation. Three decades after most children's homes and orphanages were closed down – in recognition of how detrimental institutional care is for children – they are opening again.

By the time the most-damaged and highest-needs children reach adolescence, their uncontrollable, threatening, violent, and self-destructive behaviour is so bad they can no longer live safely with their biological parents or in normal foster homes. The only suitable placement option for such children is in high-cost residential "group homes". Growth in this category of children in out-of-home care accounts for the doubling of the residential care population to more than 2,300 children and young people nationally since 2005. The increasing size, cost, and complexity of the care system is where the bulk of the evidence of the disastrous consequences of family preservation lies, and it is examined in depth throughout this book.

Another revealing piece of evidence is the growing call to

"professionalise" the care system and further develop services that have a therapeutic and psychiatric focus, to try to help children recover from the damage done by child protection failures. A system that needs to fund additional, expensive services to try to fix the children that the system itself has damaged seems to be the very definition of a failed system.

Saying this is definitely not to dismiss the hard work and commitment of many thousands of dedicated people involved across the system – including caseworkers, family support workers, and foster and other carers – who do their best to assist children, often against the odds. The criticisms levelled here are directed at the overarching philosophies that determine the overall character of the system, and which create constraints that can prevent those who have children's interests at heart from achieving outcomes that are truly best for them.

Despite the weight of evidence that child protection practices in Australia are deeply flawed, translating these insights into remedial policy action is a struggle. Cognitive dissonance plagues the field, including the raft of experts whose work on the state of the care system in Australia concedes that there are thousands of high-needs children in care who have been damaged by family preservation. Most of these experts hesitate even to whisper about the need for fundamental and well-overdue changes to current policy and practice, which the number of children with high needs in care seems to demonstrate.

Academics, advisers, and politicians routinely repeat versions of the orthodox account (that mandatory reporting has placed child protection agencies under an overwhelming burden and greater emphasis needs are placed on early intervention and family support services) whenever disasters involving known children hit the headlines. Logical and coherent, evidence-based analysis of the real problems – combined with the proposal of workable solutions to the child protection crisis – is crucial. But, of itself, this analysis appears to be insufficient to achieve policy change.

The Australian child protection system today resembles the definition of madness apocryphally attributed to Einstein (among others): repeatedly doing the same thing, and expecting a different result. This book not only describes what we keep doing wrong in the name of family preservation; it also seeks to answer why we keep doing the same things that don't work. It is not just about how and why the system performs so badly; it also asks how a system that fails to protect children keeps sustaining and replicating itself. The following chapters therefore examine the ideological factors (what is thought), the institutional factors (what is done), and cultural factors (what is felt) that create political obstacles in the way of changing the system.

Ideological factors include the now-entrenched shifts in the field of social work (first in academia, then in frontline services) that occurred since the 1970s, which prioritise parental rights and family preservation over the traditional goal of child rescue.

Institutional factors include the role that organised lobby groups play in the highly politicised process of shaping child protection policy. This especially applies to NGO charities that have a vested interest in family preservation because it helps them secure taxpayer funding for the extensive array of services that support "troubled" families.

Cultural factors, of course, include the sensitivities surrounding the Stolen Generations and forced adoption, and an awareness of the pitfalls of those past policies. The taint of these past associations accounts for a lack of political will to encourage adoption of underclass children. Cultural factors also include the legacy of the social revolution of the 1960s and the embrace of so-called progressive social values concerning "family diversity" – the idea that all kinds of families are equally good for children. Politicians display incredible timidity in relation to child protection policy failures and the manifest need for greater use of adoption to resolve situations of parental abuse and neglect. In doing so they avoid having to address, and before that to take the politically incorrect step of acknowledging, the politically and culturally inconvenient links between rising rates of single motherhood over the past 40 years and rising rates of child abuse and neglect.

Some may be disconcerted by the arguments advanced here regarding the obstacles to change and how to overcome them. This especially applies to the way the political influence of the "Big Welfare" lobby – the child and family welfare social services sector – compromises child protection policy and precludes saving children from harm. We might prefer to hold onto a rosy view of NGOs' motives, but the child and family welfare social services sector is a multibillion-dollar "industry" for which a great deal is at stake, and here you will find documented examples of NGOs' successful efforts to subvert the policy process to achieve their self-interestedly preferred outcomes.

Likewise, it could be unpalatable for some to think about child protection in left/right political terms, because this injects a partisan note into what we like to think would be a non-partisan issue solvable by applying universal principles and common sense. But, in cultural politics at least, a move to the left in thinking about and dealing with child abuse has underpinned the radical ideological and institutional changes of recent decades. This is the root of the unhealthy emphasis on upholding parental "rights" at all costs, which informs the impractical belief that government-funded support programs can fix unfixable parents.

The leftward shift has also involved assuming a non-judgemental attitude to parental bad behaviour, and tolerating parental drug abuse – attitudes that pervade child protection authorities throughout the country. Hence, in the contemporary debate over child protection policy, those who suggest drug addicts should have their children removed are upbraided by defenders of the status quo for promoting so-called "conservative" values.

Child protection has already been thoroughly politicised. Those who subscribe to self-styled "progressive" values have cast the first stone in what has become a culture war over child protection. To say nothing of the individual children involved, this war has imposed large social and financial costs on the community, through the high and ever-increasing cost of failing child protection services, and through the perpetuation of dysfunction and disadvantage in the underclass.

To say there is a culture war over child protection policy is not to set up a straw man: it accurately depicts the cultural terrain. Influential, left-leaning welfare-advocacy bodies, such as the national and state peak councils of social service (i.e. ACOSS), are orthodox to a fault when it comes to child protection "reform". In these circles, advocating for adoption is tantamount to renouncing their progressive credentials for addressing social disadvantage.

Those on the Left can be accused of sins of commission in relation to child protection. By contrast, those on the Right stand accused of sins of omission – they have been reluctant to engage with this crucial social issue by challenging the Left's disastrous monopoly on child protection policy and practice. If those on the Right don't advocate for meaningful change, who else will?

This book unashamedly argues for swinging the pendulum back towards child rescue and a focus on children's rights. This will require a concerted cultural, if not party-political, response from the Right, reasserting some fundamental but displaced traditional principles by championing greater use of adoption from care.

This is not about the Right pursuing a political vendetta against the Left for its own sake: it is about generating the political will and momentum needed to drag child protection back towards the lost centre. Taking up this challenge is also an important step in overcoming the legacy of past injustices that limits political leadership on adoption even though adoption itself has changed substantially in light of past mistakes. Politicians will be more likely to take the lead and act on child protection reform if there is already community support for a new approach.

Given the political realities, community support for change is only like to be generated by the activity of those who, like me, line up on the right of the political spectrum. I would be glad to be proven wrong if some on the Left take a clear view of what would benefit at-risk children and take up the cause of adoption, which is unlikely to appeal to their audiences, constituencies, and stakeholders.

All this is to say that Australia's child protection disaster is executed on a broader canvas than simply the wonkish details of policy, practice, programs, data, and evaluation. Here, I examine all these crucial elements to paint a picture of systemic failures. But this book is also, deliberately, a cultural and political account of the forces that create and sustain the many problematic features of the existing system. Taking this broader view was the only way to make sense of my findings and the many apparently unfathomable things I discovered about a mad system.

The inadequacies of official inquiries into child protection systems also illustrate the factors behind a failure to transcend political and cultural obstacles to creating and implementing sound child protection policy. These inquiries are said to be independent and to aim to address the systemic factors that account for child protection failures. But they tend to be called by beleaguered state and territory governments as a political diversion, usually in response to public outcries over notorious child deaths such as those of Ebony and Dean in 2007.

Since then, five of the eight states and territories have held inquiries. Going back further, between 2002 and 2010 there were reportedly at least 14 inquiries into child protection systems in various jurisdictions.[29] These inquiries have almost uniformly advised that some form of business as usual should continue. Their findings and recommendations have generally amounted to calling for more funding for early intervention and family support services, while proposing the supposed innovation of re-focusing the system around prevention – which merely dresses up a reinvention of the child protection wheel. Prevention is a politically palatable term compared to "removal" and "adoption"; it falls easily from the lips of premiers and ministers when, as night follows day, a government pledges to implement recommendations that amount to no change.

Official inquiries fail to sort fact from fiction, discount the real systemic problems, and restate the family-preservation orthodoxy because, despite their alleged independence, they are in fact high-profile political exercises. Governments are unlikely to welcome, let alone implement, recommendations that contradict the conventional wisdom in this area, and which would provoke a firestorm of protest from experts and stakeholders with ready access to the media.

Furthermore, the accepted views are promulgated and fed into official inquiries by academic specialists who almost universally endorse family preservation, which they teach at their universities as the core curriculum of the degrees completed by the social workers who staff the sector. Many academics also rely on departmental approval to conduct career-sustaining research. An academic who dissented from the orthodoxy – as well as losing standing in the field and risking professional and social ostracism – would jeopardise departmental approval (and departmental and NGO funding for research), without which they would be less likely to publish – and hence more likely to perish, to follow the adage. These additional institutional factors, which only reinforce knowledge that supports the currently prevailing view, account for why most academics, departments, and NGOs are ideologically wedded to family preservation.

When too much family support is never enough

In August 2014, South Australia became the latest state to call an inquiry (in this case a Royal Commission). It came in response to a series of child protection scandals involving the usual story of children living and dying in dysfunctional families in plain sight of the local child protection authority, Families SA. The announcement of the inquiry prompted a leading child protection academic in the state to assert that the South Australian child protection system was supposedly operating on a "1960s solution, of investigation and removal" and had failed to follow other states in switching to a family support–based early intervention and prevention model.[30] The chief executive of a leading NGO echoed this advice, and made the claim – replete with warnings about creating another Stolen Generation – that South Australia trailed the field and "has a relatively poor track record in investing in programs to prevent child abuse and neglect."[31]

The dominant voices in the child protection debate repeated the same orthodox proposals for "reform". In response, the minister in charge of Families SA said the government had tripled the department's budget and doubled its workforce so it could do more to assist families. The minister also claimed there was no simple answer to child protection, which was "why the best thing we as a community can do is find ways to better support families". This, the minister further explained, was why the Families SA Redesign project was already underway and "focusing more on targeted, early intervention so that fewer children are in the situation where they have to leave their parents."[32]

Families SA clearly believed it was already practicing family preservation, because its chief executive publicly defended the department's policy of not necessarily removing a child due to parental drug and alcohol abuse, "because of the potential difficulties of placing it in a nurturing, caring, loving environment outside of that biological family". The premier also stated that removal sometimes did more harm than good, due to the difficulties children face in the care system. He went on to say that, regardless, calls for more children to be removed from abusive and neglectful families were impractical. It was, in fact, allegedly impossible, because there were not enough resources to investigate all the child harm reports received, and that even if that was possible, removing children was "undesirable [as] we'd have 20,000 kids in our care not 2,000."[33]

For those with the ability to make or influence the direction of child protection policy, too much family preservation appeared never to be enough. This was despite, as the premier admitted, the thousands of abused and neglected children remaining in unsafe environments. But the notion that family preservation is the only logistically possible and affordable policy option is wrong-headed.

Removal would indeed be desirable for these children, and would do them more good than harm, *if the use of adoption from care were not taboo* and could be used to place removed children with safe, stable, and permanent families. It would then also be affordable, because adoptions would transfer most of the cost of caring for children off government budgets, and eliminate the financial disincentives to rescue children from abuse and neglect created by the ever-increasing size, cost, and complexity of care systems in all states and territories.

Despite claims to the contrary, Families SA was clearly practicing family preservation. The system's operation was already based around a self-justifying and self-perpetuating culture of non-intervention, which was clearly failing to protect children. The calls made to reinvent a palpably failing system in South Australia, by "switching" to a model based on prevention and family preservation, did not gel with the facts. They merely distracted attention from the real issues and challenges facing the system.

The calling of the South Australian Royal Commission coincided with a coronial inquest into another tragic but avoidable child death.

Four-year-old Chloe Valentine died from horrific internal injuries sustained when her single mother and the mother's de facto partner repeatedly placed her on a motorbike and filmed her repeated falls on their phones while they were drunk and high on ice. Families SA had received 21 reports about the family, and failed to respond at all on many occasions. These non-responses were interspersed with insistence that Chloe's development was on track and she was being properly looked after. An outcome of Family SA's involvement was that the department approved a case plan allowing the mother to use drugs provided a "sober adult" cared for Chloe. The mother spent half of her welfare payments on drugs, spent all of the $5,000 Baby Bonus payment on drugs, and her first words after Chloe's birth were about how glad she was not to be pregnant anymore, "so I can get pissed again". Yet the department and a number of charities supported the mother by purchasing food and providing home cleaning, supported accommodation, and financial assistance, to make sure Chloe stayed with her.[34]

Evidence given at the coronial inquest reveals how dangerous and deceptive the family preservation orthodoxy can be for children like Chloe. The inquest established that Chloe suffered from severe parental neglect manifested in a range of ways, including serious underdevelopment, as well as in imminent danger of the kind of fatal harm she ultimately suffered.[35] That a case such as hers could be assessed as requiring family support and not statutory intervention is appallingly significant. It illustrates the dangers inherent in the orthodox advice about raising the reporting threshold and creating dual tracks. It shows how in reality, to justify family preservation, this advice overlooks the dangers of chronic parental dysfunction and downplays the risk of cumulative harm (development deficits caused by chronic child neglect).

Other evidence given at the inquest also demonstrated the extraordinary level of dysfunction that Families SA was prepared to set aside to keep the family together. Chloe and her mother had lived in a supported accommodation facility in the suburb of Hope Valley, which was leased from the Salvation Army. The Salvation Army case manager responsible for managing the mother's case told the inquest that the trash-strewn, rat-infested property "was uninhabitable, it was filthy, it was absolutely not a suitable environment for a child". The case manager also told the inquest that based on the state of the property, she did not think the mother "had the capacity to provide Chloe with a safe, stable home environment." This appeared to state the obvious, given the photos of the squalid, filthy condition of the house that were submitted to the inquest.[36]

To her credit, the case manager had reported her concerns for Chloe's safety to Families SA based on the state of the property and the mother's failure to engage with the support services offered. Departmental caseworkers subsequently failed to take action to remove the child, and instead persisted – as obliged by the department's policy of family preservation and removal as the last resort – with efforts to keep the family together by referring the case to a more intensive kind of family support service.[37] Yet when the mother's lease was not renewed after 12 months and she was evicted, the Salvation Army case manager still wrote a remarkably positive letter of reference that congratulated her on "what she had achieved with Chloe". Put on the spot when the South Australian coroner, Mark Johns, asked why she had done this, given the mother's track record, the case manager replied that the mother "had a lot of potential", and that "as her support worker, I did not feel it was appropriate to condemn her".[38]

This statement is indicative of the radical ethos of non-judgementalism about "troubled" parents evident across the social work profession and child protection workforce, which underpins the preoccupation with protecting parental "rights" and the virtually limitless efforts that are made to ensure family preservation, even when child safety concerns are well-founded and on-going. This is an important part of the explanation for why Families SA took what the coroner described as the "path of least resistance", which put the mother's interests ahead of the child's.[39] Understanding the source of the apparent unwillingness to condemn or stigmatise, and thus to "victimise" and "punish" parents, helps explain the department's otherwise inexplicable insistence that "from their point of view there was nothing to suggest that Chloe was not being cared for appropriately"[40] – a point of view that prevailed right through until the time of her death, despite the obvious and overwhelming evidence that this was a serious case of chronic neglect and parental dysfunction.

Hypocrisy and double standards

The cases of Ebony, Dean, and Chloe are hardly one-offs. Rather, they are the worst, fatal examples of how child protection authorities repeatedly get it in wrong in virtually identical cases involving known underclass children.

In October 2014, another Adelaide couple pleaded guilty to endangering the life of their four-year-old son, who police found starving and dehydrated behind the locked door of a filth-filled bedroom. The graphic news report of their trial told a familiar tale. The court heard that:

- The boy had been left in the room for 3–4 days before his rescue, and was found by chance after police responded to a call about domestic violence.
- Officers battled through knee-deep rubbish, including rotting meat, to find the boy naked in his bedroom, surrounded by soiled nappies, plastic plates, and his own faeces.
- The boy was hospitalised for a month after being taken from the house, and suffered from a litany of development issues including language, motor, and social delays. He

needed surgery to remove a significant number of teeth because of decay.
- The mother was utterly unprepared for and incapable of performing of any of the long-term basic duties of being a mother.
- The couple had been on an alcohol bender, and had no routine to feed or care for the boy.
- There had been more than six attempts from government authorities to check on the boy's welfare, but no one had actually seen the child in any of at least the past five visits.

The evidence moved the magistrate, incredulous at the lack of action by Families SA, to state the obvious about this and similar cases: "you would not have to be an expert to realise there was something wrong."[41]

Yet, today's child protection practice means almost the opposite is true. The practice of family preservation denies obvious facts and risks when it comes to parental dysfunction, and downplays the harm done to the children. The determination to not remove children is conceived of as a virtue by those who promote and practice the ideology of family preservation. Preserving professional self-regard by appearing non-judgemental about dysfunctional parents in effect overrides child welfare.

By its nature, child protection depends on making judgements about parental capacity. If child protection authorities deem it inappropriate to judge some parents inadequate, then child welfare laws might as well be struck from the statute books. The ideology of family preservation and the accompanying inverted morality of non-judgementalism masquerade as empathy for the disadvantaged and a "progressive" form of social justice, but they are actually a perverse form of moral vanity, suffused with a sense of self-righteousness in defiance of common sense and community standards. Choosing not to condemn child maltreatment and intervene to stop it distorts priorities and impedes the proper protection of children. This is especially true of the permissive attitudes child protection authorities frequently display towards parental drug abuse, regardless of its impact on child well-being; this is the most perverse and wicked form of non-judgementalism that plagues the field.

It is hard to read about the troubled and abusive background of Dean Shillingsworth's mother, to take one example, and not feel sympathy for this woman – who had little chance of ever being a capable parent. But for child protection authorities, that sympathy should not entail the belief that she and other similarly dysfunctional parents should keep custody of children, since all Australian child welfare legislation employs the child's best interest as the paramount principle to judge all child protection cases. Knowledge of the contemporaneous facts and timelines (not in hindsight) of the "starved girl" case, the "boy in the suitcase in the lake" case, and the "girl on the motorbike" case rightly provokes outrage that no action was taken *for Ebony's sake, for Dean's sake* and *for Chloe's sake*. Despite the clear and immediate danger to their welfare, the shibboleths of family preservation got in the way and stopped them from being saved.

In addition to moral vanity, child protection is also beset by the vice of hypocrisy. The politicians, academics, bureaucrats and social workers who preach and practice non-judgementalism in the guise of family preservation are ultimately condemning vulnerable children to lives of disadvantage. This would be less hypocritical if the same people were not rightly protective of the bourgeois advantages they, their children, and their grandchildren enjoy. The comparison sometimes made between adoption from care and the forced adoptions of the past, which presumes that both involve taking children from poor families to give to rich families, is false. The truth that all children need and deserve good and stable families to protect their rights and opportunities is, or at least should be, self-evident. But instead, double standards apply in child protection that favour safe and well-cared for well-off children and discriminate against the poorest and most deprived underclass children.

Another obvious truth, which should be the bedrock of sound child protection policy, is that childhood is fleeting. This time of life must be optimised for children's sake, and for the consequent good of society, because bad early experiences have lifelong consequences. Because today's child is tomorrow's citizen, modern countries usually place a premium on the care, education and socialisation of children. A universal aspiration, shared by all civilised societies, is that adults should have a duty to nurture and not damage children. That Australians allow this social norm to be transgressed in our prosperous country, is what's so shocking about the harm done under the rubric of child protection. The wrongs hereby perpetrated are of biblical proportions. Doubly wicked are those who protest otherwise but must know, in their hearts, minds and consciences, that what they say is false.

Flawed child protection policies prevent underclass children from receiving the fair go all Australians should expect as their birthright, and destine these children to remain underdogs, chained by their childhoods to the lowest rung of society. Equity, equality of opportunity, and social inclusion are terms that form the currency of politics and animate discussion of a host of public-policy issues, and underpin billions of dollars of spending, across the whole of government, in the pursuit of eradicating social disadvantage. Yet attention rarely, if ever, focuses on the role that child protection failures play in perpetuating inequality. So long as Australian child protection systems continue to harm the most deprived children and deny them a decent family, which is the basic building block of full opportunities in life – then so long will the fair go be only a myth for many children.

If these children's lives are to change, the system that claims to protect them must change. If the system is to change, minds and then policy must change with respect to adoption. Policymakers and social workers must see through the fog of misleading claims about what is supposedly best for children, and replace the misconceptions with the goal of making adoption from care standard practice across the country. If the child protection system is to be worth its name, we must end the madness of replicating decades of policy failure that has perpetuated dysfunction and social disadvantage through multiple generations. The taboo on adoption by decent families must be broken, so that underclass children can be rescued from ruined prospects and wasted lives.

The last bastion of Aboriginal self-determination

Indigenous children are massively over-represented in the child protection system, due to the extraordinary levels of dysfunction and disadvantage found in some Indigenous families and communities. One of the many contentious issues this book discusses is the extremely controversial subject of how Australia should deal with the legacy of the Stolen Generations when considering how Indigenous children should be cared for and protected. It is important that, at the outset, I declare my views on this crucial and highly contested issue.

I disagree with those who deny the existence of the Stolen Generations, and who complain that "myth" and "political correctness" is preventing child protection authorities from rescuing Indigenous children from abuse and neglect. The Stolen Generation is no myth: child protection was done badly in the past. Before the 1980s, thousands of Indigenous children were removed from their families with the aim of assimilating them into white or mainstream Australian society, which entailed preventing any further and ongoing contact with their kin and traditional culture. Past child removal practices often had a devastating impact on the identity of Indigenous people, and this contributed to a sense of loss, confusion, and isolation resulting from the separation from families and communities.

Recognising these failings and the importance of cultural identity means that, ideally, every Indigenous child unable to live safely with their parents would be placed in "kinship care", to maintain contact with kin and culture. This would be consistent with the Aboriginal and Torres Strait Islander Child Placement Principle (ACPP), a nationally agreed on policy, included in child welfare legislation in all states and territories, which makes placement with relatives, local community members, or other Indigenous people the preferred option for Indigenous children in need of care.

Unfortunately, as the evidence compiled in this book suggests, kinship placements are in short supply. Making use of them is not always realistic, and cannot always be reconciled with child welfare due to the social problems in some Indigenous communities. In some cases, "culturally appropriate" placements that are far from safe or conducive to child well-being and development still proceed because of the well-meaning desire to prevent a repeat of the Stolen Generations. Spurred by the desire not to repeat past mistakes, child protection authorities make great efforts to exhaust all potential kinship options – to the point where the intent to preserve traditional culture and identity can outweigh basic concerns about a placement's safety and suitability. Because of the priority given to cultural considerations, some Indigenous children end up receiving substandard care in kinship placements that non-Indigenous children would not be placed.

At present, efforts to address the legacy of the Stolen Generations threaten to undermine what should be the overarching objective of the reconciliation movement, which is to achieve true equality of opportunity regardless of race, and in so doing eradicate the shameful disadvantages and abject poverty suffered by too many Indigenous Australians, particularly children. Indigenous-specific child protection practices such as the ACPP threaten to undermine the bipartisan national commitment to "closing the gap" between social outcomes for the most disadvantaged Indigenous Australians and other

Australians. This is the "kinship conundrum" – what is done in the name of preventing a repeat of the Stolen Generations risks creating another "lost generation" of Indigenous Australians, trapped in disadvantage and dysfunction, especially in remote "homeland" communities and in Indigenous communities on the social fringes of rural and metropolitan areas.

Given the memory of the Stolen Generations, it might appear unthinkable to change today's culturally appropriate child protection practices. One different approach could include making Indigenous children who cannot live safely with their parents available for adoption alongside non-Indigenous children on a non-discriminatory basis. This might be said to be unthinkable because it would be tantamount to stealing children all over again and destroying Indigenous culture and identity. But would this really be so? Such an argument cannot be sustained when all dimensions of the issue are considered. What this emotive (if understandable) response fails to appreciate adequately is the way political considerations, as distinct from child welfare considerations shape how the child protection system treats Indigenous children.

The "separatist" Indigenous child protection regimes that operate in all Australian jurisdictions are not only a legacy of well-meaning efforts to right past wrongs. They are also an important legacy of the political campaign for Aboriginal rights that emerged in the 1970s. A common misapprehension is that the ACPP was developed in response to the emergence of the Stolen Generations as a prominent national issue in the late 1990s. The release in 1997 of the Human Rights and Equal Opportunity Commission's (HREOC) *Bringing Them Home: Report on the National Inquiry into the Separation of Aboriginal and Torres Strait Islander Children* generated a wave of national sympathy, expressed chiefly through the rise of the popular Sorry Day movement, which demanded a national parliamentary apology for the Stolen Generations. However, there is more to understanding the ACPP than the well-meaning desire to express sorrow for past misdeeds.

In reality, as is detailed here in Chapter 6, the development of the ACPP was a product of the *politicisation* of the Stolen Generations issue, which was initially taken up as an important part of the political movement for Aboriginal rights. The ACPP was introduced in the 1980s, and it needs to be understood as a product of the political agenda of the 1970s, which sought Aboriginal self-determination – political, legal, social, and cultural – in all areas of Indigenous policy, based on the idea that Indigenous advancement required separate development so that traditional culture and Indigenous identity could be retained.

It is now generally recognised that policies of self-determination have failed to improve outcomes for Indigenous people. That recognition has led, in recent years, to the "mainstreaming" of Indigenous health, education, employment, and other policies, with the aim of ensuring all Australians receive the same standard of service and, hopefully, achieve the same outcomes in health, education, employment and other areas.

Even though much has changed in other areas, Indigenous child protection policies are still dictated by 1970s-style separatist thinking, particularly concerning the need for continuous contact with traditional culture to maintain identity. This is despite the changing nature of modern Indigenous identity. The large majority of Indigenous Australians are now city-based and have high rates of intermarriage, and their social welfare indicators are largely the same as their non-Indigenous peers. Many have little contact with traditional customs and lands, but this is no barrier to their identification and acceptance as Indigenous people. This is because Indigenous identity and belonging is no longer based solely on race or culture, but is increasingly an ethnic identity based on self-identification, recognition, and family history and descent.

These observations are not made here to enter a debate about who is or isn't Aboriginal.[42] Individuals are free to identify as they wish, and communities are free to determine who belongs to them. But the trend towards viewing Indigenousness as an ethnic identity suggests a way out of the kinship conundrum. Adoption for Indigenous children wouldn't necessarily mean creating a new Stolen Generation, because the idea that continuous contact with traditional culture is the source of Indigenous identity has been superseded.

This is in no way to suggest that questions of culture and identity are unimportant in Indigenous child protection and should be ignored. If Indigenous child protection was mainstreamed, and non-discriminatory Indigenous adoption became policy, the promotion of Indigenous identity and cultural awareness would remain crucial, and new ways of achieving this would need to be developed.

Current practice in overseas adoptions is that adoptive parents are educated about their children's heritage and made aware of the need to inform children about it and cultivate that identity. To formalise emulation of such arrangements, and to reconcile the preservation of culture and identity with the need to protect children's welfare, this book proposes that Indigenous organisations be funded to run cultural support and education programs that inform Indigenous children who are adopted about their heritage and cultivate traditional identity.

Despite the changing character of Indigenous identity, the major barrier to mainstreaming Indigenous child protection is sure to continue to be the perception that this would represent a betrayal of the Stolen Generations. This book, therefore, sets out the reasons why people should feel comfortable with (or at least not threatened by) the possibility of supporting a different approach.

Introducing a policy such as non-discriminatory Indigenous adoption would not be a repetition of past mistakes: the need to avoid that is clear. Mainstreaming is, rather, about correcting the political and policy missteps since the 1970s have that caused harm to Indigenous Australians in spite of good intentions. Unfortunately, misguided good intentions are not the only thing getting in the way of properly protecting Indigenous children. The outdated political legacy of 1970s-style Aboriginal politics, which perpetuates disadvantage in the name of Aboriginal self-determination, is an additional barrier.

My conclusion that Indigenous child protection should be mainstreamed follows the volumes of analysis, criticism, and commentary that have appeared in roughly the last decade and half and sparked the mainstreaming revolution in other areas of Indigenous policy. The lesson of this literature is that the problems that cause and contribute to Indigenous disadvantage are as complex as the solutions, largely because separatist policies have had unintended consequences that materially contribute to Indigenous suffering.

The welfare of individual Indigenous Australians, particularly of women and children, has been and continues to be sacrificed in the service of a political ideology that, to the nation's shame, has ill-served the most disadvantaged members of Australian society. This book contributes to the revisionist literature on Indigenous affairs by examining the relatively neglected subject of separatist child protection policies. The analysis offered here is motivated by the belief that critical and constructive analysis of a policy area stuck in the 1970s is the first step in the ending the long-standing politicisation of the Stolen Generations issue.

As in Australian child protection policy and practice more generally, the most alarming issue with Indigenous child protection is it routinely puts child welfare behind political or ideological considerations. The comparatively limited scrutiny that the ACPP and other forms of culturally appropriate Indigenous child protection policy have hitherto received has allowed the political goal of Aboriginal self-determination to continue to take precedence over the best interests and basic welfare of children. In Indigenous child protection, as in other areas of Indigenous policy, the "politics of suffering" must end in order to end the suffering of children.

For underclass Indigenous and non-Indigenous children alike, what is truly in their best interests must dictate better policy and practice in the future. The ideological, institutional, and cultural interests of adults should no longer take precedence over those of children.

2

UNDER-RESPONDING:

THE MARGINALISATION OF CHILD RESCUE

From statutory intervention to family support

Underclass children caught up in the child protection system live in homes that are unimaginable to most Australians. In these chaotic worlds of unchanged nappies, putrid kitchens, and garbage-strewn rooms, fridges are full of grog and parents feed drug habits while pantries and children's bellies remain empty. There is regular violence between adults instead of consistent care and loving, nurturing interactions with children.

No one needs to be an expert to know there is something wrong in these families and that children would be better off out of these environments. It is mainly police, doctors, nurses, and teachers, with a range of expertise in assessing family problems, who make the bulk of the risk-of-harm reports that detail concerns about the health and safety of underclass children. But in far too many cases, the action these professionals expect will be taken to remove children from harm's way does not occur, and child protection authorities permit children to remain with their dysfunctional families.

When a report of suspected child abuse and neglect is made, children enter what is known as the "statutory intervention" part of the child protection system, which consists of two interrelated processes. Reports of suspected harm are meant to trigger a "statutory investigation" by the specialist government agencies, located in each state and territory, that have been granted the legal power and responsibility under child welfare statutes to inquire into allegations of child maltreatment and determine what action is needed to protect children. Departmental caseworkers trained in social work or related fields conduct investigations, and are required to visit the family home, interview parents and children, and make an assessment of the family situation and of child well-being.

If these inquiries establish that the report of maltreatment is true, that report is said to be "substantiated". A substantiated finding of child harm may lead child protection authorities to initiate the legal process of "statutory removal" – court-approved removal of children from the custody of their parents as authorised by child welfare laws. If removal occurs, children move from the statutory part of the child protection system into what is known as the "out-of-home care" part of the system, and are placed "in care", in foster homes or in kinship care placements with extended members of their own families, or, in some cases, in residential care facilities ("group homes").

For most of the past 150 years, the core role of the organisations responsible for child protection in Australia was to rescue maltreated children from abusive and neglectful parents by taking them into care for their own protection. But in 21st-century Australia, this is no longer the case. Today, child protection authorities practice family preservation because child protection experts almost uniformly believe that children are better off at home with their parents. This has led to a significant expansion of the third part of the child protection system – the "family support" system.

The change in emphasis, away from statutory intervention and out-of-home care towards family preservation and the provision of family support services, is the root cause of the systemic problems with the Australian child protection system. Many children do not even have reports of suspected harm properly investigated. Worse, even when an investigation is conducted and a report of harm substantiated, in too many cases action is not taken to remove children into care. Instead, child protection authorities opt to leave children in abusive and neglectful homes and refer families to a range of social services that help parents. What does and doesn't happen to protect maltreated children these days reflects the radical ideological, and accompanying institutional, shifts in the field of child protection over the last 40 years. These shifts have revolutionised the way child protection authorities respond to cases of child maltreatment in the nation's expanding underclass of welfare-dependent and dysfunctional families.

Ideology

Until the 1960s, child protection in Australia was a private endeavour undertaken by charitable societies dedicated to the eradication of cruelty to children. The role and functions of these societies dated from the late 19th century, and reflected the origins of the field in the liberal, humane and philanthropic child rescue movement that developed in Britain and spread to the United States and Australia from that time.

However, by the 1970s, all Australian states and territories had enacted legislation that empowered child protection authorities like NSW DoCS to investigate reports of child maltreatment and remove children from abusive and neglectful parents. By the 1980s, child protection had been transformed from a community responsibility into a government responsibility in all Australian jurisdictions. The work of child protection came to be carried out by university-trained social workers employed in the centralised government agencies set up to receive and respond to reports.

Definitions of child maltreatment were also transformed. The original child welfare acts of the late 1800s were designed to rescue children from cruelty, severe physical abuse, and extreme neglect. Changing standards of appropriate care, broadened conceptions of child welfare, and, most importantly, wider social changes associated with the destructive behavioural consequences of the rise of welfare dependence in recent decades, led to expansion of the scope of child welfare legislation, and significantly changed the way governments and child protection agencies approach child welfare. Child protection authorities have broadened their mandate, and now attempt to protect children from a wider, less specific range of acts and behaviours that damage their development. Especially influential in these developments in legislation and practice has been the recognition of the cumulative harm done to children by chronic parental neglect and abuse in welfare-dependent and dysfunctional families and communities.[43]

However, the changing scope of child welfare laws was accompanied by corresponding ideological shifts in the field, which led to a revolution in child protection policy and practice. The core principle of traditional child protection work – that the state has a duty to intervene to remove and protect vulnerable children in the child's best interests – has been replaced with a new and radically different approach to protecting children. This new, prevention-focused credo has promoted the idea that the best way to protect vulnerable children is to keep families intact and provide support services to address risk factors such as parental mental-health issues and drug abuse.

The move towards supporting families rather than separating them originated with the radical school of social work that emerged in the 1960s. This school was critical of supposedly bourgeois institutions, such as marriage and the nuclear family, and of official policies that reinforced the hegemony of these institutions, such as adoption – especially forced adoption of the children of unwed mothers.

When subjected to radical left-wing scrutiny, child removal and adoption, and child abuse in general, were portrayed as a structural feature of an unfair society. All were seen as caused by poverty, or rather, by inadequate government support for parents who struggled to care for their children. Parents' responsibility for properly caring for their offspring was thereby transformed into the right of struggling parents to receive adequate transfer payments and appropriate social-support services. Removal of abused and neglected children into care came to be considered inappropriate, and permanent removal by adoption was especially condemned as unjust. Child removal was portrayed as punishing the poor, and all adoptions – even when court action to legally sever parental rights was deemed necessary for child protection purposes – were viewed as forced, marking a failure to address the lack of support that allegedly caused child maltreatment.[44]

The reorientation of child protection work away from child rescue and towards family preservation became entrenched as the new orthodoxy through the influence of university social-work faculties, where the new approach was the foundation of social-worker training. On the ground, family preservation quickly became institutionalised as the standard policy and practice employed by state-run child protection authorities, where non-interventionist and virulently anti-adoption attitudes held sway.

In agencies such as NSW DoCS and its counterparts in other states and territories, child protection services were, and remain, sub-departments of much larger community services departments. These departments employ a variety of social workers, psychologists, and drug and alcohol-abuse and other counsellors who have little interest in traditional child rescue, and who have greater interest in keeping dysfunctional families together so that taxpayer-funded "alternative services" can be provided. This has led to traditional child protection work – the assessment and investigation of reports, followed by legal action to remove and rescue children if necessary – being crowded out by other forms of social work and social services, especially drug and alcohol counselling, that focus on working with parents and preserving and reuniting families. In addition, the outsourcing of family support to NGOs in recent times has created a class of influential institutions that depend on maintaining of the family-preservation status quo.

Reconceptualisation of the core role of child protection authorities as essentially preventive was accompanied by an equally significant cultural change. The importance of respecting parental rights to retain custody of children was elevated and granted priority over the traditional and long-established right of children to be protected from harm. In practice, this radical parental rights agenda meant that opting to keep families together, even when children were at serious and imminent risk of harm, became a core feature of child protection casework. This move to a family-centred, rather than child-centred, approach to dealing with child abuse and neglect occurred despite child welfare legislation insisting that the "best interest of the child" must be paramount and override the interests of parents.[45] Child protection authorities have reinterpreted these legislative obligations, with considerable presumption, to mean that supporting dysfunctional parents is in the best interests of a child, "in the context of its family as the client for Family Services."[46]

These developments in the field were underpinned by a shift in moral sentiment, or in the moral framework applied to dealing with the perpetrators of child maltreatment. Perpetrators of neglect and abuse were transformed and de-stigmatised, becoming "clients" instead. The collective determination by social-work academics and practitioners was that it is not appropriate to judge or stigmatise disadvantaged people as bad parents.

The new line of thinking about the role of child protection and the need to support, not judge, parents was consistent with wider social-policy trends that discouraged making moral judgements about personal behaviour. This has principally involved rejecting, as a relic of the Victorian era, the traditional categories of "deserving" and "undeserving" poor – the concept that some people's circumstances are impoverished due to no fault of their own, while in other cases these circumstances are a product of people's own behaviour.

Ironically, the demise of the concept of the undeserving poor and the triumph of non-judgementalism has coincided with the rise of welfare dependence and the consequent downward behavioural spiral, which has in fact made the old Victorian concepts highly relevant to the social-policy challenges associated with the emergence of the underclass. Traditionally, parents who abused and neglected their children were categorised as bad – as in morally corrupt – for beating or depriving children. The disadvantaged, abusive, and neglectful parents of the new underclass that has emerged in recent decades are not necessarily bad in the traditional moral sense, but they are certainly unfit parents who chronically fail to meet their children's vital needs. Yet, the enthusiasm for preventive approaches to child protection, and for working with rather than against parents, has allowed social workers to avoid having to make hard but necessary judgements about the behaviour and capacities of dysfunctional parents, with respect to whether removal is in the best interests of a child. Instead, a misplaced egalitarianism has underpinned family preservation.

The belief that parental ability has been unfairly distributed across socio-economic groups motivates the desire to redistribute it via government-funded family support programs, on the questionable basis that this will keep children safe. This preferred sociological explanation is overlaid by the radical social justice credo, which simplistically claims that poverty causes child maltreatment, and that traditional child protection work and adoption victimises the poor by denying their "right" to parent children.[47]

Dominant voices, orthodox recommendations

When the results of family preservation-based child protection practice hit the headlines, we are typically confronted with yet another case of a "known" (previously reported) child dying in plain sight of the child protection authorities that failed to protect them. The experts – led by leading child protection academics and practitioners – routinely claim that the real problem isn't that we do too little statutory investigation and removal and too much family preservation. To the contrary, they argue – and argue with remarkable effectiveness and influence – that Australian child protection systems are operating on a 1960s model that is over-reliant on statutory services, and under-reliant on a family support–based early intervention and prevention.[48]

For a deeper look into the topsy-turvy world of child protection policy debate, we can examine the recent history of the highly politicised process of child protection "reform" in NSW.

In response to the deaths of Ebony and Dean, and to the resultant outpouring of community concern about the state of the child protection system, the NSW government of the day stuck to the standard crisis-management script. Like many state and territory governments before and since, it commissioned an inquiry. The Special Commission of Inquiry into Child Protection Services in NSW, headed by former NSW Supreme Court Justice James Wood, delivered its three-volume final report (the Wood Report) in November 2008.

The dominant voices in the child protection debate – prominent specialists – had moved quickly to stamp their preferred narrative on the search for answers. The Wood Report basically accepted the orthodox account these specialists gave of the alleged problems with the system. Wood's main recommendations claimed that the major structural challenge facing child protection services in NSW and throughout Australia was "sufficiently resourcing flexible prevention and early intervention services so as to reduce the numbers of children and young people who require the state to step in to keep them safe."[49]

The NSW government accepted 106 of Wood's 111 recommendations, which formed the basis of the $750 million Keep Them Safe program to redesign child protection service delivery in March 2009. Keep Them Safe amounted to a doubling down on the unsuccessful family preservation status quo. This transpired despite the Wood Report containing ample evidence that contradicted its own recommendations. The key piece of this evidence was the extraordinary level of re-reporting in NSW, which clearly showed how the current emphasis on family preservation was failing children.

The Wood Report and its aftermath illustrates how the "ideology"[50] of family preservation continues to trump the evidence that the system is failing, and provides a case study of how the orthodoxy manages to salvage itself. That the evidence did not guide policy ensured that the Wood Report and Keep Them Safe program perpetuated the systemic problems that stopped Ebony, Dean, and other children from being protected. The NSW "reforms" marginalised, yet again, the traditional child rescue approach to child protection that left thousands of vulnerable children in harm's way in abusive and neglectful underclass families.

Needles and haystacks: over-reporting?
In what proved an influential joint submission to the Wood inquiry, Professors Judy Cashmore and Dorothy Scott, and NSW Children's Commissioner Gillian Calvert, argued that NSW DoCS was unable to respond effectively to high-risk reports of child abuse and neglect because of the unintended consequences of introducing mandatory reporting.[51] Cashmore, Scott, and Calvert attributed the crisis in NSW child protection services to allegedly inefficient mandatory-reporting requirements – the legal obligation for doctors, nurses, police, and teachers to report children suspected to be at risk of harm. These requirements, they claimed, overloaded and overwhelmed DoCS with supposedly less-serious and inappropriate reports of child maltreatment. Instead of mandatory reporting promptly identifying the most serious cases of abuse and neglect as intended, DoCS' centralised telephone reporting service, Helpline, had instead been

inundated with over 300,000 reports. The administrative burden created by "over-reporting" had "imposed very heavy demands on DoCS to identify and respond appropriately to children in serious jeopardy" and made it impossible for the swamped department to fulfil its core responsibility – investigating higher-risk reports concerning families in crisis and children most at risk.[52]

The Cashmore submission said that "By overloading our statutory child protection agency with the responsibility to prevent and assess all cases of child abuse and neglect, we have diminished its capacity to perform its core and unique functions,"[53] This is the 'needle in the haystack' theory of child protection failure. The submission went on to say that "the mass screening of socially disadvantaged families to identify a very small minority where a threshold for statutory intervention is reached, displac[es] the core statutory role of bringing serious cases before the court for determination".[54]

The merits of Cashmore, Scott, and Gilbert's orthodox take on the problems in the system depended on whether their submission had appropriately defined and classified different kinds of reports, and whether the differentiated responses they claimed were necessary were actually appropriate. Problematically, Cashmore, Scott, and Gilbert acknowledged that many less-serious reports involved disadvantaged families with complex problems.[55]

These days, the majority of reports to child protection agencies in Australia concern parental and family dysfunction, not intentional physical abuse and neglect.[56] This is because the families most likely to be involved in reports, and most likely be over-represented in proven cases of child abuse and neglect, experience multiple, chronic, often intergenerational, entrenched and difficult-to-resolve behavioural problems. These problems include welfare-dependency, domestic violence, mental illness, drug and alcohol abuse, and the burdens of single parenting, and account for their chronic failure to meet children's physical, emotional, and developmental needs.[57] Cashmore, Scott, and

Gilbert did not believe that an overly sensitive mandatory-reporting system was inappropriate because concerns about child welfare were unjustified. Instead, they claimed that the expectation these reports should trigger a statutory child protection response was unwarranted, because "the concerns [about these struggling families] may not be such to justify statutory investigation or intervention."[58]

Consistent with the standard pro-family-support position, the Cashmore submission suggested that less-serious reports involved families and children judged to be "in need" as opposed to in crisis and "at risk". The supposed difference is that families in crisis were involved in reports where the risk of serious and imminent harm to children was high, and a statutory investigation was therefore required, with a view to statutory removal to halt or avert severe maltreatment. A report concerning a family in need involved a lower risk of imminent harm.

Families in need, it was claimed, did not warrant a full child protection response because the reported concerns were unlikely to reach the legal threshold for statutory removal.[59] Instead, the allegedly appropriate first response was to refer these families to preventive and early-intervention programs, and to other health and welfare services, to help parents overcome the problems that limited their capacity to properly care for children.[60]

The realities of NSW's struggling system appeared to support the logic of this approach. Given the workload created by the sheer volume of reports, it appeared wise to find different ways to support problem families, and provide alternative services, because the default response in many cases was no response at all. As Cashmore, Scott, and Gilbert pointed out, DoCS appeared highly unlikely to follow up on a less serious report and investigate because of heavy competing demands.[61] At the time, as the Wood Report would establish, an alarmingly small proportion of all reports – just 13% – judged as warranting further assessment were followed by a detailed investigation that included a home visit. More than 50% of all reports judged to require further assessment either received no attention (21%) or received attention that fell well short of a home visit (33%).[62]

It seemed little wonder that Ebony and Dean had been missed: the problems in the system weren't cracks so much as yawning chasms. This tallied with the damning criticisms of the NSW Ombudsman in the annual review of the death of known children. In the years preceding the Wood inquiry, the Ombudsman had repeatedly found that DoCS failed to effectively follow up reports of children at risk of harm, including high-risk cases that were closed prematurely and no further action taken without comprehensive assessment or evidence, due to workload pressure or "competing priorities".

Examples of other poor and unsafe practices included the urgency ratings assigned to cases not matching the seriousness of the reported risks, and assessment records being created simply to close a case without any information being gathered or assessed. When further assessments were conducted, the information collected was "too limited to make well-informed decisions" or "did not appear to inform decisions to close a case."[63] The Ombudsman had also identified failures to respond appropriately to chronic and ongoing child safety and welfare concerns in families with extended histories of neglect and reported risk of harm. This included caseworkers failing to conduct a home visit to "sight" (physically see) and ascertain the health and well-being of children who had been the subject of reports of serious maltreatment.[64]

No one disputed that the system was failing vulnerable children. What mattered was the interpretation of the causes. Cashmore, Scott, and Calvert's interpretation was that the problems in the system could be traced to mandatory over-reporting, or "the very significant gap between the legal threshold of suspicion for mandated notifiers to make a report to DoCS and the threshold for DoCS initiating statutory intervention."[65] Child protection authorities could not, and would never be able to, adequately respond to all of the hundreds of thousands of reports received. The situation, according to the Cashmore submission, "demands urgent change both to reduce the number of cases requiring child protection intervention and to manage the current demand more effectively."[66]

It followed, apparently as a matter of logic, that the gap between the mandatory-reporting and statutory-intervention thresholds should be addressed by raising the mandatory-reporting threshold. This would mean that child protection authorities would only receive and follow up reports for further assessment and investigation in the most serious cases, said to be more likely to trigger statutory intervention. The reduction in workload would reduce the chances of high-risk cases falling through the cracks.

Reducing "unnecessary reports to DoCS" would also require a dual-track or alternative reporting and referral pathway, which would stream the genuine statutory child protection cases from those involving "children who might otherwise be notified but who would be unlikely to receive an investigation because they are seen as being of lower risk".[67] The Cashmore submission also suggested that families in less-serious cases could instead be referred to family support services, the delivery of which could be outsourced by the government to child and family charities.[68]

Double standards and cumulative harm

Cashmore, Scott, and Calvert, like many supporters of the dual-track model, asserted that it is appropriate to limit the number of children who receive statutory intervention on the basis that "only a relatively small proportion of reports are substantiated". At the time, only 40% of investigations conducted by DoCS resulted in a proven finding of abuse or neglect.[69] In 2013–14, only around 1 in 5 reports across the country were substantiated (54,438 substantiations of out 304,097 total notifications).[70]

The rationale for a dual track is that most reports do not result in a proven finding of neglect or abuse, and among the substantiated reports even fewer involve abuse and neglect of sufficient severity to result in a statutory investigation and removal of children into care.[71] Yet the assumption that most reports do not therefore warrant statutory intervention is unsafe. The data on substantiations was (and remains) meaningless when, as in the example of NSW, so few reports received a full investigation.

The lack of statutory intervention in many cases of substantiated findings of abuse and neglect is also questionable, as decisions not to substantiate and/or not to remove children may not have been appropriate.[72] Yet the federal government's 2009 reform blueprint, the *National Framework for Protecting Australia's Children*, blithely assumes that any report not substantiated is less serious, and means "a child protection response was *not required*." It recommends a greater focus on providing early intervention and preventive service because "child protection services cannot provide a response to all vulnerable children and their families."[73]

Another problem with separating out "less-serious" reports is that they are not necessarily less serious at all. When made, child protection reports are assessed and ranked in order of priority. This is done by evaluating the initial information received (literally on paper) against a standardised checklist of safety and risk factors, to determine which reports are more or less serious. But these classifications are inherently artificial. Because child harm occurs on a continuum, even though some reports are more serious, less-serious cases can also involve families with serious problems that raise real concerns about child welfare. Downplaying the real risk of chronic child maltreatment in these dysfunctional families is to assert that a child protection response is not necessary and a response focused on family support is sufficient. But this is problematic for the reasons outlined in the Wood Report.

NGOs contracted by DoCS to support families allegedly in need complained about the "less-serious" cases referred for family support services. Once these organisations started working with these families, they found that many cases ended up involving a higher level of risk and needed more urgent attention. Family support service providers found themselves having to carry out child protection work in what turned out to be genuine statutory cases.[74] The flaw in dual-track systems is that it is not possible to safely conclude there is no serious risk to child welfare without an investigation.

One of the biggest issues in relation to the appropriateness of a family support first response is that the family's participation is voluntary, and there is a significant probability that families will disengage. Because many of the parents these services are involved with have serious, ongoing, and hard-to-change behavioural problems, they may be unwilling or find it difficult to stay voluntarily engaged with support services; they are liable to drop out of programs and reject further assistance. The children in these families are then no longer observed at close quarters, and are at risk of experiencing cumulative harm and permanent developmental problems caused by chronic parental neglect and abuse. A statutory child protection response is the first appropriate response to chronic neglect and cumulative harm cases, because parents have no choice: statutory child protection services have the legal power to get through the front door and keep coming through the front door. A statutory response guarantees that a proper investigation, including a home visit and sighting of the child, can occur to fully assess the family history and risk of neglect, abuse, and harm.

Failing to investigate to establish baseline observations on the family and child, and then to monitor the situation on an ongoing basis, means that crucial opportunities to collect evidence are lost.

This may either delay or prevent statutory removal, because if legal action is needed, the evidence used to make that determination must be presented in court. This is why child protection caseworkers should act as lead agency case manager for all reports detailing well-founded concerns about child welfare. This also means they should be responsible for determining, based on investigation and assessment, whether it is appropriate to refer families in need for additional family support and other services.

The danger of raising reporting thresholds and establishing dual-track reporting pathways is that double standards are created in responding to child maltreatment, and many children are denied the face-to-face statutory response needed to keep them safe.

Provider of last resort

The Wood Report accepted that over-reporting was the chief obstacle to making child protection services more efficient and effective. On the basis that "too many reports are being made to DoCS that do not warrant the exercise of its considerable statutory powers," Wood recommended that mandatory-reporting requirements be relaxed to include only children considered at "risk of significant harm". Wood further proposed (as recommended by Cashmore, Scott, and Gilbert)[75] that new units be created in key government departments to help mandatory reporters (the health, police, education, and other professionals legally required to report child safety concerns) assess whether reports should be made to DoCS and ensure that only serious cases meeting the risk-of-significant-harm threshold were referred to the Helpline.

Wood also recommended the establishment of new NGO-run Regional Intake and Referral Services to link families deemed to be the subject of less-serious reports to family support and other community services. And he advised that within three years DoCS should no longer operate its own early-intervention and prevention programs, instead completely outsourcing all family support services to NGO providers to whom families in need could be directly referred from either the regional intake services or the DoCS Helpline. This would allow DoCS to concentrate on its core responsibility of providing timely assessment and investigation of higher-risk reports concerning children allegedly most in need of statutory investigation and removal.[76]

The redesigned reporting and referral structure Wood recommended strongly resembled the dual-track model established in Victoria in 2003, which had been widely heralded as leading the way for other jurisdictions. Under Victoria's Child FIRST (Family Information Referral and Support Teams) strategic framework, child protection reports are made to regional intake centres principally staffed by NGOs. After reports are assessed using a "common assessment framework" – a bureaucratic tool used to filter or prioritise reports – troubled families assessed as in need are referred to family support services and to other health and welfare services. Child protection caseworkers are also placed in the centres to help assess reports and refer higher-risk cases for further investigation. Family support services in the state are entirely outsourced to NGOs.[77]

Wood argued that raising the mandatory-reporting threshold and creating a dual-track reporting pathway would allow DoCS to operate as the "provider of last resort."[78] It would serve that role only for families in crisis, where the risk of potentially severe abuse and extreme neglect is high and imminent, and based "on the likelihood of needing statutory intervention."[79] Wood recommended that only an estimated 10% to 20% of reports, "assessed as being a report that a child or young person is at risk of significant harm should be investigated by DoCS if the matter is urgent or the risk is high or the child is young."[80] This meant that under the revised regime, approximately the same number of reports, a mere fraction, would continue to receive a child protection response and investigation.

Wood recommended that the remaining reports, where the risk of significant harm was deemed "less than high", should be referred to family support services delivering a broad array of assistance, from home visiting programs to parent education programs, to drug and alcohol services, to domestic violence services. This vast community-service apparatus would case manage the complex needs of parents, and thereby allow them to retain custody of vulnerable children. This service system would even cater for "frequently reported families" by offering:

> An integrated case management response to these families ... together with [a] mechanism for identifying new families and for enabling existing families to exit with suitable supports in place.[81]

The objective of the Wood Report was not to ensure more reports were investigated and more children rescued. Consistent with the orthodox advice fed to the inquiry, the report recommended the system be restructured or reoriented so that the vast majority of child protection cases would be dealt with in the family preservation/family support way preferred across the child and family welfare sector. A 2009 report by Allen Consulting Group, which endorsed this style of reform or "redesign" process as the best way to enhance child protection systems, also accurately described the ideological and political dynamics of the sector – or, rather, the scramble to determine how roles and funding are carved up between government and non-government players. The report noted that after consultation with a broad range of stakeholders, it seemed that reorienting child protection systems more strongly around preventive early intervention and family support services "could be perceived by some players in the statutory child protection system as a loss." But it also noted that this position was not broadly representative:

> [it] does not reflect the views of [other] stakeholders consulted for this project who were wholly supportive of this goal. That said, child protection agencies generally see a role for their agency in providing secondary prevention services. This role shift would not necessarily result in a net loss for the organisation. This is opposed to the view of some family support NGO stakeholders and commentators that child protection agencies are not an appropriate organisation for providing support to vulnerable families.[82]

This orthodox view – that the statutory part of the system should shrink and the family support part of the system expand, with NGOs having an enhanced role – triumphed in NSW in the wake of the Wood Report. The NSW government's Keep Them Safe "action plan" raised the threshold for mandatory reports to "risk of significant harm" and created a new reporting and referral pathway system partly along the lines recommended by Wood. To ensure that statutory intervention "only occurs for those children who really need such protection", six new Child Wellbeing Units staffed by child protection specialists were established in six government agencies: Area Health Services and the Children's Hospital at Westmead, NSW Police, and the departments of Education and Training; Housing, Ageing, Disability and Home Care; and Juvenile Justice.[83]

Keep Them Safe shared many similarities with the Victorian Child FIRST dual-track model across the state. The role defined for NSW's Child Wellbeing Units was to help mandatory reporters determine (using a common assessment tool) whether a report meets the risk-of-significant-harm threshold and should be referred to the Helpline for further assessment and investigation. If the report is less serious, it now should be referred to family support and other services that can provide assistance. If the risk of harm is imminent, reporters in these departments can make reports directly to DoCS.

Mandatory reporters outside of these departments and other members of the community continue to make all reports to the centralised Helpline. For political reasons (public-sector union influence and the protection of departmental jobs), complete outsourcing of family support to NGOs was not supported, and DoCS continued to operate its own in-house early-intervention programs. However, funding for NGO family support and other services was significantly boosted, with an additional $300 million over the five-year lifespan of Keep Them Safe earmarked to build the "service capacity of the non-government sector".[84]

The only problem was that the "reforms" did nothing to address the real problem with child protection services in NSW: chronic under-responding to the thousands of frequently reported children hiding in plain sight of the department.

Re-reporting

The introduction of mandatory reporting in NSW in 2000 led to a fourfold increase in reports.[85] Taken at face value, this huge increase supported the notion that mandatory over-reporting had created workload problems for DoCS. Cashmore, Scott, and Calvert claimed that unnecessary reporting accounted for 40% of reports.[86] The Wood Report reached the conclusion that DoCS was receiving "too many reports" because 30% of reports were deemed not to require a statutory investigation under the existing risk-of-harm threshold. This figure was based on a breakdown prepared by the department, which showed that 13% of reports were either trivial or not genuine risk-of-harm reports as defined in the relevant NSW child protection legislation. The commission arrived at the figure of 30% of reports falling into the less-serious category by adding the 17.8% of reports that were closed after an initial assessment or were referred elsewhere for family support and other assistance.[87]

These figures were incomplete. They did not adequately capture what was actually occurring within the system with respect to the seriousness or otherwise of the reports received. The more important statistic was the fact that despite the introduction of mandatory reporting, the increase in reports had not been concentrated in less-serious categories. Since 2000, NSW had recorded little change in the proportion of reports assessed at the Helpline as requiring further assessment by a DoCS caseworker, which had remained relatively constant at around two-thirds of total reports.[88] As the Wood Report noted, the proportion of reports requiring further assessment had increased slightly since 2001, to 69.2% in 2007–08.[89] This represented considerable growth in the number of reports involving children requiring a child protection response.

Most significant of all was the level of re-reporting in NSW. Re-reporting data is a key performance indicator, especially in child protection systems oriented to family preservation–based practice. Re-reports indicate that interventions designed to prevent child abuse and neglect, such as family support and other services, may not have been effective, and concerns about child welfare persist. They also indicate that decisions not to undertake statutory interventions may not have been appropriate, given that child welfare concerns remain unresolved.

Remarkably, detailed annual re-reporting data (showing the number, proportion, and rate of children re-reported in the same year) is not publicly available in any Australian jurisdiction. One can presume it is not published because child protection authorities do not want to draw attention to data that shows the failure of their preferred family preservation approach to dealing with child abuse. The 2007 evaluation of the Victorian Child FIRST system claimed it had been effective because reports had stabilised and substantiations had fallen.

This could have been evidence of a reduction in child abuse, but it could equally have been a function of the dual-pathway system leading to serious cases being missed. Significantly, the evaluation was silent on the crucial issue of re-reports, even though the justification for the reforms was that many families subject to re-reports and re-substantiations were receiving insufficient support.[90]

In NSW, however, re-reporting data was available to the Wood Report, because DoCS was undertaking a special project studying frequently reported families. The data DoCS collected showed approximately 75,000 reports, or a quarter of the 300,000 reports received by DoCS, had concerned an estimated 2,100 families. The data also showed 7,500 families had accounted for approximately 150,000 reports, or nearly half of all reports.[91] In other words, a small proportion of families accounted for the large proportion of reports, due to high levels of re-reporting.

The same 2,100 families had been reported on average more than 35 times each, and the same 7,500 families had been reported on average around 20 times each. In terms of who and what was generating the bulk of DoCS workload, this meant, as the Wood Report explained, that 3% of reported families accounted for a quarter of all reports, and 12% of reported families accounted for half.[92]

The Wood Report also revealed that 59% of reports involved children already known to DoCS in 2007–08, compared to 45% in 2002. And the "percentage of children and young persons who were the subject of a substantiated report in the previous year and were the subject of a further substantiation within the following 12 months (another default KPI) has almost doubled since 2001–02 and increased by about 20% between 2005–06 and 2006–07."[93] In 2006–07, 24% of substantiated reports were in this category, compared to 13% in 2001–02.[94]

We can see, then, that a staggeringly high percentage of reports concerned a relatively small "hard core" of repeatedly reported underclass families. In the following year, 2008–09, 60.6% of reports received by DoCS were re-reports, amounting to an average of 1,600 re-reports each week.[95] The re-reporting figures confounded the image of a system overwhelmed by less-serious reports, which had been endorsed in the final Wood Report. The level of re-reporting also undermined claims that mandatory reporting was inefficient and caused over-reporting.

Since mandatory reporters accounted for around three quarters of all reports in NSW,[96] it was reasonable to presume that a high proportion of re-reports was being made by mandatory reporters. Doctors, nurses, teachers, and police are frequent reporters because their professional duties put them in regular contact with the most disadvantaged communities. Mandatory-reporting regimes were designed to maximise reports and protect as many children as possible through early identification and prompt response by agencies responsible for stopping child abuse and neglect. The NSW re-reporting data suggested that mandatory reporting had succeeded in identifying cases of maltreatment. Through heightened surveillance of an expanding underclass of welfare-dependent dysfunctional families, mass screening had captured increasing levels of parental and family dysfunction and an increased incidence of child maltreatment. What was manifestly lacking, though, in relation to this wealth of information received about child well-being in NSW, was a prompt statutory response by DoCS to ensure child maltreatment ceased.

The re-reporting data showed that the problem in NSW wasn't mandatory over-reporting, but rather that family preservation policy and under-responding to reports of harm had left more children at risk of lifelong damage by chronically abusive or neglectful parents.

The data matched anecdotal accounts by mandatory reporters of the need to report children again, and again, and again to try to get an appropriate response. Mandatory reporters were forced to re-report the same hard core of dysfunctional families 20 and 30 times because no action, or inadequate action, was taken in response to their initial report of serious child health and welfare concerns. As the Wood Report euphemistically noted, there had been "much dissatisfaction expressed to the Inquiry from mandatory reporters that they received no, inadequate or delayed feedback. A frequent response by them to that unhappy situation was to report the same incident repeatedly in an attempt to receive action from DoCS."[97]

In other words, DoCS failed to make the statutory intervention mandatory reporters expected, because the preferred approach was to practice family preservation and provide family support services instead. As a result, reporters felt compelled to keep reporting in an attempt to prompt action they believed necessary and overdue. Because the case-plan goal for these children is to preserve the family, DoCS may classify additional reports as "information only", not even triggering an additional investigation and home visit despite the indication that children are still struggling and maltreatment is continuing or perhaps escalating. Re-reporting data therefore captured the facts that a large number of dysfunctional parents retained custody of their children despite being continually re-reported, and that a large number of vulnerable children were exposed to an increased risk of severe and potentially catastrophic harm because intervention, if it was needed, might never come or come too late.

The problems in NSW also afflict child protection services in all other states and territories. Official inquiries in other jurisdictions have established that more than half (in the Northern Territory) to over two-thirds (in Victoria) of all child safety reports received each year are re-reports of known children already reported in the same or in a previous year.[98] There are also the same accounts of mandatory reporters in other states and territories being forced to report children repeatedly due to the lack of response to initial reports.[99] Since, in 2013–14, mandatory reporters accounted for 65% of all reports that received an investigation nationally,[100] it is also likely that mandatory reporters also make the bulk of re-reports.

While detailed re-reporting data showing precisely how many children are involved in how many re-reports is still not publicly available, the data published by the AIHW shows a significant difference between the number of notifications and the number of children involved. In 2013–14, 198,966 children accounted for the 304,097 notifications received by Australian child protection authorities. This indicates that over one third of all notifications nationally were re-reports of children who were the subject of multiple notifications in the same year. The proportion of repeat reports as a percentage of total reports across the states and territories ranged from 48% in the ACT, 42% in NSW, 39% in the Northern Territory, 35% in South Australia, 35% in Tasmania, 31% in Victoria, 16% in Western Australia, and 13% in Queensland (figure 1).

New national data available for the first time in 2015 has also provided a telling insight into the level of re-reports. Analysis contained in the AIHW's *Child Protection Australia 2013–14* report, for the first time, broke down the number of children subject to a child protection investigation into two categories: "new clients", meaning children who had never previously been the subject of a child protection investigation in a previous year, and "repeat clients", meaning children who had been the subject of a child protection investigation in a previous year. The available data (covering six out of eight jurisdictions excluding Queensland and the Australian Capital Territory) showed that of the 78,980 children who were the subject of an investigation of a child safety notification in 2013–14, only two out of five (38%) were new clients, and three out of five (47,992 children or 61.5%) were repeat clients.[101]

It is ironic, amid so many genuine policy and practice failures, that the part of the child protection system that works well – mandatory reporting – is singled out as a failure by the orthodox account of the system's supposed flaws. Mandatory reporting attracts criticism not because it works poorly, but because it works too well and demonstrates the failure of family preservation.

Official inquiries into public-policy issues should establish the facts and make recommendations based on evidence. Yet, inquiries do not operate in a vacuum and are subject to political influences, including subjective and calculated judgements about what will be acceptable to governments and other stakeholders. Inquiries are also, understandably, susceptible to influence by expert opinion, particularly when the cultural stakes are high and the issues are contentious – as they are in child protection. Due to these factors, the outcome in NSW was that the Wood Report deferred to the orthodox account that child protection services were burdened by over-reporting and that services needed a redesign to reorient them around early intervention family support and prevention – even though the evidence detailed in the final report disputed that account.

The evidence instead showed the system's most serious problem is that there was no adequate statutory child protection response to at least half of all risk-of-harm reports, which had consistently identified and re-identified the most at-risk children in the community. Though having these facts at hand, the Wood inquiry fell into line with the proponents of family preservation and endorsed the ideology that says the system should focus even more heavily on expanded family support services and less on statutory investigation and removal. The recommended cure was a bigger dose of the disease that had infected Australian child protection in the final third of the 20th century.

"Early intervention" and "prevention"

Advocates of a family support–oriented system claim government spending on these services represents an "investment". The claim is that increased support will reduce demand for child protection services by preventing families spiralling into crisis and severe child maltreatment that requires statutory investigation and removal.[102] This is an attractive theory – it promises savings on costly statutory investigations and on the most expensive part of the system: providing government-funded out-of-home care for removed children. But the evidence that family preservation combined with support services can keep children safe at home by transforming the hard core of dysfunctional parents – whose children are most likely to need out-of-home care – into capable parents is weak and unconvincing.

The literature on redesigning child protection services is keen to reassure us that "meta-analyses regarding the results of early intervention typically point to the effectiveness and utility of such programs in addressing identified risks and vulnerabilities."[103] Such opaque statements encourage the belief that family support services are effective, and that increasing access to these services is the key to keeping families intact and better protecting children. But the story that emerges upon closer inspection is far from reassuring.

There is no systematic research to support the effectiveness of the three main types of prevention programs – parent education, home visiting, and preservation programs.[104] The few studies that have been conducted have produced mixed findings on effectiveness, with significant variations across interventions, especially concerning the effect on the dysfunctional families in which child abuse and neglect are concentrated.[105] On top of a range of methodological issues (including the majority of the studies' failure to use rigorous evaluation methods such as randomised control groups), the other problems with the evidence base include:

- Parent education programs are designed to "build capacity" in families by imparting parenting skills and information to participants. At best, studies have found that "strength-based" programs can increase parental knowledge and modify negative parental behaviour, but these studies demonstrate no clear, positive effect on parenting skills.

- Parenting programs have succeeded with well-educated parents. Few programs have been available for severely dysfunctional parents at high risk of seriously maltreating children.

- There is some evidence that home visiting programs may be effective when targeted towards at-risk families, and may have a positive impact on the risk factors associated with child maltreatment. However, most studies of parenting and home visiting programs have measured the process and impact of the intervention on the skills and knowledge of participating parents. Very few have directly measured the key outcomes. Most have not directly examined child health or child protection data to establish if there has been a reduction in child maltreatment.

- Typically, and inexplicably, even the acclaimed Australian Triple P (Positive Parenting Program), which has been the subject of a supposedly rigorous evaluation, "did not include an outcome measure" such as the number of reports of child maltreatment before and after the program. Thus, "it is not clear whether the impact of the program ... would translate to a reduction in the prevalence of child maltreatment."

- Similarly, the evaluation of the Australian Community Child Health Nurse home visiting program for newborns "did not assess the program's impact on the incidence of neglect ... researchers are unable to determine whether these programs achieved more favourable outcomes for children by reducing the occurrence of child maltreatment."[106]

Select studies have directly measured and demonstrated some positive outcomes in reducing child maltreatment. However, important qualifications also apply to these findings. Many of the studies have had small sample sizes and experienced high attrition rates. The studies do not reveal whether short-term benefits were maintained over the longer term, and the results are unreliable because the parents most likely to drop out would be those in greatest need and with the greatest risk of inflicting child neglect and abuse. In other words, the preventive effect may have occurred with only the most easily resolved cases, rather than the hard core of dysfunctional families who should be the target.[107]

Another reservation is that, in general, preventive programs have been shown to have a "modest and short-term" impact.[108] Family preservation services may place at-risk families in a holding pattern by temporarily delaying abuse or neglect, but without ultimately preventing it. When services remove their support, the recurrence of abuse and neglect by dysfunctional parents may be next to inevitable, as entrenched behavioural problems re-emerge. Speculation about the cause of the modest and short-term impact of prevention programs has tended to accentuate the positive. It is suggested that the evidence has yet to show what works because more sustained and intensive interventions than first anticipated are needed to change the established and complex patterns of behaviour that contribute to child maltreatment. Not only does this cast doubt on the alleged cost reductions that come from investment in preservation and prevention; the view that more sustained interventions will produce better results is also underpinned by a "culture of optimism" – an unwarranted belief that dysfunctional people can be transformed into capable parents.

A 2009 US review of the empirical evidence on whether early intervention programs can reduce rates of child abuse and neglect found "limited evidence" that they work,[109] and confirmed earlier evaluations of family support services,[110] which were that early intervention programs fail to substantially reduce child abuse and entries into care. Yet while the existing literature is mostly silent on the factors that limit the success of prevention programs, these reasons are alluded to where it is admitted that strength-based approaches to promoting positive parenting are likely to be ineffective in working with the families most at risk, due to a lack of existing strengths and skills on which to build.[111]

The gap between what these programs promise and deliver is a consequence of overlooking the realities of personal dysfunction and the limits of individual capacity to overcome it. These programs are designed to work with families at the greatest risk of severe neglect, abuse, and child removal. They aim to address the range of behavioural factors that limit some people's ability to parent, establish that the challenges associated with parenting are normal, and ensure children's proper development. For these programs to succeed, entrenched patterns of dysfunctional behaviour have to be undone for the underclass parents whose children are frequently reported and re-reported.

Transforming dysfunctional people into competent parents is extremely difficult, because very often these people have not had appropriate parental role models, may have been permanently damaged by suffering abuse and neglect as a child, and are often dependent on drugs. Estimates are that up to half the families involved in child protection matters include parents with substance-abuse problems.[112] Most have lost or never had the discipline and responsibility associated with regular work, and do not live ordered, well-structured lives.

These members of the underclass lack basic life skills and cannot cope with the normal demands of rearing children. Their own development has been so disturbed, and their lives are so troubled, chaotic, and marred by irresponsibility, that early intervention (initiated once a child has attracted official notice by way of a report) is likely to prove too late to help. For many damaged and dysfunctional parents, their confidence, capabilities, and resilience have been sapped by the destructive behavioural consequences of welfare dependence and associated problems.[113] Prevention programs, especially those that are strength-based, are highly unlikely to transform damaged people into competent parents and make dysfunctional families functional. Such is the terrible truth at the heart of the child protection crisis: dysfunctional people stay damaged, and go on to damage their children.

Reinventing failure

The lack of evidence concerning the effectiveness and impact of family support services on child abuse and neglect has not halted the family preservation juggernaut. Official inquiries continue to recommend greater investment in family support services and to dress it up as an innovative strategy. It is described as a "public health" approach, or "inverting the pyramid", meaning universal and secondary services, such as home visiting, parent education, and skills training, which involve early screening to detect and address the risk factors for child maltreatment, should constitute the bulk of the child protection system.

This flawed take on how best to restructure the system around "prevention and early intervention" – which remains the approach to reform endorsed by the federal government's National Framework[114] – implies that the existing structure is too heavily oriented around statutory intervention, and is too quick to remove children into care instead of supporting families. This is a fallacy. The reality is that family preservation has been standard and mainstream practice for decades. Moreover, family preservation is the root cause of the systemic problems that plague child protection systems across the nation.

The latest inquiry to have recommended "a new framework",

but which actually recommends reinventing the existing failed system, was the 2013 Queensland Child Protection Commission of Inquiry, headed by Tim Carmody QC (the Carmody Report). The Queensland government agreed to implement the Carmody Report's major recommendation and increase spending on prevention and early intervention services to reorient a child protection system that supposedly "focuses too heavily on coercive instead of support strategies".[115] This was despite mounting evidence of the abject failure of the prevention approach.

The 2012 report of the Protecting Victoria's Vulnerable Children Inquiry (the Cummins Report), headed by former Supreme Court judge Philip Cummins, detailed the impact of the redesign project undertaken almost a decade before. This time, re-reporting data was assessed. The Cummins Report established that in 2010–11, 64% of child safety reports in the state were re-reports concerning known children, and this percentage had remained largely the same since 2004–05. Such were the meagre fruits of a decade of operation for the "gold standard" dual-track, family support–oriented Child FIRST system, which was so unsuccessful that the Victorian government had been forced to commission another inquiry into the systemic problems in the state's faltering child protection services.

The Cummins inquiry's damning findings highlighted the failure to deliver the core benefits that had been promised – better prevention of child maltreatment and better-targeted statutory responses to notifications of child harm. The continued high level of re-reporting, along with other measures of lack of success, led the Cummins Report to conclude that "despite increased investment" in family support services, there had been no "marked change in Victoria in the incidence and impact of child abuse or neglect or overall outcomes for vulnerable children taken into out-of-home care."[116]

This conclusion was reinforced by the Victorian auditor-general's 2015 report *Early Intervention Services for Vulnerable Children and Families*, which found that "there has been a significant increase in the number and complexity of the cases being referred" to Child FIRST services, with the implication being that NGOs were meeting demand for what were really families and children in need of a statutory service response.[117] More damning was the finding on the effectiveness of early-intervention family support services:

> There are isolated examples of vulnerable children and families being better supported. However, the department does not know whether the services provided are effectively meeting the needs of vulnerable groups seven years after the establishment of Child FIRST. This is because there are significant limitations in the service performance data and a lack of outcomes monitoring at the system level … The department's monitoring of services focuses on outputs – such as the number of cases and service hours – rather than requiring service providers to show positive outcomes for families. … The department does not have a framework for measuring the effectiveness of services for vulnerable children and families.[118]

It is a similar story in NSW, in the wake of the Wood Report. The evaluation of the NSW Keep Them Safe program released in late 2014 found there had been a reduction in the number of reports in the state. This finding was expected, as the reduction coincided with the change in the reporting threshold to "risk of significant harm". But after the initial decline, "the level of reporting has remained the same for non-aboriginal children and slightly increased for aboriginal children." In other words, the investment in early intervention appeared not to have prevented abuse and neglect, if this was measured by the children continuing to enter the statutory part of the system. This was because the expected longer-term reduction in reports "has not happened."[119]

Moreover, the evaluation found that more than half the children reported to be at risk of significant harm (ROSH) "are still re-reported within 12 months", and 60% of reported Aboriginal children and 75% of reported non-Aboriginal children "are not seen by a case worker."[120] Not only had the investment in prevention failed to deliver a reduction in child abuse, but the promise of more statutory investigations for children in crisis situations had not been realised. Only a quarter of the more than 98,000 ROSH reports that were made had received an investigation involving a face-to-face visit, meaning fewer children were seen by caseworkers than before the Wood inquiry.[121]

The evidence from Victoria and NSW is compelling, and is a warning that it is futile for all jurisdictions to continue to reinvent the same failed approach. But evidence alone – even compelling evidence of the systemic failure of large-scale, well-resourced redesign projects in two major jurisdictions – does not seem to be enough to force reassessment of the dominant ideology favouring family preservation and end the marginalisation of the traditional child rescue approach to child protection services.

This is not surprising: a propensity not to notice the evidence of failure that contradicted the prevailing ideology, had dogged the NSW "reform" process. The Wood Report had observed that in NSW, three quarters of children who had been the subject of a substantiated finding of neglect or risk of neglect did not enter care, and that "even fewer entered care" in cases of psychological harm, physical harm, sexual harm, and risk of harm. "The question as to what happened to these children and young persons is important and largely remains unanswered,"[122] said the report. But the evidence of the "system abuse" visited on children due to lack of statutory investigation, and delayed statutory removal as a last resort, was hardly difficult to find – it was lying in DoCS' own case files.

In January 2009, some months before the announcement of Keep Them Safe, the NSW Ombudsman answered the question of what happens to children left in harm's way in the name of family preservation. A case-study review of children aged 10 to 14 in out-of-home care detailed the damaging impact of under-responding to child abuse and neglect:

> For many of the children with extensive care and protection histories, the child protection case work goal in their earlier years was to support the family to retain the care of the child. This was attempted through a range of casework intervention strategies, including the provision of family support and restoration following periods of care. However, some of the children we reviewed who were reported early in their lives, initially received limited assessment and/or support.
>
> Significantly, of the nine children identified as having high needs at the time of our review, eight had extensive care and protection histories. The ninth child – who had severe developmental delay and autism – did not have an extensive care and protection history but on the basis of assessment on his entry into care, should have.
>
> For these eight children, the evidence from our reviews demonstrates that the focus on family preservation and reunification has meant that they have experienced high levels of adversity and disadvantage. Now in middle childhood and receiving extensive support, it is difficult to see how some will move through adolescence without further significant problems. In this regard, it is relevant to note that those children we reviewed who were initially reported to DoCS at age one or younger, were more likely to have additional needs – such as developmental delay, mental-health issues or educational issues – in middle childhood than the group as a whole.[123]

These findings are consistent with a range of similar studies that also reveal the type of history shared by large numbers of damaged children in care in Australia (see Chapter 4, "System Abuse"). Evidence such as this, which demonstrates the lifelong effects of abuse and neglect on children who could have and should have been rescued but were not, should be enough to change child protection policy and practice. But it is not.

Tragically, ideological commitment is not the only thing that blinds, deafens, and closes minds to the evidence of the fundamental problem – the damage done to children by prolonged efforts to achieve family preservation. That traditional child rescue has continued to be marginalised, and the best interests of children set aside, is also due to the politics and vested interests of the child and family welfare social-services sector.

3

Advocacy: The Political Economy of Child Abuse

Bottom feeders

There is nothing wrong with family support services, in principle. Supporting struggling families always has been, and always should be, part of modern child protection services. In many circumstances, it can be appropriate to give parents an opportunity to address the behaviours that compromise child welfare before making decisions about statutory removal. But family support services become problematic, and harmful to children, when in too many instances they involve a prolonged and futile quest to fix unfixable families.

There is also nothing wrong with outsourcing family support services to NGOs, in principle. The family and community service departments that grew and grew as social work became a professionalised government responsibility in the 1970s crowded out the philanthropic and charitable community organisations that had traditionally assisted families. These departments were (and still are) plagued by the waste and other problems typically found in heavily unionised, politically-cosseted public-sector bureaucracies. Since the mid-1980s, the recommended policy response to government social-service failures has been to outsource the delivery of social services to NGOs. But outsourcing has proved problematic in the child and family welfare social-services sector because the tail has been allowed to wag the dog, and the political influence NGOs wield contributes significantly to the continued marginalisation of child rescue.

Yesterday's solution has become today's problem. The theory

was that outsourcing would be a more efficient and cost-effective approach that would infuse taxpayer-funded programs with the volunteer ethic of the charitable sector. In practice, the culture of the bureaucracy has infected the charitable sector, which has become top-heavy, distracted from its mission, and dependent upon government financial support.[124] According to the economist Henry Ergas, the attempt to revitalise civil society has empowered "self-appointed, but taxpayer-funded, guardians of the public interest, whose only difference from other rentiers is that they are more vocal and intransigent."[125] This is especially true regarding child protection, as the experiment with outsourcing has created new political complications that frustrate sound reforms, work against the balanced provision of statutory and family support services, determine policy, and distort funding priorities in ways that impede effective child protection.

To understand the role NGOs play as institutional impediments to reform, consider this counterfactual. What would happen if child protection authorities undertook statutory interventions to rescue the thousands of most vulnerable, frequently re-reported children, via early removal and preferably by means of adoption? Not only would eliminating a substantial proportion of child protection reports significantly reduce the demands on the statutory part of the system, there would also be less justification for using taxpayers' money to provide family support and other counselling services to dysfunctional parents in the name of protecting children from harm. There would be less need for the services NGOs provide, and possibly less need for the NGOs themselves.

NGOs thus have a vested interest in family preservation, which we see in the NGO sector's strong support for dual-track reporting systems. When NGOs and peak organisations advocate for this model, they are lobbying for the future of their own services, given that millions of dollars in program funding are at stake. Dependence on taxpayer funding also means NGOs do not contradict the orthodox departmental line on removal only as a last resort. Due to fear that funding may be withdrawn, most NGOs would hesitate to criticise the departmental culture of inadequate intervention in family situations, and are reluctant to draw attention to faults in the system that compromise child welfare. This is how the organisations that should be an independent voice advocating for children's best interests are silenced.

Such are the brutal realities of the political economy of child abuse and neglect, and of the multibillion-dollar child and family welfare services "industry". The NGOs, alongside academics, social workers, and other members of the "helping" professions in general, work to shape the system to suit their interrelated ideological and institutional agendas.

The relevant peak NGO lobby group in NSW, the Association of Children's Welfare Agencies, endorsed the main recommendations of the Wood Report and the major thrust of the Keep Them Safe program.[126] This was hardly a disinterested contribution to the debate on child protection policy, given the financial windfall at stake. Of the $750 million allocated by the NSW government to fund the roll-out of Keep Them Safe, 40% ($300 million over five years) was earmarked for NGOs as part of the redesign intended to provide additional family support services to families in need and to deal with reports assessed as less serious.[127] Little wonder that the NGO sector in NSW enthusiastically welcomed Keep Them Safe for making child protection services a "shared responsibility."[128]

Child protection is ripe with opportunities for "bottom-feeding" activities: benefiting from the misfortunes of those on the lowest rungs of society. Key stakeholders and their attendant political considerations drive government decisions to undertake flawed "reform" initiatives that exacerbate existing defects in policy and practice. The (perhaps unconscious) desire of NGOs to see the services they offer continue to be needed, and to receive funding, is put before the interests of abused and neglected children who would benefit if permanently removed from dysfunctional parents. Moreover, NGOs also benefit from funding flows for outsourced out-of-home care services when damaged children end up requiring long-term care placements.

The vested interests of the "Big Welfare" lobby – the child and family welfare social services sector – compromise child protection. Many readers will find this argument difficult to believe. A likely response, especially by those unfamiliar with the workings of government, will be that the role "politics" is said to play in determining child protection policy must be overstated. Surely this can't be correct, given we are talking about saving children? The following case study from Victoria suggests that my account of the politics of the sector is hardly exaggerated.

The message has been heard

Keep Them Safe in NSW was modelled on the Child FIRST dual-track reporting system that had been implemented in Victoria. Child FIRST had been widely praised as the best system in the country, and the model for other states to follow.[129] But the Victorian system did not deserve this acclaim.

The one certain but unintended benefit of the dual-track model is that, once implemented, the excuses routinely used to explain away child protection failures lose validity. Authorities no longer have the excuse that they are flooded with less-serious reports that distract them from responding to reports concerning those children in greatest need. Prompted by numerous complaints about the performance of the Victorian equivalent of DoCS, the Department of Human Services (DHS), in 2009 the Victorian Ombudsman undertook an own-motion investigation into child protection services. The Ombudsman's damning report found that streaming child safety notifications and pouring resources into family support services had failed to improve the statutory response to the most serious cases.[130]

Only a quarter of notifications to the DHS were found to have received an investigation, because selective screening was used to eliminate reports and many cases were closed prematurely despite warranting further investigation. Of the notifications singled out for further attention, 20% of the children were still not allocated a caseworker, and no investigation was conducted.[131] Review of the quality of the department's work also uncovered other shortcomings in "core practices for ensuring the safety and wellbeing of children."[132] These included lack of timely follow-up, inadequate investigations, and failures to sight children.[133] In a number of cases the Ombudsman reviewed, the department had not intervened and the interests of children were not protected.[134] Children were left in situations in which the risk of harm was unacceptable,[135] leading, in some cases, to assault, serious injury, and death.[136]

The Ombudsman's report was highly significant: its findings indicated that the redesigned Victorian system was a dead end, not a shining light, in terms of improving child protection policy. The serious gaps and defects identified in the Victorian system were virtually identical to those identified in the NSW system by the NSW Ombudsman.[137]

To underline the point, under-responding continued despite the dual-track Child FIRST system. Only a quarter of "significant harm" reports were investigated in 2008–09. Another major problem identified was the impact of the raised mandatory-reporting threshold, which meant that many streamed notifications assessed as less serious and allocated to family support services turned out to be genuine child protection cases concerning children in crisis situations or suffering serious cumulative harm due to chronic neglect. Some Victorian NGOs had found themselves in the same position as other reporters, discovering that reporting and then re-reporting children failed to prompt the appropriate statutory response.[138]

The independent scrutiny of the Victorian Ombudsman identified the real problems with the Victorian system – the huge gaps in core statutory services and practices. But rational analysis did not lead to rational policy solutions. The findings were swept aside and policy outcomes were subverted by interest group–driven politics. The Victorian NGO lobby, which ostensibly defends the best interests of disadvantaged children, sabotaged the policy review process initiated by the Ombudsman.

In the lead-up to the release of the Ombudsman's report, the Victorian Centre for Excellence in Child and Family Welfare sent an email addressed to "All Member CEOs". The Centre for Excellence, formerly the Child Welfare Association of Victoria, is the peak lobby group for 93 community service organisations in the child, youth, and family services sector of Victoria, including Anglicare and the Brotherhood of St Laurence. Here is an excerpt from the email:

> Over the last few weeks, the Centre has been involved in a range of activity relating to the pending Ombudsman's Report (anticipated date of release Thursday Nov 26) ... Over the past two weeks, supported by the Board and member CEOs external to the Board, the Centre has had the opportunity to discuss the pending Ombudsman's Report with the Premier's Senior Policy advisor, [the] Minister, [and Shadow Minister], DHS and Editor-in-Chief of The Age. I am also aware of discussions held with the Editor-in-Chief of the Herald Sun and we are still aiming to talk with some radio media. Further to this the Centre along with a number of key sector representatives also participated in a Round Table Forum to be published in The Age this week.
>
> Primarily our key message has been focussed on prevention,

early intervention, the need for more family services and not expanding mandatory reporting.

A strategy that was also developed was to place a paid advertisement in both The Age & Herald Sun—an invitation to participate was circulated over a week ago and resulted in about 25 organisations 'signing up.' The advertisement was to appear early this week however after further consideration this is no longer going to take place. The advertisement was aimed at demonstrating to government the views of a large number of CSOs—designed as a letter to the Premier. At the end of last week through the strategic sharing of the planned advertisement a number of conversations continued. Consideration of the letter as an appropriate strategy continued until late last week when in brief it was determined by those individual CSOs who had initiated the letter and the Centre Board that continuation with the strategy was 'redundant for now'—the message had been heard by Government and the Centre will now continue to work on the heightened level of interest to pursue our key points.

Next month the Board is anticipating that [the Director of DHS] will be attending the December Board meeting and a request to meet with the Premier and Treasurer has been issued. As you may recall last year the Centre was successful in meeting with the Treasurer, which greatly supported our then Budget Campaign. The timing is right for us to repeat this. An early morning briefing on the day the report is released with the Centre is anticipated and we will issue media comments accordingly to positively influence the debate on behalf of members.[1]

The uninitiated might think the Centre for Excellence is an independent think tank or university research unit. It is anything but

---

[1] Several minor corrections have been made to this text to avoid overuse of "sic" as a marker for mistakes that appeared in the original.

that. The email detailed the centre's efforts to "positively influence the debate on behalf of members", with the lobbying undertaken spanning the Victorian government, the opposition, senior policy advisers, the Victorian Department of Human Services, and the media. A key paragraph in the email is the one that states, "our key message has been focused on prevention, early intervention, the need for more family services and not expanding mandatory reporting." In policy terms, the message delivered to the government was that the failed dual-track system must not be tampered with by expanding the scope of traditional child protection work, including lowering the mandatory-reporting threshold.

The email also detailed the centre's media strategy, the first arm of which was to bring together friendly experts in a forum that generated the desired media splash by warning of the potential dangers of creating new Stolen Generations.[139] However, the most telling section is the explanation for why the second arm of the media strategy – a newspaper advertisement in the form of a letter to the premier signed by 25 member organisations – was "redundant for now." The "strategic sharing of the planned advertisement" had paid off. The ad was pulled, the email explains, because "the message had been heard by Government." The Victorian government pre-emptively caved in to the lobbyist's tactics to avoid criticism and embarrassing headlines.

The subject of better protecting the most vulnerable children – on whose behalf one would think that children's charities ought to be advocating – failed to feature in the centre's missive. Instead, the focus was on ensuring that charities retained current funding and on parlaying the influence achieved over the government into bigger budget allocations.

The email suggested the leadership of the DHS was working closely with the NGOs. So much for proper governance.

The contribution to the policy debate by the public official whose statutory role is to provide an independent voice for children, the Victorian child safety commissioner, was to repeat the orthodox claims and blame the problems on less-serious reports swamping the department.[140] So much for robust accountability.

The email from the Centre for Excellence was placed in the hands of the opposition, but the response was silence. So much for parliamentary scrutiny.

When the Ombudsman's report was released, the Victorian government issued a barrage of media releases about the extra millions of taxpayers' dollars it planned to throw at the flawed system.[141] So much for evidence-based policy.

Big welfare

One of the strategies proposed to restore the role of traditional child rescue within child protection systems, and to break the connection between family preservation and the interests of "Big Welfare" social-services departments and NGOs, is to create stand-alone child protection agencies. The thinking behind this is that, ideally, these agencies would be staffed and led by child protection specialists, and be responsible for rigorously assessing and investigating child harm reports to determine if statutory removal of children is required. These stand-alone agencies would also operate as the lead agency for coordinating, supervising, and monitoring the response to child protection matters. This would include buying in targeted support services, if appropriate, to assist parents with their problems, based on best-practice decisions concerning the family situation and the needs of children.

A stand-alone Child Safety Department was established in Queensland as recommended by an extensive 2004 report by the Crime and Misconduct Commission.[142] But the forces of Big Welfare are resistant to change, wield considerable influence over their political masters, and are strategically positioned inside the bureaucracy and the political beltway to stymie reforms that are contrary to their own interests and predilections. The major thrust of the 2004 Queensland reforms was eventually reversed when in mid-2009 the state government announced that the Child Safety Department was to be placed back under the control of the Department of Communities.[143]

The additional institutional obstacle to reform is the extent to which NGOs with ready access to the media and politicians' offices and advisors drive policy formation. As in other policy areas, many ministers and shadow ministers and their offices confuse inclusive and consultative policymaking with thinking it is their job to satisfy the key stakeholders in their portfolio. To achieve leverage over child protection policymaking, peak NGO organisations conduct intensive lobbying campaigns – often in the midst of another headline-making child protection scandal – that repeat the major orthodox untruths about the problems in the system. In doing so, they make numerous promises about the benefits of a family support-oriented system, which fly in the face of the evidence and are based on the myths that serve their own agendas.

Part of the reason lobbyists' claims are not properly scrutinised is that oppositions are always looking for easy ways to embarrass governments in complex policy areas. They are prone to listen to the largest and loudest stakeholders, and to defer to the NGOs by uncritically recycling what they are told about the need for more government funding for outsourced family support services. The result is that much government and opposition commentary and policy resembles a press release from the peak lobby groups, especially in crises, when politicians invariably default to the standard spin about doing more to support families.

Politicians who support a family preservation–based approach also avoid having to address the difficult systemic issues that surround frontline child protection work, such as adoption. They keep the loudest and best-organised voices in the debate happy, and minimise negative and critical media coverage that entertaining unorthodox thoughts would generate.

This style of politically risk-averse and stakeholder-driven policymaking ensures that child protection policy remains captured by an iron pentagon – between academia, bureaucracy, social workers, the NGO sector, and politicians. The governmentalisation of child protection since the 1970s has centralised not only power over the system but also control of knowledge about the way it should (or should not) be run. A dearth of informed debate is the result, and myths such as those about over-reporting fill the vacuum. Few individuals or groups are actively engaged in genuine advocacy on behalf of the children in greatest need.

The politics of moral embarrassment also hang heavily over child protection policymaking. There is a powerful perception that the current failings of the child protection system are small mercies, given the harm past practices did to removed children and their families. Those who endorse the alternatives to family preservation will inevitably confront the accusation that adoption from care will repeat past mistakes associated with forced adoption and the Stolen Generations.

Separation from birth parents can undeniably cause pain. There is no doubting the seriousness of breaking the bond between parent and child, which is fundamental to personal identity and sense of belonging. But when framed by the legacy of historic malpractices, the debate about child protection policy mainly occurs on another plane removed from on-the-ground realities, which include unsatisfactory outcomes for children. It is inadequately appreciated, in the many scandals involving child protection services, that there are worse things than separating children and parents. What's worse is that children are being abused and neglected while the massed ranks of the child and family social services sector hesitate at the front door of the family home.

To say that children may die, be injured, or endure long-term neglect while veritably surrounded by a host of family support workers is no exaggeration. Professor Chris Goddard, director of Child Abuse Prevention Research Australia, and Joe Tucci, chief executive of the Australian Childhood Foundation, have pointed out that in the name of family preservation, dysfunctional parents "can have drug and alcohol workers, domestic violence workers, mental health workers, homelessness workers, family support workers" – every conceivable service except a skilled child protection worker to monitor the family situation in the best interests of children.[144]

The maltreatment industry

Despite the wealth of family support services available and the difficulty mandatory reporters face in triggering a home visit or statutory intervention, the Big Welfare lobby claims that child protection services in Australia are unbalanced *in favour of statutory intervention*. The argument is that funding for allegedly less-costly early intervention and prevention services is insufficient because resources are inefficiently allocated across statutory, family support, and out-of-home care services. High spending on the out-of-home care part of the system is especially singled out, to indicate that the system too heavily focuses on statutory intervention and too little on helping families before they reach crisis and children need to be removed. These claims might sound logical based on the numbers alone – based on the relevant data on growth in the size and cost of the care system – but these claims, and the statistics, require close scrutiny.

The strong growth in the number of children in care in all Australian jurisdictions in the last decade and half is the most revealing single fact about the state of child protection systems across the country. As these systems are oriented, and increasingly so, around services designed to prevent removals into care, they have failed their own test of effectiveness. This failure is obscured by the claim that systems are supposedly focused on a "1960s model of child removal". This is the meta-myth of the child protection debate.

This myth draws its strength from failure. The higher the number of children in care, the more relevant it appears to be, and the more attractive "investing" in supposedly lower-cost preventive services is to misinformed politicians faced with paying for the ever-rising cost of care amid limited budgets and competing priorities. Who wouldn't want to hear there are cheaper ways to keep children safe at home? But the truth is that the numbers in care have increased despite spending more on family support, and the care system has ultimately cost more due to the damaging impact of family preservation on child welfare.

The total number of children across Australia who are unable to live safely with their parents and require government-subsidised out-of-home care has doubled since the year 2000. On 30 June 2014, 43,009 children were in care nationally, up from 18,241 children nationally in 2000–01. All states and territories recorded strong increases, ranging from 84% in Tasmania to an astonishing 454% in the Northern Territory (figure 2). The increase in the total number of children in care has continued to far exceed population growth, with the national per capita rate of children in care rising to 8.1 per 1,000 population in 2013, from 3.9 in 2001 (figure 3). This reflects an increase of more than 135% in the national out-of-home care population since 2001.

Understandably, given the rising number of children in care, total real (adjusted for inflation) spending on care has also continued to increase in all jurisdictions since 2000–01. South Australia (455%) and Queensland (389%) lead, with Victoria recording the smallest increase, still substantial at 161% (figure 4). Total real national out-of-home care expenditure has more than tripled, increasing by 272% and rising by over $1.5 billion, from just under $600 million in 2001 to over $2 billion in 2013. Growth in the cost of out-of-home care has far exceeded the still substantial growth in real cost of statutory services (179.4% since 2001), which topped $1.1 billion in 2013–14 (figure 5). Only in Western Australia and Tasmania have spending on statutory services grown faster than spending on out-of-home care.

However, growth in spending on "intensive family support services" has far exceeded the growth in spending on statutory services and out-of-home care. During the last decade, all Australian jurisdictions have established programs targeting families deemed at imminent risk of child removal. State and territory community service departments usually outsource provision of these services to NGOs. The services, designed to keep families intact by providing extra assistance, are meant to be a less-costly alternative to out-of-home care – by avoiding the need to remove children from families. As their name suggests, the development of these intensive services constitutes an intensified commitment to the principle of family preservation in the cases of children who otherwise might have been removed. In practice, this commitment pushes child removal further into the background as an even more distant last resort.

Between 2001 and 2014, national expenditure on intensive family support services grew by 312%, at a higher rate than spending on out-of-home care (271.7%) and statutory services (179.4%). Efforts to keep children with their families have intensified despite the great risk of severe and permanent harm to children that staying in a neglectful or abusive family poses, and despite "the lack of good quality research about the effectiveness of family preservation services."[145] In all jurisdictions except South Australia and Queensland, real expenditure on intensive family preservation services has grown faster than spending on either statutory or out-of-home care services. However, all jurisdictions have recorded substantial real increases – more than 200% in each case – in spending in this segment of the child protection system. Some of the increases recorded since 2001 have been extraordinary – 1795.9% in Tasmania and 1081.2% in Victoria (figure 6).

Over this 2001–2014 period, across Australia the proportion of child protection spending consumed by out-of-home care services, compared to statutory and intensive family preservation services, has remained above 50%. This share has increased by just over nine percentage points from 2000–01, to reach 60% in 2013. Over the same period, the proportion of spending on statutory services has fallen to 32% in 2013–14, down from 39% in 2000–01. The proportion of child welfare spending consumed by intensive family preservation services has increased from 7% to 8% (figure 7).

If the significant investment in extended efforts to achieve family preservation were successful and had kept more children safely at home, the expectation would be that these proportions of spending might have changed more, with intensive family preservation services representing a high proportion of total costs due to its beneficial impact in substantially reducing out-of-home care spending.

This is not to say spending is incorrectly distributed. Since 2011, the AIHW has been publishing expenditure data (excluding South Australia) for early intervention and prevention "family support services". Nationally, in 2013–14, more than $375 million was spent by the states and territories on early intervention and prevention services. When this is combined with the $300 million spent nationally on "intensive family preservation services" it changes the relative proportions of spending across the system.

The expenditure explicitly devoted to all forms of family preservation services currently consumes 17% of the $4 billion national expenditure on child protection compared to statutory intervention (29%) and out-of-home care (54%) (figure 8). In 2013–14, the Northern Territory spent the highest proportion (27%) of total spending on child protection on family preservation-focused services. The NT was closely followed by Victoria (24%), then NSW (18%) and Tasmania (16%). South Australia (6%) and ACT (7%) spent the smallest proportions of their child protection budget on family preservation services, along with Western Australia (13%) and Queensland (12%).

It needs to be noted that these figures understate actual spending on services that provide support for struggling families. This is because the leading edge of contemporary statutory child protection practice is focused on working with families and case-managing problem parents to achieve family preservation. The same applies to many services officially classified as out-of-home care, which focus on reuniting children and parents.

The new data that shows the high level of spending on all forms of family support services makes more explicit what we already knew about the official emphasis on practicing family preservation. But do different levels of spending on family support and preservation explain variations across jurisdictions such as different growth rates in the number of children in care? Victoria, for example, spends a higher proportion of its child protection budget on family support and preservation than NSW, and the number of children in care has not grown as fast. Yet the number of children in care in Victoria has "only" increased by 100% (compared to 134% in NSW) since 2000–01.

Rather than the higher proportion of spending on family support and preservation, the more likely explanation for the relatively smaller increase in the number of children in care in Victoria is probably the state's smaller Indigenous population and lack of remote communities compared to other states and territories. That the number of children in care has kept growing strongly in Victoria should also be interpreted in light of the findings of the Cummins Report, which, to repeat, could find no evidence that "increased investment" in family support services had a positive impact on "the incidence and impact of child abuse or neglect or overall outcomes for vulnerable children taken into out-of-home care." [146] This is striking evidence that greater spending on a more elaborate family support service system amounts to throwing good money after bad.

The policy significance of the distribution of spending across the child protection system needs to be emphasised. High and growing spending on family support and preservation services is consistent with the orthodox policy advice provided to governments by the overwhelming majority of social-work academics and NGOs. These figures on spending show that orthodox policy advice has gained traction but has not produced the promised results, especially in terms of reducing out-of-home care expenditure.

The increase in spending on family support has failed to produce the promised return on the investment in so-called alternatives to statutory and out-of-home care services, because the entire cost of the child protection system is growing, including the cost of statutory and out-of-home care services. The plain fact is that if family support and preservation doesn't work and fails to keep children safe at home, spending more on it will never substantially rebalance spending across the system by reducing spending on out-of-home care.

One indicator of the real and perverse impact of higher spending on family preservation is the rate of "re-substantiations". "Substantiation" is the technical term for a proven case of child abuse and neglect. A report of risk of child harm is said to be substantiated if an investigation by child protection caseworkers establishes that maltreatment has occurred. "Re-substantiation" is when a subsequent risk-of-harm report about the same child is also found to be proven, following an additional investigation.

Re-substantiations data is significant because it suggests the investments that have been made in family preservation may be extending the time some children spend experiencing abuse and neglect in the family home, as well as adding to the statutory investigation caseload while ultimately ending with child removal despite extended efforts to avoid that outcome.

Nationally, the number of children subject to a re-substantiated finding of abuse or neglect within 12 months increased by 119% between 2001–01 and 2012–13 (latest year available), from 3,607 children in 2000–01 to 7,902 in 2012–13 (figure 9). Performance across the states and territories has varied over the period (figure 10):

- In South Australia, the proportion of re-substantiations after 12 months fell, but over a fifth of children are still having cases of abuse and neglect re-substantiated within 12 months.
- In Queensland, re-substantiations after 12 months also fell slightly, but almost 20% of all children were still re-substantiated in 2012–13.
- In Victoria, re-substantiations fell, but 13% of children were still the subject of a re-substantiated finding of abuse or neglect within 12 months in 2012–13.

In most other jurisdictions, there were significant increases in the proportion of children experiencing repeat, proven abuse and neglect within 12 months:

- In New South Wales, the proportion of re-substantiations has doubled, from 11% to over 22%.
- In Western Australia, re-substantiations also rose, from 9% to 13%.
- In Tasmania, re-substantiations have increased from 8% to 22%.
- In the ACT, re-substantiations have more than doubled to over 28%.

- In the Northern Territory, the proportion of re-substantiations has tripled, with over 22% of children having reports of harm re-substantiated within 12 months.

Only recently (since 2012–13) has the AIHW reported the proportion of children who were the subject of multiple substantiations in the year. In 2013–14, there were 54,438 substantiated findings of child abuse and neglect nationally, and almost 1 in 5 children who had a report of abuse or neglect substantiated were the subject of more than one substantiation. This means that 20% of the 40,844 children subject to a substantiation were also the subject of repeat findings of abuse and neglect. Rates varied across the states, with the proportion of children subject to two or more substantiations being highest in NSW (38.5%). This compared to re-substantiation rates of 23.5% in ACT, 19.2% in South Australia, 14.1% in Northern Territory, 9.9% in Queensland, 9.3% in Tasmania, 6.7% in Western Australia, and 4.7% in Victoria (figure 11).[147]

Re-substantiation data is almost certainly an underestimate, given the gaps in statutory practice that see large numbers of reports and re-reports not receiving an investigation. Nevertheless, like the re-reporting data, the high levels of re-substantiations recorded suggest family preservation generates significant demand for statutory services. The amount of repeat demand increases the cost of statutory services, and makes it harder to provide sufficient resources to undertake full and proper statutory responses to all reports. Caseloads would be more manageable, and the perpetual shortages of frontline caseworkers would be alleviated, if early and permanent removal and adoption were standard practice in hard-core cases. Significantly reducing the demand placed on the system from re-reports, early removal would allow a higher percentage of reports (ideally 100%) to receive a proper investigation including a home visit.

The increasing size, scale, and cost of the care system also indicate that record numbers of children are still ending up in care despite high levels of spending on family support services. Moreover, spending on care is increasing because of the increasing number of damaged children in care and the increasing length of time they spend there. It is not that the system removes children into care too quickly that drives expense and complexity up, but rather leaving them with abusive and neglectful families too long, which causes greater damage and generates a need for additional services to help children recover from the effects of maltreatment.

High levels of spending on family support are a bad investment because they have the perverse effect of prolonging the time children suffer abuse and neglect in the family home, after which they languish in unstable care placements while awaiting attempted family reunions (see Chapter 4, "System Abuse").

The data suggests that Australian governments spend more than 50% of a growing child protection budget on out-of-home care services not despite spending at least a fifth of that budget on family preservation-based support services, but because of it. Ever-larger sums are being spent on family support and preservation without it yielding the promised reductions in demand for statutory and out-of-home care services – because Australian child protection authorities refuse to face up to the failure of family preservation.

Too much is spent on every part of the child protection system because there is too little early removal and adoption. There is too much family support, too much out-of-home care, and there are too many reports, because there is not enough of the right thing. Children are not removed from unfixable families in a timely fashion, and these children are not provided with safe and stable adoptive families.

The pejorative term "industry" is used to describe an area of government activity that generates its own reason for being and thrives off policy failure. A damaged child who requires out-of-home care and additional therapeutic services until they are 18 is a lucrative proposition for NGOs delivering outsourced care services, and literally represents hundreds of thousands of dollars of funding over a period of multiple years. Barnardos has estimated that if a three-year-old was adopted rather than stay in care until 18, the saving to the NSW government would be over half-a-million dollars.[148] Child maltreatment in Australia is a multibillion-dollar growth industry that provides middle-class employment and lifestyles for many who are fortunate enough to live off the Big Welfare system while entrenching disadvantage in those on the lowest rung of society.

The political economy of child abuse and neglect, and the institutional framework that permits and perpetuates child maltreatment, rests on left-wing ideological foundations that are an affront to common sense, defy basic community standards, and defend the indefensible. Yet these highly questionable foundations have proved remarkably resilient, in part because few on the Right, with some notable exceptions, have been willing to challenge the ideology that sustains the institutional status quo.

The Left and the "right" to drug-addicted parenting

In 2005, the House of Representatives Standing Committee on Family and Human Services conducted an inquiry into adoption in Australia that found adoption was being underused to provide safe and stable alternative families for children who could not safely live with their parents. Based on the international evidence comparing adoption to family preservation and foster care, the inquiry concluded that at-risk children who are removed early, speedily, and permanently have better outcomes than children who are removed later and cycled through multiple temporary foster placements and failed family reunions. Adoption for child protection purposes promotes child welfare because, as studies have shown, it produces better outcomes for abused and neglected children by providing them with the certainty and stability of a permanent family.[149]

The committee's conclusion, together with the recommendation that greater use be made of adoption from care, implicitly criticised state and territory child protection authorities for over-relying on family preservation as the primary response to child abuse and neglect. In 2007, the chair of the adoption inquiry and of a subsequent inquiry into the war on drugs, Liberal MP Bronwyn Bishop, made national headlines when she called for the children of drug addicts whose parents' drug use is the subject of a child protection report to be removed permanently and put up for adoption.[150] Bishop told the ABC's *Four Corners* program the evidence from both inquiries showed child protection authorities paid only lip service to the "mantra that everything is done in the best interests of the child." Bishop argued that not only did a permissive, non-judgemental attitude pervade the way drug-addicted parenting was viewed, but the application of a strict "biology-first principle" ruled out the option of adoption.[151]

The truth of Bishop's claims was borne out when, appearing on the same program, the Victorian child safety commissioner defended the sector and justified current practices that put parental rights before children's interests. He told *Four Corners* that parents' drug use need not lead to permanent family break-up, because some people who used drugs could be better parents than non-users. This confused the real issue and raised the obvious question: what about when parenting was the worse for drug use? But the commissioner maintained that because "there is nothing in my experience worse than a child who's sentenced to be without their parents for the rest of their lives ... we need to work with families to make them the proper place for children to be raised."[152] Significantly, the minority report by Labor members of the war on drugs inquiry expressed similar concerns about the view that "addiction alone should determine whether a child is separated from their parent".[153]

The foray into the cultural politics of child protection by a significant figure on the right of Australian politics was subsequently critiqued by the left-wing orthodoxy that dominates the standard literature in the field. In an article published in June 2009, in the *Australian Journal of Politics and History*, three academics and leading anti-adoption activists, Kate Murphy, Marian Quartly, and Denise Cuthbert accused those who frowned on drug-addled parenting of supporting the "conservative family policy of the Howard era."[154]

In the context of families that are the subject of child protection concerns, substance abuse profoundly impairs parenting ability. Substance abusers are also highly prone to relapse. Given these two realities, there are good grounds for earlier and decisive statutory intervention to stop child maltreatment by parents who abuse alcohol and illicit drugs.[155]

Murphy, Quartly, and Cuthbert's exercise in cultural politics and minimisation of a serious social problem would have been bad enough if it only reflected the dated ideology pervading the sector, which is that removing children punishes poor parents who are helpless victims of impersonal social forces and structural socio-economic injustice. But the authors' views did not merely faithfully reflect the Big Welfare orthodoxy that the best way to keep vulnerable children safe is to construct a vast social-service system to assist dysfunctional parents. They also expressed the major themes of the rights-obsessed culture that has developed since the social revolution of the 1960s, which has debased personal responsibility and elevated self-fulfilment above traditional social obligations, especially in relation to family life.

The idea that personal behaviour shouldn't be judged in the context of the family first applied to marriage and child-rearing. The traditional expectation that people get married before having children and stay married for the sake of the children was culturally enforced by frowning on and stigmatising certain behaviours deemed antisocial, such as pre-marital sex, ex-nuptial births, and cohabitation.

This expectation has withered in an age when divorce, de facto relationships and single motherhood are socially accepted as realities of modern, diverse, and "progressive" society.

New social ethics have underpinned the non-judgementalism that is the key feature of contemporary social work, and have profoundly undermined effective child protection. This is most starkly illustrated by the extension of non-judgemental attitudes to parental drug abuse. There is a big difference between a professional de facto couple that smokes marijuana recreationally and a single mother who is addicted to heroin or ice. Yet the social-work fraternity deems all families equal regardless of the relative circumstances, and considers it "conservative family policy" — with "conservative" being distinctly pejorative — to reject the notion of family diversity and judge one family differently to another.

The permissive attitudes towards parental drug abuse in the child protection context also reflect the postmodern values that have seeped into mainstream thinking in the field. Under the influence of the postmodern turn in social analysis, the discipline of social work has cast anxieties about child welfare as a moral panic deployed to authorise the social surveillance (via mandatory reporting) and cultural oppression of the powerless and excluded. According to this account, the purpose of "conservative family policy" isn't to establish the social and behavioural norms that create good families and functional communities, but is a form of power and knowledge used to impose social control on marginalised groups. The far-fetched notion, which is encapsulated by the Murphy, Quartly, and Cuthbert article, is that child welfare laws hold parents to socially constructed behavioural standards to buttress the hegemony of traditional bourgeois family values.[156]

The social and intellectual trends of the last 40 years have blown child protection so far off-track there is a dire need to restate what should not need restating: treating parental drug use in a non-judgemental and relativist manner – as if drug-addled parenting is somehow a legitimate, alternative lifestyle choice – is wrong and dangerous because it denies the role drug addiction can play in child abuse and neglect.[157] The idea that welfare-dependent drug addicts have a "right" to keep their children in squalor reveals a terrible ideological and moral confusion about the purpose of child protection laws, which are meant not to preside over family chaos, but to police it out of existence for children's sake.

The preoccupation with preserving parental custody is, alas, typical of the woolly thinking about "rights" – unmoored from common sense and traditional community standards of behaviour – typically found on the contemporary Left. It suggests that the moral judgements that sound child protection must depend upon are beyond the comprehension of those who subscribe to the family preservation orthodoxy.[158]

The role of the Right in child protection reform

Before the social revolution, the common-sense idea that parental drug abuse breached fundamental obligations towards children would not have been controversial. Criticism of such bad behaviour would simply have reflected universal social values, held across the political spectrum, and would never have been portrayed in party-political terms as a question of "conservative family policy". That defenders of permissive attitudes to parental drug abuse choose to politicise the issue in this way demonstrates how those subscribing to self-styled progressive values have cast the first stone in what has thereby become a culture war between Left and Right over the child protection crisis.

The cultural issue at stake in the contemporary debate over child protection policy is the need for the Right to advance what should be core and indisputable social values, rather than let the morally suspect and ideologically dubious perspectives of the Left continue to dictate practice in as important a policy area as child protection. To say this is as much to criticise sins of omission on the Right – a failure to engage sufficiently with this crucial social issue – as it is to criticise the Left's sins of commission.

Child protection reform should be on the agenda of those on the right of the political spectrum for practical, principled, and political reasons. The practical reason is that child protection reform is important to reduce the size of the welfare state. The principled reason is that child protection reform is consistent with truly liberal traditions of the role of the state, which formed the intellectual foundation for the development of the child protection field in the late 19th century. The political reason is that the debate about child protection reform needs greater involvement from the Right to fill the gap in advocacy for change in the best interests of children.

Restraining Leviathan

The first, practical reason child protection reform should be on the Right's agenda is that those on the Right live in a world they did not make. The Right did not champion the right to welfare that has increased joblessness and entrenched poverty and dysfunction in disadvantaged communities. But those on the Right, and all other taxpayers, have to live with and pay for the destructive personal, social, and political consequences of the rise of the welfare dependence, which include its terrible impact on the lives of increasing numbers of underclass children and the large financial cost to the community.

Flawed child protection policy and practice lie at the centre of the process by which welfare dependence and its associated dysfunctions are replicated through the generations. After children are exposed to prolonged maltreatment at home and then cycled in and out of care, prospects for the future are often bleak. The lifelong consequences of child abuse include unemployment, welfare dependence, mental illness, homelessness, substance abuse, crime, prostitution, and incarceration.[159]

As the Senate Community Affairs References Committee rightly warned in a 2005 report, *Protecting Vulnerable Children*, "the social and economic costs of not addressing these issues will only escalate in the future."[160] The lifetime costs imposed across the whole of government are substantial, and as the underclass expands so does the size of the welfare state. Estimates suggest the direct and indirect annual costs of child abuse and neglect to Australian governments could now be approaching $50 billion a year.[161] In the UK, the 120,000 most troubled families cost the public purse approximately £9 billion per year in 2011, with expenditure spanning areas including child protection, health, welfare, and justice.[162] A subsequent study in 2014 revealed the true extent of the problem, and established that 500,000 dysfunctional underclass families cost British taxpayers more than £30 billion – £75,000 ($147,000) per family per year in benefits and other services.[163]

There is no reason not to think the costs associated with struggling families are similar in Australia; they are almost certainly higher given the additional costs associated with extraordinary levels of Indigenous disadvantage in this country. The 2015 federal-government-commissioned Review of Australia's Welfare System stated the obvious when it noted that long-term welfare dependence was a significant cost to the public purse, was intergenerationally transmitted in disadvantaged communities suffering complex social problems, and was strongly associated with family dysfunction linked to poor developmental outcomes among children.[164] For those concerned about the size of government and maximising the freedom of all citizens, breaking the intergenerational cycle of neglect and abuse is essential to contain the growth of the welfare state and the extra-state entities that prosper off the misery and waste of potential created by child protection policy failures.

Lost tradition: on Mill and children's rights

The second, principled reason child protection reform should be on the agenda of the Right is because in this policy area, as in perhaps no other, the ideals of the welfare state run up against the realities of human nature. The logic of the welfare state is that material resources are unequally distributed across society, and should be redistributed via government programs to promote economic well-being. With regards to the protection of children from abuse and neglect, the contemporary welfare state applies a different version of the same logic: since parenting ability has also been unequally distributed across the socio-economic spectrum, it too must be redistributed via government-funded family support programs. The flawed operating assumption is that individual character is infinitely malleable, and even highly dysfunctional people can be rehabilitated and unfixable families fixed as desired by the visible hand of taxpayer-funded social-service interventions.

The seeming contradiction this creates is that greater state intervention is needed in the lives of dependent and dysfunctional members of the community – more court-approved removals, severing parental rights and freeing underclass children for adoption – to break the cycle and save future generations from lifelong dependence and dysfunction. This makes child protection a difficult issue, for philosophical reasons, for some or perhaps many on the right of the political spectrum. Those who strongly identify with liberal traditions of social and political thought prefer limited state intrusion into the lives of individuals. They also defend the sanctity of the private world of the family and are wary of the potential abuse of power by capricious welfare authorities in violation of parents' legitimate rights.

I understand these reservations because critics challenge me on these points of principle. Critics ask: how it is possible for me to reconcile greater use of adoption with my disposition to otherwise support smaller government and less state intrusion into social and economic affairs? Some even suggest it is hypocritical to hold these two seemingly contradictory views.[165]

But those on the Right should not be troubled by misplaced doctrinal reservations about making judgements about the rights of parents as against the rights of children. This does not represent yet another inappropriate expansion of the prerogatives of the state. It represents a return to founding liberal principles and a recalibration of the state towards its legitimate role of defending those who can't defend themselves. When the welfare of children is at stake, it is neither illiberal nor too judgemental to hold parents accountable for bad behaviour in circumstances that obviously fit John Stuart Mill's famous principle that liberty should only be interfered with to "prevent harm to others." As Mill himself argued, it was in the case of children "that misapplied notions of liberty are a real obstacle to the fulfilment by the State of its duties."[166]

Mill was one of the 19th-century progenitors of the progressive idea that a child had the right to enjoy his or her full liberties and opportunities as a future citizen. In *On Liberty*, he argued that parents who failed to fulfil their "sacred duties" towards their children were guilty of "a moral crime both against the unfortunate offspring and against society ... if the parent does not fulfil this obligation, the State ought to see it fulfilled."[167] The international child protection (anti-child-cruelty) movement of the late nineteenth century in Britain, the United States and Australia, was – like the movement to emancipate women – a project inspired by the enlightened ideas found in the writings of Mill.[168] Concerned citizens motivated by humanitarian instinct and the pursuit of the common good joined together to form philanthropic societies devoted to advancing the care and protection of children from bad and inadequate parents.[169] The state empowered these voluntary associations of citizens by setting out the legal framework for their activities – the original child welfare laws – which permitted child protection societies to actively seek out and rescue children from unsafe homes.[170]

Historically, liberal philosophical traditions and the promotion of child welfare were strongly connected, until in the 20th century the links were broken by the ascendancy of the Left and the coterminous growth of the welfare state that crowded this tradition out. In child protection, too much has been left to the new class of left-leaning social workers and other professionals employed in government departments and NGOs, who identify and treat abused and neglected children in their preferred family-centred fashion – badly, and at great cost to children and society. Because the Left dominates so many areas of contemporary social policy, the Right's long, if interrupted, history of social activism on behalf of vulnerable members of the community, including the defence of the independent rights of children, is often overlooked – including by those on the Right.

Restoring the lost centre: recover, reclaim, rescue

The third, political reason child protection reform should be on the Right's agenda is that it presents an opportunity to challenge the institutional reality of a system based on leftist thinking and captured by the vested interests of service providers in the sector. To challenge the institutional reality, the Right must challenge the ideology that underpins the current system, by reasserting the intellectual foundations of the child protection movement and by recovering the liberal heritage of enlightened social activism on behalf of children.

This is not about pursuing a partisan political agenda against the Left for its own sake. Rather, the political challenge, to update Mill, is to ensure that instead of prioritising the rights of bad parents to keep and regain custody of children, child protection prioritises and protects the rights of the child to enjoy the full opportunities of their citizenship. Recovering the ideas and motives behind the liberal tradition of child rescue and deploying the precepts of this tradition in contemporary debate would start the process of reclaiming child protection from the Left and inject genuine advocacy for children who need to be rescued into the political and policy formation processes.

The concept of a culture war over contentious public-policy issues is sometimes criticised as a figment of overheated ideological imaginations, and as a straw man deployed to blame the ills of the world on those who don't share the same political disposition. Yet, unfortunately, the culture war is no figment.

There is no shortage in this country of left-leaning, influential welfare-advocacy bodies that are vocal about addressing social disadvantage. This includes the peak national and state Councils of Social Services who, when it comes to child protection "reform", are orthodox to a fault. For example, the submission to the South Australian Royal Commission by the South Australian Council of Social Services calls for "progressive change" in the familiar direction of shifting the focus away from statutory services and towards an early intervention and prevention "family service model".[171] Advocacy for greater use of adoption does not feature in the child protection policy advocacy of any Council of Social Services anywhere in the country. In these circles, advocating for adoption is tantamount to renouncing one's "social justice" credentials and placing oneself outside the charmed circle of approved progressive approaches to addressing social disadvantage.

Given the cultural terrain, if those on the Right don't advocate for adoption and counteract the influence on the child protection policy debate of those who are resolutely hostile to adoption, who else will generate the political will and momentum required to drag child protection back towards the lost centre?

Reclaiming child protection from the Left will require those on the Right to tell, and keep telling, the truth about the difficult questions that surround the issue. Child protection policy is currently made largely by insiders blinded by ideology, self-interest, and political calculation. Policy should no longer be made, regardless of the evidence, in an echo chamber that more or less excludes the potentially dissenting voices of outsiders who challenge the conventional claims about how best to protect children. If more people, with clean hands and unclouded minds, started arguing back against the idea that the drug-addled have a "right" to raise children "with appropriately funded support services", it would help change the political dynamics behind the system. Political leadership is usually a misnomer. Politicians tend to lead only where public opinion is already willing to travel. Meaningful child protection reform needs to be driven from below if politicians are to finally acknowledge that family preservation does more harm than good and should be replaced by early removal and adoption.

Children are being damaged and disturbed due to the ideological and institutional eclipse of the traditional approach to child protection. The entire community also pays for child protection failures, including the good money wasted on the bad practice of family preservation. Nowhere are the costs imposed by the "industry" so high, in financial terms and in terms of the impact on the well-being and futures of children, than in Australia's ever-expanding out-of-home care system.

4

SYSTEM ABUSE: RE-INSTITUTIONALISING OUT-OF-HOME CARE

False economy

The orthodox account of the alleged solutions for the crisis in Australian child protection rests on three conventional myths. The first myth says child protection authorities are too quick to remove children without properly supporting families. The second myth says children are almost always better off with their families because removal into costly out-of-home care placements does more harm than good. The third myth says it therefore makes sense to invest in allegedly cheaper family support services that supposedly allow children to live safely with their parents.

The growing numbers of children in care, and other troubling features of the out-of-home care part of the child protection system, might at a glance suggest these myths are true. After all, the number of children in care nationally more than doubled to more than 43,000 children since 2000. Worse, care placements are often lengthy, with over two-thirds of children in care in 2013–14 (almost 30,000 children) having been there for more than two years. Instability – many moves in and out of care and between different foster carers – is also very harmful to children, and the literature on out-of-home care in Australia reveals that time spent in care is often highly unstable for many children. The literature (discussed later in this chapter) also reveals that most children in care have some level of "high needs" – developmental, behavioural, or emotional problems that can be partly linked to their unstable experiences in care.

Contrary to the many myths, the challenges and strains facing out-of-home care systems in all states and territories – "increasing numbers of children needing care, greater demand from children with high or complex needs, a consequent rise in the real cost of services, and a shortage of foster carers"[172] – stem from the systemic problems in the child protection system that come from the overemphasis on family preservation. The truth is actually counter-intuitive: we have increasing numbers of high-needs children in care because of too much support for families, not too little, and because of overextended efforts made to keep families together. The extensive literature detailing the crisis in out-of-home care in Australia – examined at length in this chapter – conclusively establishes this. A good indicator is the rising cost and complexity of the care system, which is also driving demands to further professionalise out-of-home care and deliver additional therapeutic services for children damaged by child protection failures.

Paradoxically, more children with higher needs are entering care as a last resort than in the past because of the emphasis placed on supposedly preventing abuse, neglect, and entry into care. The increasingly complex needs of the children in care, together with the growth in the number of children in care, the extended length of time in care, and the multiple occasions of care that many children experience, show that tens of thousands of children and young people have been abused by the system that is meant to protect them. These sufferers of "system abuse" have been damaged, disturbed, and distressed by family preservation.

The expanding size, scale, and cost of out-of-home care in Australia shows that despite near-universal support among policymakers, social workers, academics, and NGOs, family preservation is a flawed approach to promoting child safety. The prolonged efforts made to try to fix extremely dysfunctional families and prevent maltreatment and entry into care is doing more harm than good. Statutory intervention is coming too late, and the delay is exposing children to significant abuse and chronic neglect. Family preservation also represents false economy in public expenditure because of the demand, financial, and associated pressures that are ultimately placed on the care system due to the higher needs of children in care today.

Cost and complexity

Total real (adjusted for inflation) recurrent national expenditure on out-of-home care in Australia topped $2.1 billion in 2013–14, an increase of over 270% since 2000–01. The out-of-home care system continues to consume a more or less stable proportion of the $4 billion in total annual national expenditure on child protection services despite much higher government spending on the alternative family support and preservation services that are failing to prevent child abuse and entries into care. As a result, limited and overstretched state and territory budgets are struggling to fund the care placements required to provide sufficient alternative accommodation for every child and young person who is unable to live safely with their parents.

A national shortage of families willing to act as foster carers also imposes real constraints, and makes it logistically and financially impossible for governments to assume guardianship of all the children in need of protection. Increased selectivity in care placements[173] and higher thresholds for entry into care mean that many children who once would have been removed for health and welfare reasons remain in harm's way in the family home. In other words, despite the high and increasing numbers in care, there are thousands more children who should be in care because of "serious deficit in parenting capacity", but are not, because this is impossible given the constraints of the current system.[174]

The increased cost of the care system partly reflects the significant growth in the number of children in care nationally over the period.

The factors that generally account for the large volume of children in need of care and protection includes increased prevalence of parental problems in the underclass, the consequent increase in levels of child abuse and neglect, and greater awareness and reporting of child maltreatment due to mandatory reports.

A further factor contributing to the financial pressures created by the rising demand for care is the longer times children are spending in care after entering the system, which means fewer children are exiting than entering care each year.[175] In Victoria, for example, the proportion of children in care for under a year decreased from 49% in 2002 to 26% in 2013, while "the proportion being returned home after 5 years or more in care increased from 2.4% to 12.1%."[176] Lengthening stays, and longer times taken to reunify children with their families, account for why the 8,409 children discharged from care Australia-wide in 2013–14 did not offset the 11,085 children who entered care.[177] However, the story of rising costs is more complicated than this.

In 2013–14, the vast majority of children in care lived either in foster care placements or kinship care placements. Approximately two fifths of all children in care lived in foster care, around half lived in kinship care, and 1 in 20 lived in residential care facilities.[178] Residential out-of-home care is non-home-based care in "group homes" where multiple non-related children are cared for by paid staff. Foster out-of-home care is home-based care provided by volunteer foster and kinship carers who agree to take non-related and related children respectively into their family home and act as substitute parents. State and territory governments are responsible for the funding and regulation of out-of-home care, but in many jurisdictions the management of home-based placements and the provision of residential services are outsourced to NGOs.

Of the 43,009 children in care in June 2014, 14,991 were Indigenous, with Indigenous children over-represented in care at over nine times the rate of non-Indigenous children. Half of all Indigenous children in care live in kinship placements. This is consistent with the Aboriginal Child Placement Principle (ACPP), which aims to ensure that child welfare agencies, where possible, place Indigenous children with extended family members, the child's Indigenous community, or with other Indigenous people to maintain cultural traditions and preserve cultural identity.

Without the expanded use of kinship placements for both Indigenous and non-Indigenous children that has occurred over the last decade or so, it would have been impossible to meet the increased demand for care, and the care system would have collapsed. The foster system could not have coped with all the new children entering care after the closure in the 1980s and 1990s of nearly all large-scale state and charitably run children's residential care institutions (orphanages), which housed 40% of the children in care in the mid-1980s.

The foster system is crumbling due to difficulties recruiting and retaining suitable carers and increasing concerns about the quality of foster placements.[179] In many cases, acute shortages mean children are placed in foster homes not much better than the dysfunctional homes they were removed from. Foster carers themselves can even be welfare-dependent, and the prime motive for taking foster children may be the additional income they receive, not the welfare of those children. This has led (with implicit official sanction of the look-the-other-way kind) to the baby-farm type of foster home, in which multiple foster children are kept in filthy and crowded boarding-house-style accommodation.[180] Hence, over 20% of children in foster care nationally are placed in foster homes alongside three or more other foster children.[181]

Different placement types attract different amounts of government subsidies, which vary in value across jurisdictions and the level of care provided. Volunteer foster and kinship carers receive the same base fortnightly allowance to partially offset the cost of raising children. Full recompense does not occur, as is consistent with the philanthropic origins of the foster system, which developed as a charitable form of community service. Kinship and foster carers may also receive additional payments, known as loadings, based on the assessed needs of children with personal problems and other difficult behaviours. However, the overall cost of kinship care tends to be lower than for foster care because kinship carers tend to receive less screening and training, and less follow-up supervision and support.[182] Non-home-based residential care costs the most per child; it absorbs a disproportionate amount of total out-of-home care funding because the full cost of caring for children, especially staff wages, is borne by government.

The apparent anomaly is that spending on care has soared, due not only to increased demand but also to a significant increase in the real cost of out-of-home care services per child – which currently ranges between $44,000 and $91,000 per child per year across the states and territories. This is despite the historic decrease in the use of expensive residential care and much greater use of lower-cost kinship care. The explanation for the rapid growth in the real unit cost of care is the growing complexity of the out-of-home care population.

The major source of the stress on the care system – as the 2005 Senate Community Affairs References Committee report *Protecting Vulnerable Children* established – is the rising proportion of high-needs or "complex" children in care. These have challenging behavioural, emotional, health, social, educational and other psychological problems, including depression, hyperactivity, ADHD, anxiety, post-traumatic stress disorder, sexual deviance, conduct disorder, aggression, delinquency, and poor peer relationships and social functioning.[183]

The policy response to the increased complexity of the children living in care has been to expand the provision of additional (largely NGO-provided) specialist support service packages for children with high or complex needs. This expansion extends to both home-based and non-home-based settings ("treatment" or "therapeutic" foster- and residential care programs), and is combined with a significant and alarming shift back to greater use of higher-cost residential placements for highly disturbed children and young people. The extensive range of multidisciplinary specialist counselling and other services involved in foster and residential care these days can include assertiveness training, self-esteem building, anger management, social-skills training, grief management, behaviour management, and mentoring support, plus clinical, psychological, and other mental-health services.[184]

Damaging and disturbing

The rising cost and complexity of the care system plainly reveals the many damaged, disturbed, and distressed children that are victims of system abuse. The first 2006 national comparative study of high-needs children and young people by Alexandra Osborn and Paul Delfabbro found that these children share a common history. They have a long record, often from birth, of dealings with child protection authorities regarding serious welfare concerns;[185] they have been eventually removed as a last resort at older ages after extensive contact with support services;[186] they have been harmed by chronic abuse and neglect by highly dysfunctional families;[187] and they have had multiple placements because of complex problems[188] and multiple episodes of care following failed family reunions.[189] Overall, the study also confirmed that only children with the most serious needs and severe problems are placed in care nowadays, and that these children, particularly when they enter care at older ages, have already experienced trauma, often severe trauma, in the family home.[190] As Osborn and Delfabbro concluded:

> Almost all the children had been subjected to traumatic, abusive, and highly unstable family backgrounds ... [and] it is almost certainly true that many of the children displaying

significant emotional and behavioural difficulties when they are older had already suffered significant, possibly irreparable, physical and psychological harm during their early years.[191]

As a major 2005 National Child Protection Clearinghouse report on the problems facing out-of-home care in Australia, by Bromfield and others, also observed:

> Child welfare services are recognising the importance of family support and early intervention. Out-of-home care is viewed as a last resort, and the preference is always for children to be reunited with their birth parents if possible. This shift in the "hard end" of child welfare practice has meant that children who enter out-of-home care are likely to have chronic child maltreatment and family disruption prior to entering care, and therefore have more complex needs than children entering such care in the past.[192]

Crucially, the literature that confirms the negative impact of family preservation on children also tells us (again contra the orthodoxy) that high-needs children do not end up in care because they lacked access to early intervention and family support services. They end up in care despite being "most likely" to access a "wide variety of services and interventions" before entering care, which failed to resolve family problems that necessitated eventual removal into care.[193] A subsequent analysis of the care system by Ciara Smyth and Tony Eardley, published by the University of New South Wales Social Policy Research Centre three years after the National Child Protection Clearinghouse report, also noted:

> It is children who are beyond the scope of early intervention programs, or for whom early intervention has failed, who are the most likely to enter care. Provision for high needs children is limited and in most cases the only placement option is with foster or kinship carers. However, many carers struggle to meet the demands of caring for these children,

leading to an increase in placement breakdowns and carers leaving the system.[194]

The high demands placed on carers indicate that family preservation also contributes to how unstable, and thus harmful, time spent in care proves for many children, as well as contributing to longer times being spent in care by many children.

Children are staying longer, sometimes indefinitely, in "temporary" care because child protection authorities wait for their parents to be rehabilitated and family circumstances to stabilise sufficiently to attempt reunions. In the interim, foster placements involving children with high needs are more likely to break down due to those children's challenging trauma-related behaviours. When children are finally returned home, often at the first and premature sign of parental improvement, living arrangements become even more unstable because unrealistic reunions often break down.[195] When parental problems re-emerge, re-damaged children re-enter care.[196] The difficulties of caring for high-needs children, together with the heartbreak when children have to be returned to dysfunctional parents, are major contributors to the shortage of foster carers. Frustration and burnout lead existing carers to drop out, while reports of negative fostering experiences discourage potential carers from volunteering.[197]

Good parents would appreciate how bad current policy and practice is for the welfare of children caught up in the care system. Children need security and consistency to thrive – established routines and loving attention from trusted carers. It is not surprising that children become disturbed when they are shuffled in and out of family and foster homes, and are denied the stability and attachment every child requires. There is, moreover, a large and uncontested international literature on the importance of permanency – of stable and secure living arrangements with at least one devoted carer – for a child's psychological development.[198] "Attachment deprivation", a syndrome associated with parental inattention to their children's basic needs and broken attachments associated with periodic moves from one placement to another, impairs children's cognitive, behavioural, and emotional development, including development of the capacity to bond, trust, and form close relationships throughout life.[199] Not surprisingly, foster children subjected to numerous placement moves also lament this instability and cite a trusting relationship with carers as vital to their well-being.[200]

Uncertainty and disruption, particularly at younger ages, are major contributors to poor behavioural, developmental, educational, health, and social outcomes in childhood and later in life.[201] Stability is a strong predictor of better outcomes.[202] The longer children linger on the removal–reunion treadmill, the greater is the harm done due to a snowballing effect. Unstable living arrangements due to placement breakdowns and failed reunions severely disrupt schooling and seriously compromise educational opportunities. Frequent school changes and non-attendance mean children fall behind. These educational deficits are compounded as children grow older and struggle to cope as they proceed through school, increasing their likelihood of dropping out permanently.

The emergence of an extensive literature on the importance of permanency (routinely cited in academic research and reports on the child protection system)[203] was closely linked with the identification in the 1980s of the problem of "drift" in care, where children experience multiple temporary placements over many years. This led to the introduction of Permanency Planning legislation in the United States. Similar legislation, which formally recognises how vital stability is to child welfare, has been enacted in other countries, including in Australian jurisdictions. The permanency planning provisions of the NSW *Children and Young Persons (Care and Protection) Amendment (Permanency Planning) Act 2001* required DoCS to draw up a long-term plan to provide a child or young person with a stable placement that offers long-term security. "Stability planning" is also a requirement of the Victorian *Children, Youth and Families Act*. However, these statutory obligations are honoured more in the breach than in the observance, due to authorities persisting with efforts to ensure that children in care are reunified with their parents.[204] A 2014 study of the experiences of a representative sample of children in care found that the "stability planning framework … has failed to achieve the timely decision making that was intended." Only 61% of children had a "stability plan", and 32% of these plans were not completed within the statutory timelines.[205]

Permanency planning legislation is designed to set time limits on temporary care placements and mandate timely decisions about permanent living arrangements, within a realistic and child-centred timeframe, especially for younger children. In the United States, the aim is to expedite the process of securing normal living arrangements for children in a stable family setting (as opposed to institutional or unstable foster care) by formal adoption from out of care by suitable families or by de facto adoption by foster carers granted permanent care orders (guardianship) until the child is 18. In Australia, permanency laws have proven ineffective and adoption remains officially taboo.[206] Here, the importance of achieving stability and restoring children to a family setting has been interpreted differently by child protection authorities:

> The presumption [is] that separation [from biological parents] should be temporary wherever possible and every effort must be made to reunite children with their families of origin. In contrast to the United States, then, the emphasis in Australian child welfare policy is on family reunification ahead of placement permanency.[207]

Yet here, as in other parts of the system, child protection authorities are reluctant to own up to the results of putting preservation before permanency. The publication of high-quality out-of-home care data – such as the average number of placements per child each year[208] — would reveal the level of churn in the system and exactly how many children bounce in and out of care, of multiple placements, and of failed family reunions. It would also reveal the number of children languishing in care and lacking permanent homes who might be made available for adoption if it were allowed. The only official time-series data currently available to the public are the number of placements during the time spent in care for each child that exited care each year.

The nationwide proportion of children exiting after 12 months or longer in care with three or more placements has almost doubled from 26.8% in 2001–02 (the first year for which data is available) to 53.1% in 2013–14 (figure 12). The worst performing states, with the highest increase in instability, are NSW, Victoria, and Queensland. The Northern Territory and ACT recorded smaller but still substantial increases in instability.

The literature on out-of-home care admits that unstable placements are "not unusual for foster children" and concedes that instability is linked to the numbers of children with high needs who "pose insurmountable problems for generalist foster carers."[209] However, the information available on the frequency of placement disruption remains patchy, historical, and sometimes anecdotal. But it is well informed: according to the NSW Foster Care Association, "most children who are sent home come back to care more damaged ... [and] might have 20 foster placements because of their behaviour as a result of what they have suffered."[210] The evidence confirms large numbers of children in care experience a disturbing level of churn and instability.

Evidence of churn and instability

A longitudinal study in South Australia by Delfabbro, Barber, and Cooper (2000) found 20% of the surveyed children had been placed once or twice in foster care; 20% had between three and five placements; 20% had between six and nine placements; and almost 25% had 10 or more placements.[211]

A **Victorian Department of Human Services report (2003)** found just 7% of children in care had only one placement, while 65% had four or more placements.[212]

A **Queensland Crime and Misconduct Commission inquiry (2004)** found that before leaving care, 37% of children had experienced four or more placements.[213]

A **NSW DoCS option paper (2006)** revealed that in 2004–05, only 32% of foster children had one placement in their current period in care, and 16% had four or more placements.[214]

The **Wood Report (2008)** into child protection in NSW found that in 2006–07, 29% of children entering care had a previous care episode, suggesting that "the decision concerning restoration may not have been comprehensive." Wood also found that in each year between 2005 and 2008, more than 50% of all children in care had two or more placements, with the likelihood of multiple episodes and placements increasing with age and time spent in care.[215]

In Victoria, the **Looking After Children Outcomes Data Project Final Report (2009)** found that the average number of placements for children was 4.6, but suggested this was likely to be an underestimation: many children "could not quantify the number of carers because the number was too high to record accurately. For example, some of the responses to this open-ended item were 'Too many', 'Lots' and 'More than 20'."[216]

According to the **Bath Report (2010)**, "In the Northern Territory, a child could be the subject of five or six daily care and control or short term parental responsibility orders covering ten to twelve years and during which no planning can be commenced for long term placement outside the family."[217]

The Cummins Report (2012) found, "The average time taken between a child's first report and their ultimate permanent care order, at just over five years, is too long. For children who have been abused and known to statutory child protection services at a young age, it takes too many years for a permanent care order to be granted when this is necessary to ensure their safety and well-being. During this time, many children are subjected to multiple placements, compounding psychological harm."[218]

The Carmody Report (2013) detailed concerns about "the high number of children and young people subject to multiple short-term [care and protection] orders because this could indicate that many children are 'drifting' in care without achieving either reunification with the family or long-term out-of-home care".[219]

Revival of residential care

Some studies have suggested that approximately 80% of children in long-term care may eventually be able to find stable placements. Good foster care, involving a permanent placement and a one-on-one relationship with trusted carers – helps repair disturbed children.[220] Hard-working, patient and dedicated carers help these children make up some lost ground, and achieve small but significant improvements in social and psychological outcomes, though their futures remain compromised by their childhoods. The remaining 20% of severely damaged children, who will never find stable placements, are children with the highest needs, who experience additional harm due to frequent and ongoing placement breakdowns caused by parental abuse and challenging neglect-related behaviours.[221]

Many studies have confirmed that children in care do exceptionally badly, compared to peers who grow up in a stable family home. Educational outcomes are worse,[222] and the incidence of emotional, psychological, behavioural, and other health problems is much higher. More than half of Australian children in foster and kinship care have a significant, clinically diagnosable mental illness, a much higher rate than in the general population.[223] This is understandable to an extent, given the trauma these children experience in the family home;[224] but, in addition, bad experiences in care worsen the effects of parental abuse and neglect. Children who suffer harm due to disruption are identified as those having had two or more placement breakdowns in the previous two years due to their behaviour.[225] The extended periods of instability experienced by children who cycle in and out of care, in and out of multiple placements, and in and out of failed family reunions, is an independent and additional cause of harm that exacerbates behavioural and other problems. Studies show that as the "unconscionable" number of detrimental placement breakdowns becomes higher, the higher becomes the level of disturbance observed.[226]

Two broad groups of children and young people make up the out-of-home care population. The first is damaged children, usually aged 10 and under, who have suffered parental abuse and neglect. The second is disturbed teenagers (invariably on long-term care orders) who have suffered highly disruptive childhoods. The two groups represent the same children at different stages of life.[227] The second group are the "hard to help" adolescents whose traumatic childhood experiences at home and in care are played out through challenging behaviours (risk of suicide, mental illness, substance abuse, and death by misadventure) at older ages.[228] For this severely disturbed group of young people, it is no longer safe to live in the family home. Nor is it possible for them to live safely with normal foster families, because their uncontrollable, threatening, violent, and self-destructive behaviours necessitate round-the-clock supervision. The only suitable placement option is very-high-cost residential care facilities.[229]

Today's residential care facilities tend to be smaller-scale NGO-operated group homes with no more than six residents. However, these facilities have a strong psychiatric care focus and include "secure facilities" for the most antisocial children. These are the modern-day asylums used to lock up disturbed teenagers whose behaviour poses a threat to themselves and to others.

The increasing size and cost of residential care in Australia is a crucial measure of the poor performance of child protection services. Ironically, 30 years after the vast majority of residential care institutions (state and charitable children's orphanages) were closed down because of the detrimental impact of institutional care on children, Australian governments have been quietly re-institutionalising the care system by reopening residential facilities to cater for all the children damaged and disturbed by family preservation.

Nationally, the proportion of children in out-of-home care who are living in residential care is relatively small – 5.5% in 2013–14 – and has fallen from 6.5% in 2000–01. However, the actual number of children in residential care throughout Australia has doubled (figure 13).

Decades of falling numbers of children in residential care have been reversed, with the residential population bottoming out in 2004–05 at 939 children and then growing to 2,356 by 2013–14.[230] The total population of children in residential care has held steady in Victoria and Western Australia, declined by a third in Tasmania, and increased by 49% in NSW, 677% in South Australia, 710% in Queensland, 900% in the Northern Territory, and 138% in the ACT (figure 14).

The re-institutionalisation of out-of-home care to house children with the highest abuse and neglect-related high needs appears to have had major financial implications for the cost of the care system.

Since 2000–01, except for a small decline in the ACT (−5%), real out-of-home care spending per child has increased in all states and territories, ranging from increases of over 100% in South Australia and Tasmania, 70.6% in Queensland, around 40% in NSW, just above

35% in Western Australia, and about 15% in Victoria (figure 15). Not all states and territories report out-of-home care expenditure by placement type. In the states and territories that do report, the rise in real costs has grown far faster for residential care compared to (still substantial) increases in the real cost of non-residential care, with the exception of Western Australia (figure 16).

Not surprisingly, therefore, residential care has also consumed an increasing percentage of total out-of-home care expenditure in these jurisdictions (figure 17). This reflects the fact that average real expenditure per child on residential care has increased at a much faster rate than average real expenditure per child on non-residential care (figure 18). The escalating cost of residential care, and its impact on the overall cost of the care system, appears to have been driven by more than a volume effect or simply by the growth in the number of children living in residential care facilities. The rising real unit cost of residential care is a reflection of the complex needs of the increasing numbers of damaged children who require intensive assistance and specialised services. The costs of residential care, already high at the start of the period, are now quite extraordinary and run into multiple hundreds of thousands of dollars per child – above $200,000 in South Australia and the ACT, almost $400,000 in Victoria, and in excess of $600,000 in Western Australia.

Expansion of kinship care: silver lining or dark cloud?

The other side of the story of changing placement patterns and cost structures for out-of-home care in Australia is the more pronounced trend of decline in the use of foster care and towards greater use of kinship care placements. This is demonstrated by the increasing proportion of children in kinship care, which has become the leading placement option.

Nationally, over half of all children in care were in foster care in

2000–01, whereas currently just less than half are in kinship care, up from 38% in 2000–01 (figure 19). This is due to the fact that since 2000–01, the total number of Indigenous and non-Indigenous children in out-of-home care in Australia who are placed in kinship care has grown much faster than the (still substantially growing) number of children in residential care and foster-care placements. The numbers of kinship placements nationally have grown at twice the rate of foster and residential care placements since 2000–01, as is demonstrated by changes in the proportion of all children in care in different types of placements. Foster care has been squeezed on both sides by increased use of residential care since the mid-2000s and, more significantly, by strong growth in kinship placements (figure 20).

The shift from foster care to kinship care has occurred in most states and territories (figure 21):

- In 2000–01 in Victoria, 56.6% of children in care were in foster placements. By 2013–14, this proportion had fallen to 27.7%, with kinship placements increasing from 27% to over 50%.
- In South Australia, foster care fell from 83% of all placements in 2000–01 to 42.3% in 2013–14, with kinship care rising from 12.5% to 44.2%.
- Similar patterns are evident in Queensland, Western Australia, and the ACT, with large falls in foster placements and significant growth in kinship placements.
- Tasmania bucked the national trend by keeping a steady proportion of foster care placements while the proportion of kinship placements fell.
- NSW also defied the trend, but off a high base. Foster-care placements increased slightly, while the proportion of kinship placements held steady at around 55% over the period.

The likely explanations for the decline in foster care and increase in kinship care include:

- increased demand for out-of-home care
- shortages of foster carers
- the unsuitability of many high-needs children for foster placements
- the belief children benefit from placements with their extended family or within their local community
- the financial constraints on state and territory governments that have used kinship care as a "cheaper" option.[231]

The out-of-home care expenditure data examined above also seems to suggest that greater prevalence of kinship care may be having an impact on the overall cost of the care system. The financial trends of smaller non-residential expenditure growth recorded since 2000–01, and recent declines in the cost of non-residential care per child in some jurisdictions, coincidences with the growth in use of kinship care, which is generally recognised to be a less-costly alternative to foster care because kinship placements tend to be less well assessed, trained, monitored, and supported.[232]

The expansion of kinship care might appear to be a positive development and a win-win situation for governments and for children and their families. Governments appear to have staved off total collapse in the face of rising demand for care, and to be sustaining and lowering the cost of the care system by using the least-intrusive form of intervention. In theory, placing children with relatives reduces the trauma of parental separation and maintains family ties, including contact with birth parents.[233] In the case of Indigenous children, placement with kin or with members of their local communities or other Indigenous carers may also ensure continuing contact with their family heritage and with traditional culture.[234]

However, there are still question marks over the greater use of kinship care. There is little information available about its quality, other than repeat findings in official inquiries and academic literature that assessment, training, support, and supervision are inferior to what foster care affords.[235] The potential for children's care to be compromised starts with the fact that initial assessment of kinship carers tends to take place after a placement has occurred; by contrast, children are only placed with foster carers after a proper assessment.[236]

Less-rigorous assessment, training, and support is especially concerning given that child protection authorities are likely to set and forget children when placing them with relatives. Hence, studies show that children in kinship care tend to "remain in care longer, are reunified with their birth families at slower rates, and are adopted at lower rates."[237] In the words of a damning 2010 review published by the Australian Institute of Family Studies, these systemic failings mean this growing segment of the care system "neglects the needs of children and young people ... which stands in opposition to a child-focused approach and serves to further subordinate children, young people and kinship carers who already suffer extreme disadvantage."[238]

There are also many unanswered questions about the impact of kinship care on children's welfare and development.[239] Because there is "little substantial research on kinship care in Australia", and because "the growth in kinship care is not underpinned by strong outcomes focused evidence", there is "no concrete evidence that this type of care produces better outcomes for children", and "no conclusive evidence that those in kinship care are more or less well-adjusted than those in foster care." The belief that kinship care is preferable for Indigenous children because it maintains connections with culture and identity is based, at best, on "limited evidence".[240] This reflects the fact that "despite the over-representation of Aboriginal children in care and associated threats to family and cultural connections, there is little published research especially on Aboriginal children in kinship care."[241]

What is known about kinship care is as worrying as what isn't known. Kinship carers tend to be low-income, less-educated, older, single women, usually a grandmother or aunt, and commonly find it stressful and difficult to cope with the complexities and difficulties of parenting again, particularly when raising high-needs children with abuse- and neglect-related developmental and behavioural problems.[242]

Though no data is available, according to a 2014 Senate committee report, it is becoming increasingly common for grandparents to accept responsibility for caring for grandchildren, and many grandparent-headed families provide children with the stable and functional homes that their dysfunctional sons and daughters are incapable of providing, usually due to drug and alcohol abuse.[243] Yet, not surprisingly, many grandparents also report that they struggle given their own financial and health challenges; they also report that training and support are inadequate.[244]

The knowns and unknowns of kinship care mean that this apparent silver lining to the otherwise dire story of child protection in Australia may conceal a dark cloud, if quality of care is being compromised. The shift towards less-costly but unproven and inadequately assessed, supervised, and supported kinship placements is due to foster-care shortages and because this option reduces financial strain on the increasingly unaffordable care system.[245] But it should be cause for concern if child protection authorities are propping up the care system and, in effect, covering up the full demand and cost implications of family preservation by consigning children, whether Indigenous or non-Indigenous, to suboptimal kinship placements.

Duck-shoving children with the greatest needs to old, poor, and sick grandparents least likely to be able to cope with the challenges posed by caring for these children is hardly a welcome development or signal achievement. Of course, grandparents want to care for their grandchildren, but whether imposing these burdens upon them is wise or conscionable is an open question. So too is the question of whether, in some cases, children are being placed with troubled and struggling grandparents, given the prevalence of multigenerational dysfunction and disadvantage in underclass families. The question this raises is whether some children, regardless of the kinship care alternatives available, would be better off adopted. Under "open" adoption arrangements, these children would gain a functional adoptive family while continuing to have meaningful ongoing contact and relationships with grandparents who were neither stressed nor overwhelmed by the challenges of returning to full-time parenting.

All the reservations that have been noted regarding kinship care are especially important for the protection of Indigenous children, due to concerns about the suitability of kinship placements for some (perhaps many) Indigenous children. This subject and the wider implications for Indigenous policy are discussed in Chapter 6.

Professionalising out-of-home care

Defenders of family preservation argue that the poor outcomes many children in care experience prove that children "are better off with families in the long run".[246] Those who cite the harmful impact of unstable out-of-home care on child well-being as evidence that family preservation is best use flawed reasoning.[247] This view does not recognise that the problems many children encounter in care are linked to the problems brought into care due to child protection policy failures.[248] It isn't removal into care that really harms children, but that the removal is too late, too temporary, and too unstable to prevent lasting damage. That this is the experience of increasing numbers of children in care is accepted in child protection circles up to a point.

Most academics who study the problems in the care system support the ideology that says family preservation is best, and dismiss the notion that this approach is bad for vulnerable children.[249] They do not candidly acknowledge the causal links between the problems in the statutory part of the system and the problems with the out-of-home care part of the system. It is obliquely acknowledged, and only in passing, that the complexity of damaged children's high needs reflects "the failure of early intervention programs to ameliorate abuse and chronic neglect in highly dysfunctional families".[250] But explicit comment or criticism is not made of the wisdom, utility, and morality of the shift in the "hard end" that exposes children to the twin and related evils of harm at home and instability in care due to family preservation. Instead of addressing systemic causes, attention is shifted to ameliorating and managing the symptoms. The "troubled teens" issue has instead led to recognition of the need for a wider range of placements using two strategies: a major reappraisal of "policies that prioritise home-based care in the hierarchy of placement options"[251] and the "increasing recognition" of the "integral" role of residential care in the care system.[252]

Academic and policy literature on out-of-home care mainly focuses on the shortage of "alternative placement options" and the lack of "specialist therapeutic services" in foster and residential care.[253] The rising number of high-needs children is cited as evidence of the inappropriateness of using volunteer foster families to care for them. The instability experienced by "difficult" children in family-based care is blamed on an over-reliance on foster care and the excessive closure of residential facilities more suited to housing such children.[254] A consensus has thereby emerged "among practitioners, policymakers, and researchers that there is a need to expand the range of OOHC options to cater for a heterogeneous OOHC population with differing needs."[255]

Overall, the advice tendered to government is that traditional foster care is outdated. The principal concern of the care system is no longer to simply provide children with normal family environments, substitute parents, accommodation, food, health care, and schooling. Given the numbers of "highly deprived" children in care, it is unrealistic and counter-productive to expect volunteer foster carers with limited training and support to manage "extreme behaviours", and the result is frequent placement breakdowns. Instead, the advice is to develop new, specialised models of out-of-home care such as treatment foster care and residential care. Skilled staff with qualifications in relevant disciplines should be employed as full-time carers or provide specialist training and support for foster carers and extra counselling and assistance.[256]

The most benign case for undertaking a modest expansion of a mix of placements is that there always has and always will be some children unsuited to traditional foster care. In the past, these children did not get the support they needed. Child protection failures will occasionally occur even in the best, most responsive and accountable systems. Some children will have experienced abuse, neglect and trauma, and they will require "intensive" care incorporating a "therapeutic component and multidisciplinary, wrap-around support services".[257]

But the arguments for the professionalisation of out-of-home care services are shallow and perverse. Analysis of the issues is limited to calling for the recruitment, training, and support of carers, and paying them a professional salary for taking high-needs children into their homes.[258]

While the literature on out-of-home care establishes the "links between the child's current behavioural and emotional functioning and their previous family and placement history", the policy advice is limited to recommending more "therapeutic interventions", as opposed to remedying the root cause of child protection failures.[259]

Official inquiries mimic academic papers and assorted research reports, focusing exclusively on the "lack of appropriate care options." The Senate Community Affairs References Committee noted "disturbing trends" – child removal as a last resort, failed reunifications, and placement instability – that indicated the care system's failure to cope with increasing numbers of complex children. Yet the committee's policy recommendations were confined to calling for greater "diversity" in placement options such as "therapeutic foster care" and "residential care staffed by highly-trained professionals."[260] Hence, the conventional policy discourse is silent on the harm family preservation does to the most vulnerable Australian children, and about the need this clearly suggests for fundamental change to current policy and practice. Instead, the discourse is preoccupied with ensuring high-needs children can access "appropriate" placement options with "appropriately trained staff." This would simply implement new models of care to make up for years of system abuse.

An unhappy but familiar truth lies beneath the inadequate policy advice given to Australian governments: stakeholders' interests trump child welfare. Under the remit of the National Framework for Protecting Australia's Children, the federal government is working with the states and territories to further the cause of professionalisation as part of the National Standards for Out-of-home Care. This has taken the form of the 2013 federal government–commissioned "review of the barriers and opportunities for developing models of professional foster care", *Professional Foster Care: Barriers, Opportunities, Options*.[261] Stakeholders in the NGO sector have naturally welcomed national leadership in this direction.[262]

This is the latest example of the way the child protection system does not operate in the children's best interests but in the interests of the professionals who staff it and the organisations they work for. The determination within the sector to only treat the symptom, and not deal with the cause, of the need to develop new models of care for damaged children reflects the fact that additional funding streams for services and employment opportunities in the out-of-home care sector depend heavily on the continuation of the current family preservation approach. This approach, as we have seen, is better at harming children than protecting them, and is best at sending a multitude of "clients" – dysfunctional parents and traumatised children – the way of psychiatrists, psychologists, therapists, counsellors, mentors, social workers, and caseworkers.

Monuments to a failed system

In all states and territories, the recruitment of an "appropriately skilled and qualified carer workforce" and the provision of "more therapeutic residential facilities" is a policy priority.[263] The paradigm shift from unskilled, volunteer, home-based care has been more or less accepted, and the roll-out of programs that expand the range and capacity of treatment-focused, usually outsourced, out-of-home care options has proceeded at different paces in different jurisdictions.[264] This reflects the fact that the old model of foster care (and the accompanying payment system based on the cost of raising a "normal" child) is viewed as increasingly redundant due to the high concentration of children with high needs in care.[265]

These developments suggest significant unmet need for treatment foster and residential care.[266] They should also be a source of national shame. But the unpalatable reality is that the overburdened care system is ill-equipped to deal with its short- to medium-term challenges. In the absence of alternative placements, general foster (and kinship) carers are struggling to give damaged children stable homes, and carers and children receive limited assistance. The brutal, inescapable truth is that damaged children already trapped in the system, who are a danger not only to themselves but also to other children, carers, and staff, will need long-term residential care because disturbed teens have nowhere else to go.

There is a distressing logic to the view that the complexity of the children in care necessitates greater professionalisation and residentialisation – and an inexorable rise in out-of-home care costs in coming years. State and territory governments are sure to come under pressure to provide additional funding and meet the particularly high cost of expanding the residential care sector. Residential demand and cost trends have important financial implications for state and territory budgets. Sound and affordable child protection should therefore concern not only child welfare ministers and shadow ministers, but also premiers, treasurers, and finance ministers.

Policymakers should not simply be resigned to constructing a more elaborate care system. In this, genuine prevention is superior to cure. Good, full-time, one-on-one foster care might allow some children to recover from childhood maltreatment. However, there is only equivocal evidence that treatment foster care is effective for damaged children, and it is tainted by the "methodological limitations of many of the studies", particularly with respect to long-term outcomes.[267] There has been no rigorous evaluation of outcomes for children in the intensive foster and therapeutic residential care models developed by states and territories.[268] But the ethics of conducting such rigorous research would be dubious: it is morally abhorrent to use abused and neglected children as guinea pigs when sound child protection policy and practice can prevent child harm and trauma.

Even advocates of treatment-oriented residential care admit the long-term prognosis is poor, and that such care "may only achieve modest changes to behaviour" because of the level of harm already experienced.[269] By the time damaged children reach adolescence, the problems are so entrenched and developmental deficits so great that the prospects for recovery are bleak.[270] When disturbed teens finally exit care, they experience high rates of social disadvantage. Transitional support services for those entering independent living as adults are patchy – another gap in the system, with significant cost implications.[271]

Policymakers should realise that a child protection system that has to spend increasing sums on an army of professionals to try to fix the children it has damaged is a failed system. As residential facilities are reopened, we should lament that we are building monuments to child protection failures. Only when these facilities are closed down again, and when we no longer have to pay taxpayer-funded professionals to try to fix damaged children, will we know we have got child protection right. The effective and affordable way to get it right is to fundamentally rethink how to provide safe and stable homes for all children, by lifting the taboo on adoptions from care.

Apology again?

In 2009, the federal parliament apologised to the Forgotten Australians who were physically, sexually and emotionally abused in institutional care from the 1920s until the 1970s. The national apology was overdue.[272] The detrimental impact, including physical and sexual abuse, of institutional care on children has been documented since the 1950s, and the case for closing the institutions and deinstitutionalising children was unarguable by the 1980s. We should never forget or repeat the trauma experienced by the members of the Forgotten Generations, who were mentally, physically, and emotionally damaged by institutionalisation.

The debate about child protection policy is rightly framed by the memory of bad past practices. But we are fooling ourselves to think that apologies, accompanied by pledges to "never again" repeat those mistakes and to instead do everything to keep families together, are sufficient to keep children safe today, when we turn a blind eye to what is really going on. Similarly, the soothing language of support, therapy, and responding to the diverse needs of "unfosterable" children, which is used to justify the expansion of residential care as a "realistic option for children and young people who exhibit major behavioural and emotional problems,"[273] simply covers up the damage done by family preservation.

Recent scandals have revealed that damaged children living in residential care in NSW had been sexually abused by carers and by each other.[274] It has also been revealed that damaged children living in residential care in Victoria have been trafficked between towns and interstate by paedophile rings.[275] These scandals have led the Royal Commission into Institutional Responses to Child Sexual Abuse to broaden its inquiry beyond past malpractices by churches, schools, and other organisations, to turn its attention to the operation of the contemporary child protection system.[276] This is a reminder that while scrutiny of the response of religious and other institutions, or lack thereof, to child abuse is well overdue, it is not only the churches that can be accused of failing children they had a duty to protect.

National apologies for past practices ring hollow when today's child protection system continues to fail children, harming a new generation of forgotten children and young people to whom a national apology will one day be owed. This time, it will be for failing to remove them from the care of abusive or neglectful parents. Perversely, it is the national apologies to the Forgotten Australians and the Stolen Generations, and for forced adoption, that have helped to reinforce and keep in place the taboo on adoption. How we choose to deal with the complicated legacy and contemporary implications of past child protection practices is one of the key cultural obstacles in the path of revising flawed current-day practices, which, in their own way, subject children to ordeals that are as damaging as being institutionalised, stolen, or forcibly separated from their families.

5

CULTURAL CORRECTNESS: THE SORRY TALE OF THE SOCIAL REVOLUTION

Adoption: the evidence

Adoption is chronically underused for child protection purposes in Australia compared to other countries, despite the international evidence that shows adoption is the better option for many children in care. As detailed in the 2005 House of Representatives' adoption inquiry report, multiple studies from both the United States and the UK have shown adoption is the tried and tested way to provide safe and stable alternative homes for abused and neglected children, and to help reverse the setbacks experienced early in life.[277]

Children adopted from care at earlier ages have been found to do better on short- and long-term personal and social indicators than children who are returned to their parents or remain in foster or residential care. Children adopted at earlier ages do better compared to those adopted at older ages, as later adoptions are more likely to break down due to children's behavioural and other problems related to prior abuse and neglect. Still, the studies suggest the vast majority of older-age adoptions are successful. Based on the findings of these studies, Patricia Morgan, a British sociologist and researcher at the UK think tank the Institute of Economic Affairs (IEA) argued in her 1998 book *Adoption and the Care of Children* that the evidence base, along with common sense, refute the claim that "children are almost always better off with natural parents". Adoption is the superior alternative for many children who otherwise would remain in unstable out-of-home care. The blanket claims that child removal does more harm than good, and that adoption is inherently harmful, are wrong.[278]

The evidence adoption would benefit children – and be preferable to drift and churn in care – continues to mount, and was confirmed by the findings of a 2011 British report by Carolyn Davies and Harriet Ward. Davies and Ward reviewed 15 research studies funded by the UK health and education departments that had examined how child protection and other government services responded to the needs of abused and neglected children. Their initial finding was there is "evidence that many children are left for too long or returned prematurely to abusive or neglectful families where their welfare is inadequately safeguarded."[279] They went on to conclude that the evidence also "suggests that maltreated children, and particularly those who are neglected or emotionally abused, may benefit by being looked after away from home ... [and] maltreated children who remain looked after find greater stability and achieve better wellbeing than those who return home."[280] This was based on the additional finding that children "who experience repeated, failed attempts at re-unification have the worst outcomes", and that repeated attempts at reunification should be avoided because this was "damaging to children's wellbeing and jeopardise[s] their chances of achieving permanence through alternative routes."[281]

Davies and Ward's view that long-term care is a "positive alternative for children and young people who have been maltreated"[282] may appear to suggest long-term foster care is as good an alternative route as adoption. The work of British professor of social work John Triseliotis answered this question by evaluating the evidence of outcomes for children who are adopted compared to children in long-term care. Based on a review of the available studies, Triseliotis concluded that the "main defining difference found between these two forms of substitute parenting appears to be the higher levels of emotional security, sense of belonging and general well being expressed by those growing up as adopted compared with those fostered long term."[283]

The major explanation for this appeared to be that adoptions were permanent in a qualitatively different sense to long-term foster care, due to the legal force of an adoption order compared to long-term fostering arrangements, which were liable to be disrupted by child protection authorities and birth parents. The "ambiguous and uncertain position" that children in long-term care found themselves in, compared to children that are adopted, appeared to "generate longstanding feelings of insecurity and anxiety in children" and to account for why adoption "provides higher levels of emotional security, a stronger sense of belonging and a more enduring psychosocial base in life for those who cannot live with their birth families."[284]

In addition, adopted children find permanent families, while many children in long-term care find temporary carers until they turn 18, and often struggle with the transition to living independently. Adoption is not just permanent care during childhood and adolescence – it provides a family for life. This is not to doubt some long-term foster care may also provide children with ongoing love and support into adulthood. Moreover, in some cases, particularly for older children, adoption may not be appropriate and long-term care will prove superior, especially if children don't want to be adopted or removed from their foster home. But the evidence does suggest that, all things being equal, adoption is more likely to generate substantial benefits and a less unpredictable, less uncertain and less ambiguous position for many children, by providing them with a genuinely permanent substitute family for life.

Adoption in Australia

Despite what the evidence indicates about the benefits of adoption, there are pitifully few adoptions in Australia each year. The small number of "local" adoptions is extraordinary, given the rising number of potential candidates for adoption currently in care. In 2014, 29,863 children had been in care continuously for more than two years. This represented 69% of the total number of children living in care,[285] a proportion that has risen from 50% in the early 2000s.[286] But despite the increasing numbers of children spending increasing time in care over the last decade or so, there were only 317 adoptions completed in Australia in 2013–14 – 114 from overseas and 203 local adoptions. Of the local adoptions, there were only 46 where the child was not previously known to the adoptive parents, and in all these cases either or both of the birth parents consented to the adoption. Of the remaining 157 "known" adoptions, 64 were "step-parent" adoptions, 4 were "relative" and "other" adoptions, and only 89 were "carer" adoptions – out of a care population of more than 43,000. To repeat, more than two-thirds (almost 30,000) of these children had been in care continuously for more than two years, a figure that is a proxy for the number of children potentially available for adoption. Moreover, 84 of 89 carer adoptions were in NSW alone. The underperformance or non-performance on adoption from care by other states and territories speaks for itself.[287]

The number of local adoptions has declined dramatically over the last 40 years. There were more than 8,500 adoptions a year in the early 1970s.[288] The massive fall is due to social changes: widespread availability and use of contraception, increased abortions, and the introduction of government benefits for single mothers. Before the 1970s, most adoptions involved the babies of unwed teenage mothers, who were adopted under the practice that has come to be known as forced adoption. But the decline in adoptions is not just a supply-side phenomenon. Many of the thousands of children in long-term care are likely to remain there indefinitely, and many, especially in light of the harm they are exposed to in and out of care, should have been adopted years earlier, and could have if not for the taboo placed on adoption by child protection authorities.

Scholars ideologically opposed to adoption maintain that the explanation for low rates of adoption lies instead in Australian attitudes to adoption:

> Domestic adoption in Australia appears to have lost appeal for parents in search of children partly because the children available for adoption tend to be older or have other special needs. Australians have, on the whole, been less willing to adopt children with special needs, including older children, than their counterparts in the United States and Britain.[289]

Note that what these anti-adoption academic activists appear to be claiming is that older children and those with special needs, who have been damaged by family preservation, are unwanted by Australian families because they are dismissed as unadoptable. This dated assessment does not reflect contemporary Australian attitudes to adoption or fully account for the reasons for low rates of adoption from care today.

Before the 1970s, those who could not have their own children but wished to be parents preferred to adopt babies. This was realistic because there was a reliable supply of infants born to unwed (mostly teenage) mothers. Many older children in care never found adoptive homes, and languished in care their entire childhoods. But this was primarily due to policy. For most of the 20th century, older children in care were classified as unadoptable because of their "history". A rough start in life was believed to have irreversibly damaged them, and meant it was believed adoption by a normal family would fail. The resulting practice of not making children in care available for adoption mirrored the official belief that parents preferred "untainted" babies. This became self-fulfilling when agencies made no efforts to recruit adoptive parents for older children, and turned away those who expressed an interest in adopting them.[290]

As a result, before the 1950s, most "hard-to-place" children were institutionalised. But after the second world war, this began to change. The negative effects of institutionalisation on children's intellects and personalities started to be recognised, which led to greater use of foster care for children who had no prospect of returning home but were still considered unsuitable for adoption. The few older children adopted from care were usually adopted by long-term foster parents, as is the case today. Attitudes and policy changed (briefly) in the mid-1970s, driven by research from the United States that showed children could be successfully adopted irrespective of age. Despite some rapid and early successes with older-age adoption, this discovery never fully translated into practice and was soon forgotten in the wholesale shift towards family preservation.[291] In the wake of the ideological upheaval, Australian child protection authorities made fewer children in care available for adoption – to the point that reporting on the number of children waiting for adoption ceased in the 1990s.[292]

The personal desire of the childless to raise children is still strong – hence the strong stock-market performance of private-sector companies providing in vitro fertilisation (IVF) services – as is the parallel social motive of wanting to give good homes to disadvantaged children. But social change has evaporated what once was a constant supply of babies in need of adoption. As circumstances have changed, the attitudes and expectations of prospective adoptive parents regarding older children have also shifted. Hence, the adoption of older children from overseas has become commonplace. Only 14% of overseas adoptions in 2013–14 (16 out of 114) involved children less than one year of age. Some of these older children would have higher needs due to suboptimal early years.[293]

The claim that Australians are less willing to adopt older children than parents in the United Kingdom and the United States does not account for the role ideology and policy play in obstructing adoption from out of care. The better explanation is that official anti-adoption attitudes are evidently much fiercer in Australia than in comparable countries. Similar anti-adoption attitudes have long been prevalent in the United Kingdom, for example. Yet in England, 5,050 children were adopted from out of care in 2013–14. Of these, 76% were aged one to four, 19% were aged five to nine, and just 4% were under the age of one. The number of children in care per capita in England and Australia is roughly similar. If Australian children in care were adopted at the same rate as in England, there would have been approximately 3,140 adoptions from care in Australia in 2013–14.[294]

On average in the last decade, more than 50,000 United States children have been adopted out of care every year by foster carers and others wanting to become adoptive parents.[295] Of the children adopted from care in 2012–13, only 2% were aged less than one, and 61% were aged four and over. Approximately 58% of the adoptions from care were by foster parents, 31% by relatives, and 26% by non-relatives.[296] The number of children in care per capita in the United States and Australia is roughly similar. If Australian children in care were adopted at the same rate as in the United States, there would have been approximately 5,419 adoptions from care in Australia in 2013–14.

Despite substantial growth in the number of children in care in recent decades, adoption in Australia is acknowledged to be "rare" (by the Australian Institute of Family Studies), primarily due to the "strong push" to restore children to their parents.[297] The plain fact is that adoption from care is so rare in Australia because family preservation-focused child protection authorities will not pursue this option and make children in care available for adoption without parental consent. They will not apply to the courts to dispense with parental consent and to legally terminate the responsibilities of parents who could contest adoptions, no matter how bad or inadequate those parents are.[298] It is sometimes claimed that the use of "permanent care orders", which eventually end drift and churn, and give children stability by placing them permanently with foster carers, has eliminated the need for adoption.[299] However, the Australian Institute of Health and Welfare's annual publication, *Adoptions Australia*, records the numbers of permanent care orders in Victoria. In 2013–14, just 302 such orders were granted.[300]

Similar histories, divergent practices

The UK and the US, like Australia, share child protection histories marred by poor practices and mistreatment of children, parents, and families. Yet the benefits of adoption, compared to the well-known and highly damaging experiences of many children in care, are still recognised in these countries today. In all countries, adoption was done badly in the past. Children were treated as blank slates and as if they had no previous heritage or identity. Hence, adoptions were "closed", meaning adopted children had no contact with their birth parents and extended families, and no knowledge of their background and culture. The result was that some adopted children experienced confusion, loss, and isolation later in life due to separation from their family.

But lessons have been learned from past mistakes, including the realisation that it is important to cultivate the identity and belonging of adopted children. Hence, contemporary adoptions are "open", meaning children's origins are acknowledged, connections with birth parents and extended family are maintained, and links with culture and identity are developed as part of the duty of adoptive parents to act in children's best interests

The change in practice that has led to open adoption processes is a product of acknowledging the negative psychological impacts closed adoptions had on some adopted children. It has been recognised that it is not in children's interests to grow up as mysteries to themselves, without any knowledge of the genetic and cultural backgrounds that are fundamental to personal identity. Closed adoptions meant, among other things, that original birth records were sealed, and there was no way of discovering even basic information about biological parents, let alone any way of making contact and having ongoing relationships with them. Some adopted children consequently struggled with the fact that there were always unanswered questions about who they were, and experienced profound and distressing feelings of loss, confusion and isolation. Changes in practice have been led by the experiences of the adopted children who undertook a literal journey of self-discovery and campaigned for the legislative changes of recent decades that have allowed adoption records to be opened, which enabled some adopted people to solve the mystery about themselves by finding their birth parents, siblings, and other relatives.

Despite improved contemporary practices, Australia remains the outlier internationally in rejecting adoption. An important part of the explanation for this seems to lie in the way the legacy of past practices has created cultural barriers to adoption that have high political potency. Adoption has been stigmatised in Australia particularly because of its association in the public mind with the Stolen Generations of Indigenous children who lost contact with kin and culture when taken away from parents. It has also been strongly and negatively associated with the experiences of the separated mothers, fathers, and children harmed by the forced adoption practices widespread throughout Australia after the second world war. In the wake of the national apologies extended to these groups by the federal parliament in 2008 and 2013 respectively, politicians fear being falsely accused of forcibly removing and stealing another generation of children. Due to the sensitivities, policymakers prefer to profess support for preserving rather than separating families, and for temporary removal only, never permanent removal.[301]

To intimidate politicians, the vocal anti-adoption movement promotes the absurd idea that reviving adoption is tantamount to a return to the bad old days of taking children for racist reasons and ripping babies from the breasts of unwed teenage mothers. The positive impact that adoption by functional families can have on the lives of underclass children is disregarded. Just as importantly, the harm done to many children in the name of avoiding repeating past mistakes is also underappreciated by those unwilling to countenance adoption in any form, even though it would be the most effective way to stop the system abuse of children.[302]

Adoption is also a cultural minefield because it goes against the grain of what many like to think are the enlightened and progressive social values of today, which also render adoption politically unacceptable. Attitudes to adoption have been shaped by changing social attitudes since the social revolution of the 1960s, especially regarding marriage, family, and children. The case for adoption struggles to win acceptance because accepting the need for greater use of adoption from care challenges the myths that otherwise prevail about so-called family diversity – the idea that all families, regardless of the marital status of parents, are equally beneficial for children. Hence the taboo on adoption as a socially acceptable practice remains in place, even though adoption is needed to address major social problems concerning the welfare of children in underclass families – which, ironically have stemmed in considerable part from the consequences of ending forced adoption and the resulting rise in single motherhood.

Senate inquiry into forced adoption

In February 2012, the Senate Community Affairs References Committee tabled a bipartisan report, *Commonwealth Contribution to Former Forced Adoption Policies and Practices*, which recommended the federal parliament issue a formal statement of apology for the role the Commonwealth played between the 1950s and mid-1970s in the routine adoption by childless married couples of an estimated 150,000 babies of unwed (mostly teenage) mothers.[303]

The Senate report mainly canvassed the experiences of unwed mothers subjected to unethical and unlawful treatment by hospital staff, social workers, and faith-based adoption agencies, which resulted in an unknown number of young and vulnerable mothers being coerced into signing adoption forms and relinquishing their babies for adoption. The inquiry, which received 418 submissions from individuals and organisations, found that many decades after these events, it was not able to "express a view about any particular cases" of alleged malpractice involving duress and uninformed or fraudulently obtained consent. Nor was it able to determine the extent to which these problems were systemic.[304]

However, there is no doubt some unwed mothers and their children experienced grief. Nor is there any doubt some of these women, by their own accounts (as revealed to the Senate inquiry), were victimised and subjected to pressure that amounted to immoral and unconscionable coercion and manipulation. When people have suffered hurt and anguish, the human instinct is to feel compassion and express sorrow, understanding and regret. No doubt spurred by this sentiment, the Gillard government announced in June 2012 that it would act on the Senate inquiry's recommendations, and offer in 2013 an apology on behalf of the nation as a "step in the healing process to acknowledge the trauma of forced adoption".[305]

That a national apology for forced adoption was deserved seems unarguable, and the national impulse to say sorry was based on good-hearted sentiments. Discredited attitudes and practices once common and condoned – such as refusing to allow unwed mothers to see or hold their newborn babies – certainly strike us today as cruel and punitive. This was especially so when efforts to ensure a clean break between mother and child involved using pillows to shield the mother's face during delivery, and shackling mothers to their bed to prevent post-natal visits to the nursery.[306] Yet it is also important to appreciate the thinking behind forced adoption if the contemporary social and child protection policy significance of the national apology is to be understood.

In the 1950s and 1960s, the attitudes and practices condemned today, together with the institutionalisation of virtually automatic adoption in response to pregnancy out of wedlock, were considered tough but humane. If an unmarried woman did not have financial support from her family, or married the father, the view before the 1970s was that the only realistic option, in the best interests of the child, was for the mother to consent to adoption. The wrench of giving up the baby she could not support financially would be less, or so it was thought, if the mother had not bonded with it.[307]

The presumption was that unwed mothers without breadwinning husbands would be unable to combine child-rearing duties with paid work. Children would therefore have to be given up for adoption, given that the meagre government benefits then available were insufficient to support mother and child. Adoption of children born out of wedlock was designed, in part, to prevent the creation of an underclass of unmarried women and their children, who otherwise would inevitably require public assistance.

By these means, traditional family values were also upheld. The widely held conviction was that it was unquestionably in the children's and society's best interests for a child to have a married mother and father, and for a child to be raised in an intact and financially self-supporting family, be it biological or adoptive. Hence, respectable social conventions stigmatised and shamed women who conceived children out of wedlock. Pre-marital sex was frowned on, and personal autonomy in sexual matters did not trump the public interest in avoiding the harm done to children and society by irresponsible sexual behaviour. Social and moral disapproval was expressed through the general acceptance of what is now considered the draconian social policy of adopting out the babies of young, unwed mothers, who were pressured by families, health and welfare workers, and by society at large, to agree to give up their "illegitimate" children for adoption.[308]

The Senate inquiry into forced adoption had little sympathy for the values of earlier times.[309] Scrutinising what were deemed (in a pejorative sense) as "conservative societal attitudes" led the inquiry to employ a broad definition of forced adoption with respect to the role of the Commonwealth.[310] The report maintained that the Commonwealth — which had no constitutional responsibility for the adoption laws and processes overseen by state governments — should apologise for financially coercing unmarried women and giving them no other realistic option than to submit to forced adoption. The Commonwealth's failure to extend the scope of social security payments to include welfare benefits for unwed mothers was deemed wrong and deserving of an apology because provision of taxpayer-funded income support would have enabled many women to keep their children.[311]

Having established that lack of sufficient government benefits was a "key factor" leading many mothers to relinquish their babies,[312] the Senate inquiry lauded as a social leap forward the Whitlam government's decision to support rather than stigmatise and discriminate against unwed mothers by introducing the single mother's ("supporting mother's") pension in 1973.[313] The inquiry rightly identified this as the moment when social attitudes to marriage, the family, and the raising of children were officially revolutionised. Unmarried women no longer needed to give up their babies for financial reasons and comply with traditional social values, as conduct previously considered antisocial now received state sanction and was reclassified as deserving of government support.

These developments were in keeping with the permissive spirit of toleration fostered by the 1960s social revolution, which rapidly altered the social conventions surrounding sex, marriage, and children. Relaxation of social attitudes led to social acceptance of behaviours previously judged personally immoral and socially irresponsible, such as pre-marital sex, divorce, and conceiving children out of wedlock. Changing community mores concerning marital status meant that divorce, cohabitation, and single motherhood were no longer subjected to the same degree of prejudice and discrimination that was hitherto applied to enforce the traditional code of behaviour.[314]

Changed conventions changed behaviour. Until the early 1970s, less than 10% of births in Australia were ex-nuptial. The number of births out of registered marriage steadily rose in the following decades, and had tripled to over 30% by 2000[315] and 34% in 2010.[316] The official statistics do not distinguish between cohabiting and single mothers. David de Vaus and Matthew Gray estimate that in the 1960s, between 5% and 6% of births were to single mothers; by the early 2000s, this had increased to over 11%.[317]

The fight to end the discrimination against unmarried women was also led by middle-class activists who defied convention and kept their babies, and who in the late 1960s mobilised single mothers into a political lobby centred on the National Council for Single Mothers and their Children. The successful campaign to establish the "right" to receive welfare soon became associated with the women's liberation movement of the 1970s. For this reason, the introduction of the single mother's pension and the greater social acceptance of single motherhood are usually portrayed as a feminist triumph that liberated women from the patriarchal institution of marriage. Women's economic dependence on men was eliminated by the state stepping in to assume the roles of father and husband via the provision of taxpayer-funded payments to fund the "independent" raising of children.[318]

Consistent with this interpretation, the Senate inquiry endorsed the idea that the social-policy developments of the 1970s and the "shift towards greater support for single mothers" to help them keep their children represented unalloyed social goods.[319] The report was in line with the standard "progressive" account of the evolution of the family over the last 40 years, which celebrates the rise of single motherhood and the decline of the institutions of marriage and the traditional nuclear family as victories for tolerance, feminism, and the status of women.[320] The report therefore praised the diversity of family types the single mother's pension made possible, and criticised previous generations for discriminating against unmarried women and making strict judgements about the best circumstances in which to raise children.[321] The intolerance and stigmatisation experienced by unwed mothers not supported by the state, and the social pressure to agree to adoption in the virtual absence of any other state-supported choice, were also singled out for condemnation by the inquiry.[322]

Family breakdown

The Senate report is an important document because it is a faithful guide to contemporary social attitudes, as mediated through analysis of past practices based on the commitment to the modern principle of family diversity. This is best illustrated by the issues the Senate report chose not to discuss. The inquiry's reflexive endorsement of progressive social values overlooked the social consequences of the changes to welfare and family policy in the early 1970s, and all that has subsequently been learned over the past four decades about the breakdown of the family and child welfare. The story of supposed social advancement outlined in the Senate committee's report did not accord with the far-from-positive relationship between the rise of single motherhood and the well-being of children.

Rather than the state-sponsored breakdown of the family having liberated and empowered women, the decision to recognise women's (supposed) "right to have a family without a husband" and right to receive "the income maintenance they needed to achieve independence"[323] has transformed the welfare-dependent single-mother phenomenon into a leading cause of female and child poverty.[324] The inquiry entirely overlooked the chief legacy of the social and policy changes that helped end forced adoption. The unfashionable truth is that welfare for the unwed has created a pathway to dependence and dysfunction for a significant underclass of single mothers and their children – and contributed significantly to the scale of the child protection problems confronting the country.

International and Australian studies show that child abuse and neglect is more prevalent in single-mother families.[325] Most families, regardless of composition, who frequently come to the attention of child protection authorities tend to share common sources of dysfunction – such as welfare dependence, drug and alcohol abuse, domestic violence, and mental illness – and a related breakdown of behavioural standards concerning the proper care of children.[326] However, these kinds of single-mother families are significantly over-represented in cases of child maltreatment in Australia.

In 2009–10, 15% of children aged 0–17 lived in single-mother households, according to the Australian Bureau of Statistics (ABS) Family Characteristic Survey.[327] In 2013–14, "single parent – female" families accounted for over a quarter (26.4%) of all substantiated cases of child abuse and neglect. The rate of child abuse and neglect in these households is almost twice that expected, given the number of single-mother families. Moreover, the available data is almost certainly an underestimate, because it does not distinguish between "never-married" households and other types of single-mother households. This means that many of the "two-parent step- or blended" families that account for 15.6% of substantiated child abuse and neglect could be rightly classified as products of the rise of single motherhood.[328]

The relationship between family structure and child maltreatment is consistent with the negative consequences of family breakdown that are verified by a wealth of studies examining family structure and other measures of child welfare.[329] These studies have consistently found that children in an intact family in which the biological mother and father remain married derive, on average, modest but consistent educational, social, cognitive and behavioural benefits. Conversely, divorce and family non-formation (cohabiting and single-parent families) have been found to be significantly associated, on average, with a range of adverse outcomes that persist into adulthood, and the "evidence on the benefits of marriage for the well-being of children has continued to mount."[330] Marriage, as the foundation of family life, seems to be in a child's best interests while the alternative – raising children outside of intact two-parent married families – appears to compromise their care and socialisation.[331]

Summarising the evidence, US political scientist Charles Murray says:

> No matter what the outcome being examined—the quality of the mother-infant relationship, externalizing behaviour in childhood (aggression, delinquency, and hyperactivity), delinquency in adolescence, criminality as adults, illness and injury in childhood, early mortality, sexual decision making in adolescence, school problems and dropping out, emotional health, and any other measure of how well or poorly children do in life – the family structure that produces the best outcomes for children, on average, [is] two biological parents who remain married. Divorced parents produced the next-best outcomes. Whether the parents remarry or remain single while the children are growing up makes little difference. Never married women produce the worst outcomes. All of these statements apply after controlling for the family's socio-economic status.[332]

Kay S. Hymowitz of New York's Manhattan Institute says the

"single-mother revolution" is a leading cause of socio-economic inequality because:

> Decades of research show that kids growing up with single mothers (again, even after you allow for the obvious variables) have lower scholastic achievement from kindergarten through to high school, as well as higher rates of drug and alcohol abuse, depression, behaviour problems, and teen pregnancy. All these factors are likely to reduce their eventual incomes.[333]

This is consistent with Australian research on family structure and child well-being. A study published in 2012 by Lixia Qu and Ruth Weston, based on high-quality longitudinal data of children born in the late 1990s and early 2000s, found that compared to children with married parents, "those living with their sole mothers appeared to fare less well in terms of social-emotional, learning, and physical development."[334] The findings that children in sole-mother families "fare much worse" supported the

> ... great deal of evidence ... suggesting that children in these families are at an elevated risk of displaying a broad range of emotional and behavioural adjustment problems and low school achievement. Factors explaining such trends include the poorer financial circumstances of sole-mother families, poorer maternal health, fewer effective parenting practices, and more limited social support networks.[335]

This literature indicates the strong class dimensions to the *on average* adverse outcomes for children in non-traditional families, which occur on a continuum[336] in which the "worst outcomes" are strongly associated with "low socioeconomic status" (a.k.a. welfare-dependent) single mothers.[337] The worst problems for child welfare appear not to stem from divorce or even single parenting in themselves, but from family non-formation in specific socio-economic circumstances involving welfare-dependent (and invariably younger and less-educated) single mothers.[338]

The sound of silence

Approximately 27% (more than one in four) Australian children do not currently live with both biological parents.[339] In 1960, by comparison, around 90% of children lived with both biological parents.[340] Rising rates of divorce and ex-nuptial births have led to substantial growth in the number of blended, step- and single-parent families. Only 7.1% of families with dependent children were single-parent families in the late 1960s, compared to 22.3% in the early 2000s, and the proportion of step- and blended families has approximately doubled.[341] The rise of single motherhood has thus had a substantial impact on community well-being, given the range of social problems and costs (to the state) associated with childhood abuse and neglect. This is on top of the billions of dollars that have been spent on transfer payments since 1973. The current annual cost to the federal budget of Parenting Payment (single and partnered) is $5.8 billion, and approximately two-thirds of the more than 360,000 recipients are single mothers.[342]

Despite the dire overall statistics, many single mothers raise happy and successful children, and are to be admired for overcoming financial and other challenges. It is also true that all kinds of families can succeed or fail to raise well-adjusted children. Many single mothers thus understandably resent the stereotypes, and the feeling they are being scapegoated for child harm and related social problems for which they are not responsible.[343]

Yet a large volume of evidence shows the key non-judgemental idea the social revolution has popularised and elevated into an alleged marker of social progress and greater tolerance – that the traditional family is just one among many equally valid and worthwhile family forms – is plainly wrong. The social sciences have repeatedly and consistently demonstrated that irrespective of class, on average marriage makes a real difference to child welfare. Nevertheless, mainstream cultural gatekeepers prefer to avert their eyes. In Murray's words:

> I know of no other set of important findings that are as broadly accepted by social scientists that follow the technical literature, liberal as well as conservative, and yet are so resolutely ignored by network news programs, editorial writers for the major newspapers, and politicians of both major parties.[344]

Murray's description of the wilful blindness among cultural elites in the United States equally applies to Australian public life and the role cultural elites play here in policing debates on contentious social issues. The default countercultural values embraced since the social revolution by the majority of university-educated elites with culture-shaping positions in key political, media, and academic institutions[345] account for the reluctance to give prominence to culturally unfashionable, socially conservative views that challenge the post-1960s "progressive" consensus on moral tolerance, personal liberation, and family diversity. This reflects the shift in moral sentiment that accompanied the social changes of the period, which has had a lasting influence on mainstream cultural values and has seen Western societies such as Australia cease to make collective moral judgements about good and bad behaviour.[346] As a result, the negative social consequences of the social revolution are rarely criticised, and key social issues are insufficiently scrutinised. Among these is the potentially harmful impact on children of adult behaviours – such as divorce and having children out of wedlock – that were previously judged immoral and irresponsible but are now socially accepted.[347]

Hence, while social change has transformed the character of Australian families, there is little community debate and discussion about family breakdown and child welfare. The issue remains on the political fringe and has little cultural salience, because cultural politics intervene before it can be talked about. Due to strong cultural resistance to a message that contradicts "progressive" social values, public discourse is self-censored in compliance with politically correct attitudes towards family diversity.

Public discussion of family matters is inhibited by acts of omission – facts not reported in the media do not exist in terms of public debate and policy. For instance, Qu and Weston's study on marital status and child well-being was not reported on by the media, despite its challenging and important finding that the children of sole mothers were doing less well than others.[348] This is an example of what social commentator and author Bettina Arndt describes as the chronic failure by agenda-setting media organisations, especially the highly influential Australian Broadcasting Corporation (ABC), to discuss family-related social issues and trends if it would challenge the progressive consensus on family diversity that cultural elites have invested much political and intellectual capital in.[349]

If one did not already know better, this is an area where one might expect the Australian child and family welfare social services sector to be leading the debate and advocating for children. Instead, the state and territory community service departments, together with NGO social services, are bastions of the non-judgemental attitudes that characterise the modern social-work profession. Progressive social attitudes and anti-traditional family values are endorsed by promoting the fiction that says all families, however constituted, are equally beneficial for children.

Endorsing family diversity chiefly entails downplaying the links between family type and child abuse – such as the over-representation of single-mother and other non-traditional families in child protection caseloads – to avoid "judgemental discrimination of certain types of families."[350] A 2012 report on family structure and child abuse, published by the taxpayer-funded Child Family Community Australia Information Exchange, exemplifies the studied non-judgemental attitude that is the norm among social workers and the organisations they work for. The authors protested against stigmatising non-traditional families, on the grounds that "much of the perceived relationship between family structure and child maltreatment can be explained by factors such as poverty, substance misuse and domestic violence."[351]

Despite the obvious sensitivity of the issue for many, the understandable desire to not unnecessarily offend some members of the community should not preclude discussion of the broader social issue of the risks certain family structures pose – on average – to the welfare of children. The social science on family structure and child outcomes, together with child protection data revealing the over-representation of certain types of families, demonstrates strong and well-recognised links between single motherhood, dependence and dysfunction, and child maltreatment. In the sober words of the NSW DoCS literature review, the stereotype is all too accurate in many cases:

> The typical neglecting family is likely to be a young, single mother who has experienced poor parenting herself, lives in an overcrowded chaotic household with several children, and is dependent on public assistance for support. She is likely to have inadequate social support, abuse substances, be depressed and, if partnered, suffer domestic violence. She is so overwhelmed by life and perhaps drugs or alcohol that she fails to adequately care for, be psychologically available to, or supervise her children.[352]

The anti-adoption movement

The ever-increasing demand for and cost of child protection services in Australia illustrates a tragic social reality. In this country, there is a growing underclass of inadequate parents who are not fit to care for children, which includes disproportionate numbers of single-mother families. It is no coincidence that the breakdown of the traditional family and the proliferation of state-supported single motherhood have coincided with the perpetual crisis that has engulfed the Australian child protection system in recent decades. Spiralling numbers of reported cases of child maltreatment have gone along with the normalisation of welfare-dependent parenting.

Australian child protection services have failed to respond appropriately to the crisis because of the shift in the past 40 years from traditional child rescue to family preservation policies. This shift has been partly driven, and partly reinforced by, the social-work profession's desire not to repeat what are now perceived as historic wrongs.[353] Permanently removing children by adoption, even from bad parents, and whether by consent or by court order, is considered akin to the discredited forced adoption practices of previous eras and the accompanying lack of support for diverse families. The reluctance to consider making children available for adoption, particularly when many dysfunctional families are headed by single mothers, reflects the social-work profession's concern not to repeat history and replicate the harm done to separated mothers and children.

The taboo on adoption for child protection purposes demonstrates how culturally and politically powerful the memory of forced adoptions is, and how the memory of these practices is exploited to shape the debate about child protection policy.

The anti-adoption movement in Australia consists of influential advocacy groups, backed by vocal academic activists, who maintain that having heard the stories told by the women who experienced forced adoption, we should learn from the past. The movement claims we now know adoption harms not only the separated mother but also the stolen child, whose genetic identity is lost by severing the connection with birth parents, and that we should "never again" repeat the same mistakes.³⁵⁴ The intention is to exploit the history of forced adoption to discredit all uses of adoption as socially and politically illegitimate and unacceptable in modern Australia, even if adoption is necessary to protect children from unfit parents. This is done by characterising any move to lift the number of children adopted from out of care as a "re-emergence of 'forced adoption'", with the argument being that all adoptions would be "forced" and allegedly caused due to inadequate government support for parents to care for children.³⁵⁵ By also focusing on an indeterminate number of adoptions that may involve unethical and illegal practices – including allegations of a trade in babies for adoption by Westerners from developing countries – a broad brush is used to tar all adoptions as illegitimate and harmful.³⁵⁶

The call for a national apology for forced adoption was a key part of the long-term campaign to ban all adoptions waged by the anti-adoption movement. The submission to the Senate inquiry by the high-profile anti-adoption advocacy group Vanish maintained:

> In the national apology to the adoption community, there must be an acknowledgment that separation by adoption causes distress; henceforth the Australian Government will dedicate its resources to keeping families together. Any apology needs to confirm that the lessons of the past have been learned; that the Commonwealth's resources are to be redeployed in the name of family integration … Without this undertaking, any national apology will be undermined.³⁵⁷

The submission went on to claim that the national apology required the phasing out of inter-country adoptions. With regard to local child protection issues, the insistence on government resources being used to keep families together was code for persevering with flawed family preservation policies and practices. The political strategy was to heighten sensitivities and make policymakers reluctant to support adoption for child protection purposes and avoid being accused of once again stealing children from grief-stricken parents and depriving them of their identity. The purpose of this powerful and morally intimidating argument was to strengthen the taboo on adoption, based on the notion that all adoptions are harmful and illegitimate, and that without a commitment to learn from the past and not repeat the same mistakes, any apology would not be sincere. This amounts to using and abusing the history of forced adoption by explicitly warning that using adoption for child protection purposes will repeat "the mistakes of the past."[358]

The Vanish submission was quoted with approval in the Senate report, in keeping with the inquiry's recommendation that "all those involved in current adoption practices [should] ... take the findings of this report into account to ensure that the mistakes of the past are never repeated."[359] Hence, the Senate report is an important document not only because it is a faithful guide to contemporary social attitudes to past practices and to family diversity, but also because it demonstrates how those attitudes shape current attitudes to adoption. The Senate inquiry's failure to discuss the social and child welfare problems caused by the proliferation of single motherhood was also compounded by its failure to consider the broader questions of contemporary child protection policy that were relevant to the national apology. The inquiry simply did not pay any attention to the implications of the way criticism of forced adoption practices can today involve outright opposition to adoption in all forms and under any circumstances.[360]

State parliamentary apologies

In 2012, five state governments issued parliamentary apologies for forced adoption in rapid succession. Western Australia had been the first state to apologise, in October 2010. Following the publication of the Senate report in February 2012, which recommended that all states make separate formal apologies, South Australia (July), NSW (September), Victoria (October), Tasmania (October), and Queensland (November) also apologised. A 2000 NSW parliamentary inquiry into forced adoption supported an apology, but no action was taken by the NSW government until after the Gillard government committed in June 2012 to delivering an apology on behalf of the Commonwealth.

The state apologies took the form of parliamentary motions, with members of parliament from all sides of politics delivering speeches in support. The sentiments expressed by state parliamentarians overwhelmingly reflected the progressive and politically correct arguments and assumptions of the Senate inquiry report. The influence the report had on attitudes to the forced adoption issue largely accounts for the uniformity of parliamentary opinion. The texts of the formal motions of apology varied from state to state, but together with members' speeches, they provide insight into social values and attitudes of the political class to child protection and adoption.

The apologies operated on four levels. In general, they expressed sincere regret, sympathy and acknowledgement for (1) the pain, suffering and grief of separated mothers; (2) the unethical and unlawful malpractices and duress to which some young and vulnerable women were subjected; (3) the societal attitudes that led to the stigmatisation of and discrimination against unwed mothers; and (4) the flawed government policies not supportive of unwed mothers, who had little choice other than to relinquish their babies.

A contemporary edge was placed on the apologies for forced adoption by the welter of criticism parliamentarians heaped on the "less enlightened" social values and welfare policies of previous eras. Politicians committed to socially progressive views seized on the opportunity to tolerate no dissent regarding complex and contentious social issues. This was typified by the speech of Alison Xamon, a member of the Western Australian Greens party, who argued the prejudice that "drove these abhorrent practices" was not "entirely dead" because:

> Discrimination against women who raise their children out of wedlock and on their own [is] still very much alive and well. Those who peddle this hurt may not be stealing the babies anymore but they are still attempting to perpetuate the thinking that led people to think that it was okay, if not preferable, to steal these babies from their mothers.

According to Xamon, discrimination included the "bogus" social science evidence that shows the children of single mothers do worse on average and are over-represented in child protection cases. This Xamon dismissed as merely the type of "thinking that remains a painful hangover from exactly the same thinking that enabled the state and the churches to tear at the very heart of the mother–child relationship and to undertake the very behaviour that we are apologising for today."[361]

More surprising was the extent to which politicians from the right of the political spectrum expressed similar "progressive" sentiments. For example, the Victorian Liberal premier, Ted Baillieu, abjectly apologised for the health and welfare policies that "did not provide or require support or attention for parents faced with a pregnancy out of wedlock."[362] The Liberal NSW premier, Barry O'Farrell, echoed Baillieu's lament for the lack of "care and support," and went further by declaring, ahistorically, that it was:

> ... hard to fathom how these practices were allowed to occur when today in the twenty-first century we celebrate motherhood and family diversity in all its forms.[363]

However, Baillieu and O'Farrell were outdone by the then Liberal leader of the opposition in Tasmania in complying with politically correct and self-congratulatory attitudes to family diversity. Will

Hodgman not only apologised for the lack of government support, but also for the "moralistic and judgmental attitudes that prevailed." He also said it was naive to think the old stigmas attached to single mothers had entirely disappeared, and hoped that repudiating such thinking was "one of the lessons from today and for the future."[364] Hodgman's shadow minister for child protection, Jacquie Petrusma, followed this up by declaring that "enough support" must be given to single mothers so that child removal occurs only as a last resort. So that the "lessons of history" were not repeated and another apology needed in the future, she said, "we must make sure that we do everything we can to keep mother[s] and babies together, especially to support, nurture and encourage young single mothers."[365]

This sampling of parliamentary opinion demonstrates the degree to which the "never again" sentiments of the anti-adoption movement were incorporated into the apologies for forced adoption. This also illustrates the cognitive dissonance that expressions of support for family diversity have involved. Apologies have been made for stigmatising and failing to provide government support to single mothers, while implicitly conceding that single-mother families commonly struggle to parent children adequately, and that they require support and "more services." The "outdated conventional wisdom"[366] about the best circumstances in which to raise children that motivated the practice of forced adoption was denounced while parliamentarians studiously avoided mention of the way the negative social consequences of our time's more "enlightened" policies have borne out the wisdom of traditional social values concerning marriage and the family. In sum, the state apologies complied with the anti-adoption movement's demand that apologies not be "undermined", because they backed the idea that governments must continue efforts to support, not separate, problem families. Endorsed alongside the family preservation approach was the taboo on adoption and the radical social-worker view of the need for state support to fulfil the "right" of problem parents to parent. Parliamentarians' comments on the issue appeared oblivious to how these flawed ideas have compounded the child protection crisis confronting the nation today.

The national apology

The national apology for forced adoption was delivered in the Great Hall of Parliament House, Canberra, on 21 March 2013. Its formal text heaped predictable opprobrium on previous generations for the "shameful practices" and harsh and outdated attitudes that had led to the separation of unwed mothers from their babies. Consistent with the "never again" sentiments of the anti-adoption movement, the apology also culminated with an implicit endorsement of family preservation:

> We resolve, as a nation, to do all in our power to make sure these practices are never repeated. In facing future challenges, we will remember the lessons of family separation. Our focus will be on protecting the fundamental rights of children and on the importance of the child's right to know and be cared for by his or her parents.[367]

In her speech, Prime Minister Julia Gillard stuck closely to the sentiments of the anti-adoption movement, and said: "We can promise you that no generations of Australians will suffer the same pain and trauma that you did – the cruel, immoral practice of forced adoption that will have no place in this land anymore."[368] In his speech, then opposition leader Tony Abbott also went to great lengths to endorse family diversity:

> There are no first- and second-class mothers. There are no first- or second-class children. Every child deserves a mother's love, and every mother has the right to raise her child. We know it now, and we should have known it then. It should never have been presumed—presumed—that some mothers

were incapable of raising their child, because, as everyone here knows only too well, there was presumption and there was coercion, by families, by charities, by peers, and by the conditions that governments placed upon people. The harder something is—and few things are harder than raising a child alone—the more people should have had our support, not our judgment. We were hard-hearted and judgemental, and that is why we should apologise. We did inflict pain on those we loved and on those we had a responsibility for. For some, we turned what should have been the wonderful experience of new life into something filled with shame. Instead of love, there was reproach; instead of support, rejection; instead of celebration, silence; and instead of justice, wrongdoing.[369]

Abbott outdid the similar sentiments expressed by his state Liberal counterparts. However, his speech was derailed when he attempted to inject some balance into discussion of the contemporary implications of the national apology for the practice of adoption today. To his credit, Abbott sought to ensure that the apology was not a repudiation of all adoptions as illegitimate. But his mention of the term "birth parents", and acknowledgement of "those adoptive parents who have tried to do the right thing by their children", provoked angry interjections. Members of the audience shouted that they were the true parents. Forced to apologise and retract, Abbott got into further trouble when he said that "whenever adoptions take place, they have to be chosen and they have to be for the right reason." This strategic, coded attempt to assert that adoption was necessary and acceptable for child protection reasons prompted further heckling, with an audience member yelling out, "All adoptions should be banned."[370]

The incident shows how easy it is to get tripped up by the cultural politics of adoption, and the risks involved in deviating from the culturally correct line. This demonstrated the power and political importance of the "never again" sentiment of the anti-adoption movement in determining what is and isn't considered acceptable to say about adoption, and hence the need for politicians to exercise caution in speaking on the subject, lest they be characterised as unfeeling throwbacks to the discredited "judgemental" era of forced adoption.

The consequences of this – the resulting unwillingness among the political class to endorse the use of adoption – has real policy implications. A discussion paper on options for reform released by the Queensland Child Protection Commission of Inquiry in October 2012 cautiously raised adoption "as one response" to provide children with stable and permanent families. The inquiry exercised caution on this subject, despite:

> Empirical evidence [that] suggests that, compared with long-term fostering, adoption is favourable because it generates higher levels of emotional security, a greater sense of belonging and a "more enduring psychosocial base in life for those [children] who cannot live with their birth families."[371]

Significantly, however, the commission was reluctant to strongly support greater use of adoption, primarily due to concerns about the "historical practices of forced adoption in Australia," and consequent doubts about whether adoption is a "socially acceptable and appropriate 21st century option for children who are unable to remain with their family."[372] The timidity displayed by the Queensland inquiry illustrates how the legacy of forced adoption makes it more difficult for the community to effectively address the serious problem of child maltreatment, and why the national apology was a lost opportunity.

How the nation said sorry, and what it said sorry for, have real implications for child protection policy, since the apology appeared to repudiate all uses of adoption, just as anti-adoption activists intended. By seeming to endorse the anti-adoption movement's view that adoption is always inherently harmful, the national and state apologies cast further doubt on the legitimacy and acceptability of adoption for child protection purposes in 21st-century Australia. Despite Tony Abbott's lone but faltering efforts, the national apology was a missed opportunity for federal parliament to exercise national leadership on child protection issues in the best interest of children by endorsing the appropriate and beneficial use of adoption from care.

The easy moralism of saying sorry

Parliamentarians have the right to be critical of policies and practices they consider the misguided products of less enlightened times. They also have the right to condemn these as morally wrong, as some have deemed forced adoption to be, in agreement with the Senate report, which recommended that the forced adoption apology contain no qualifications concerning contemporary values and judgements about children's best interests.[373] It is also understandable that politicians are morally and politically intimidated by the thought of being accused of repeating past mistakes and stealing children from devastated parents. However, members of parliament also have a responsibility to face up to the consequences of today's "moral" and "enlightened" policies, and they will be held to account by history for current child protection policies.

Given the different standards and circumstances that applied in earlier eras, apologies for past government policies should only be made when the means and ends pursued were unambiguously morally deficient. Previous generations believed that adoption of children of unwed mothers was an effective child welfare measure and method of preventing a serious social problem by averting the formation of fatherless families.[374] Looking at the social statistics on children from broken families, who can say unequivocally that our forebears were entirely wrong in consciously deciding to forestall anticipated social harms by not adding single mothers to the welfare rolls? Furthermore, the child protection legacy of the social-policy changes that led to the end of forced adoption cannot be overlooked. Expanding welfare benefits helped put an end to forced adoption by enabling unwed mothers to financially support their children. But establishing the right of unwed mothers to receive welfare also led to the very social problems that forced adoption was designed to prevent. By facilitating dependency and dysfunction, welfare for the unwed has significantly contributed to the creation of an underclass of abused and neglected children in need of removal and adoption by good families.

The spate of official apologies issued in recent times in Australia has given politicians the opportunity to pick and choose the mistakes and errors they say sorry for. The general rule is that apologies are tendered for actions taken by those who are safely dead, and for actions that can be easily labelled as conservative and discriminatory because they transgress fashionable contemporary values. This is the easy moralism that condemns previous generations for past sins while ignoring contemporary faults. The apologies for forced adoption morphed into an uncritical and self-congratulatory celebration of family diversity, and did indeed practice the easy moralism about the sins of yesterday while abrogating the duty of parliamentarians to promote social policies that advance child welfare. So-called progressive social values and welfare policies have proven anything but pure social advances, and state-sponsored single motherhood has proven toxic for child welfare – as the over-representation of single-mother families in the child abuse caseloads demonstrates.

We cannot afford to practice this easy moralism if we are going to address the social disaster of contemporary child protection. We must resist the temptation to simplistically condemn previous generations for discriminating against unmarried women while we mindlessly praise family diversity for the sake of political correctness. Given the social realities of today, contemporary evils, and not just the sins of earlier times, need to be front of mind. The negative consequences of the progressive attitudes that have prevailed since the 1970s should be acknowledged, as should the way these attitudes hamper the community response to child maltreatment. This includes honestly facing up to and addressing the real legacy of the end of forced adoption.

There is no suggestion of whitewashing the past, or simplistically treating forced adoption as a necessary means to a justifiable end. The point of reviewing the social-policy developments of the last half century is to draw attention to their verifiably bad consequences for contemporary child welfare, and to the need for current generations to take responsibility for addressing these issues today.

In the United Kingdom, this kind of thinking about the downside of the social revolution of the last half century has shaped the debate on child protection policy in the best interests of children. The Blair government's *Adoption Act* of 2000 failed to increase the number of children adopted from care as intended, due to resistance from social workers. Martin Narey, the former chief executive of the children's charity Barnardo's, who was appointed adoption adviser to the Cameron government in 2011, has stressed that responsible ministers must insist the interests of children come before the rights of parents, and must tell child protection authorities that adoption at earlier ages is in children's best interests. He has also recommended social workers resume the once-standard practice of advising struggling, welfare-reliant single mothers that consenting to adoption will give their babies the best chance in life.[375]

The reality, in Australia too, is that the child protection crisis will not be solved without increasing the number of adoptions. If this policy is to succeed, history will have to repeat itself to an extent. Single mothers, among the burgeoning underclass of dysfunctional families, will have to be told again, via the legal process of freeing maltreated children for adoption, that their children will be better off adopted. Even if acknowledging the culturally inconvenient links between single motherhood and child abuse and neglect causes discomfort by recalling the history of what unwed mothers were told in justification of forced adoption, it is still better to disturb complacent social beliefs than continue to tolerate child maltreatment the name of respecting family diversity. All families are not equal, and this myth should no longer be allowed to help keep adoption for child protection purposes taboo in this country.

It is not only the legacy of forced adoption that affects contemporary child protection practices for the worse. The complex legacy of the Stolen Generations also has an often-deleterious impact on what is and is not done to protect Indigenous children. How to rightly and properly address the legacy of past mistreatment of Indigenous Australians, but in a way that can be reconciled with the promotion of Indigenous child welfare, is one of the most difficult and contentious issues the nation faces. But we must face and address it if we are to achieve the national objectives of Indigenous reconciliation and of closing the gap between the most disadvantaged Indigenous Australians and other Australians.

6

KINSHIP CONUNDRUM: POLITICISATION OF THE STOLEN GENERATIONS

Impractical reconciliation: keeping the gaps open

Less than a decade after the National Apology for the Stolen Generations was issued in 2008 by Prime Minister Kevin Rudd, governments Australia-wide are vulnerable to the emotive charge of repeating the errors of the past if they fail to adopt "culturally appropriate" Indigenous child protection policies and practices. The legacy of the Stolen Generations raises important and well-intentioned considerations, which must form part of any discussion about child protection policy for Indigenous children. Part of dealing with that legacy, and part of achieving reconciliation between Indigenous and non-Indigenous Australians, is to understand the devastating impact of past child removal practices on Indigenous people. This especially includes the impact on the cultural identity of the members of the Stolen Generations who experienced loss, confusion, and isolation as a result of the child removal policies and practices that saw thousands of Indigenous children separated from their families before the 1980s, which were intended to assimilate Indigenous children into mainstream Australian society and prevent children from maintaining family ties and connections with traditional culture and identity.[376]

Recognition of past failings and the importance of cultural identity means that, in principle and if it was safe to do so, every Indigenous child who cannot live safely with their parents would be put in "kinship care" placements in accordance with the Aboriginal and Torres Strait Islander Child Placement Principle (ACPP). The ACPP means child protection authorities seek, where possible, to place Indigenous children who need to be removed from parents and taken into care with extended family members, the Indigenous child's community, or with other Indigenous people. This is intended to allow children to maintain contact with Indigenous culture – language, ceremonies, and traditions, including spiritual connection to traditional lands – and to thereby preserve the child's Indigenous cultural identity.

For the reasons set out in Chapter 4, there are good reasons to be concerned about the quality of kinship placements for both Indigenous and non-Indigenous children, including the quality of assessment, training, and support for carers. In relation to Indigenous children, the main issue is whether compliance with the ACPP is prioritising contact with culture and maintenance of identity *at the expense of* basic child health and safety considerations. The problem is that culturally appropriate kinship placements for Indigenous children are not always realistic because they cannot be reconciled with child welfare. Worse, in some cases, the well-meaning desire to prevent a repeat of the Stolen Generations means kinship placements can proceed despite being far from safe, suitable, and conducive to child well-being and development.

State and territory child protection policy and practice have national implications for Indigenous policy, given the bipartisan national commitment to "closing the gap" in social outcomes between the most disadvantaged Indigenous Australians and other Australians.[377] The heavy over-representation of Indigenous children in the child protection system reflects the significant gaps that exist in health, education, employment, housing, and other indicators of social welfare. The concern is that efforts to close these gaps are in danger of failing due to dealing with Indigenous children under an exceptionalist regime, which treats Indigenous children differently to non-Indigenous children in the name of preserving traditional culture and identity.

Further gaps in Indigenous children's welfare and life opportunities, opened up by culturally appropriate but poor-quality kinship care, will prove very difficult to close later in life – no matter how many public resources are poured into programs designed to address Indigenous disadvantage. Child protection policy failures, and failures to address the escalating crisis in Indigenous child welfare, will perpetuate intergenerational social and family dysfunction, and ensure child welfare remains a major problem for future generations of Indigenous people. These failures risk defeating the aim of true and practical reconciliation, which should mean equality of opportunity for all Australians regardless of race.

Efforts to address the legacy of the Stolen Generations by giving priority to cultural considerations, when it results in placing children in suboptimal kinship care, risks creating another lost generation of Indigenous Australians trapped in disadvantage and dysfunction. Impediments to securing Indigenous child welfare lie most obviously in the worthy, if often impractical, sentiments associated with the Stolen Generations, which for many people make even the mere mention of alternative approaches – such as Indigenous adoption from care – unacceptable, unthinkable, and unspeakable: tantamount to stealing children all over again. But that is not the only force acting against the interests of Indigenous children.

What is and isn't done to care for and protect Indigenous children is also a legacy of the Aboriginal politics of the 1970s, and the way the Stolen Generations issue was politicised – through the formulation of the ACPP and the creation of "separatist" Indigenous child protection regimes – as part of the push to advance the political goal of Aboriginal self-determination. The politicisation of Stolen Generations and Indigenous child protection has gotten in the way of the proper protection of children, causing child protection authorities to persist with a "culturally appropriate" approach that demonstrably fails some (probably many) Indigenous children.

Indigenous children in out-of-home care

Between 2000–01 and 2013–14, the number of Indigenous children in out-of-home care in Australia increased from 20 per 1,000 population to 60 per 1,000 (figure 22). This means that 6% of all Indigenous children are currently removed from their family for safety and welfare reasons and living in some form of out-of-home care.

In 2013–14, Indigenous children were significantly over-represented in out-of-home care, at more than nine times the rate of non-Indigenous children (5.6 per 1,000 population). In 2000–01, by comparison, Indigenous children were a little more than six times over-represented in care compared to non-Indigenous children (3.1 per 1,000 population). Indigenous children have also disproportionately accounted for growth in the number of children in out-of-home care. Since 2000–01, the number of Indigenous children in care has increased by 261.6%, compared to 78.0% for non-Indigenous children. Of total children in care in 2013–14, more than one third (14,991) were Indigenous. This compares to 4,146 (21%) Indigenous children in care out of a total in-care population of 19,783 in 2000–01 (figure 23). These figures speak of an escalating crisis in Indigenous child welfare.

The increasing number and increasing over-representation of Indigenous children in care reflects the fact that Indigenous children are "almost 8 times more likely than non-Indigenous children to be subject of substantiated reports of harm/risk of harm."[378] This reflects the high levels of social problems and dysfunction in the most disadvantaged metropolitan, rural, and remote Indigenous communities – associated with welfare dependence, drug and alcohol abuse, domestic and community violence, and concerns about child welfare.

In all Australian states and territories, kinship and other forms of culturally appropriate out-of-home care are the preferred placement options for Indigenous children who need to be removed from their families. Hence, the majority of Indigenous children in care are in some form of kinship care with either extended family members, members of the child's Indigenous community, or with other Indigenous people. This is consistent with the ACPP. In 2013–14, over two-thirds of the almost 15,000 Indigenous children in care in Australia were classified as living in culturally appropriate placements. The majority, slightly more than 50% of all Indigenous children in care, were placed in kinship care with either Indigenous or non-Indigenous relatives or kin.[379]

In response to the escalating Indigenous child welfare crisis, child protection authorities have endeavoured to conscientiously comply with the ACPP by seeking to place Indigenous children with "kin" where possible. This is demonstrated by the growth in the total number of Indigenous children in kinship care. However, despite these efforts, there has been no success changing the overall distribution of placements for Indigenous children. While increasing numbers of Indigenous children are in kinship care, it has proven difficult to provide kinship care for all Indigenous children requiring out-of-home care. Despite the commitment to avoiding the errors and mistreatment of the past, and despite the priority given to ensuring more Indigenous children receive culturally appropriate care, many Indigenous children who are removed from their families are not placed in kinship placements.

Because the number of Indigenous children in kinship, foster, and residential care have all grown strongly at similar rates (figure 24), the overall proportions of Indigenous children in kinship, foster, and residential placements has remained relatively stable. Around 50% of Indigenous children were placed with kin in 2013–14, the same proportion as in 2000–01 (figure 25).

In the states that have the largest number of Indigenous children in care, the proportion of Indigenous children in kinship care has held more or less steady. Around two-thirds of Indigenous children in care in NSW, and around a third of Indigenous children in care in Queensland, are currently placed with kin. In the state with the next largest Indigenous care population – Western Australia – the proportion of Indigenous children in kinship care has increased by about 10% but remains under 60%. Victoria and South Australia have both recorded substantial increases in the proportion of Indigenous children in kinship care, but off very low bases relative to NSW, Queensland, and Western Australia. In both of these states, approximately 45% of Indigenous children in care are in non-kinship care (figure 26).

The overall growth in total kinship placements has therefore been due to a higher proportion and total number of *non-Indigenous* children being placed in kinship care (figure 27). The stable overall national proportion of Indigenous children across all placement types is a measure of the difficulties child protection authorities face when seeking to place Indigenous children in kinship care. Practice of the ACPP appears to contain the seeds of its own failure due to Indigenous demographics and the dysfunction found in some communities.

Despite the best intentions

The obstacles to placing children in kinship care are most profound in the places with the most serious dysfunction – in the remote "homeland" communities of jurisdictions such as the Northern Territory. The extraordinary levels of social problems in some communities in turn account for the rising number of children needing care, the shortage of suitable kinship carers, and the resulting inability to place children in accordance with the ACPP.

The demographics of Aboriginal communities accentuate shortages of suitable carers. High birth rates and high adult mortality mean an estimated 70% of the total Aboriginal population in the Northern Territory is aged under 30, leaving fewer adults to care for children. "Quite simply," as the 2010 *Report of the Board of Inquiry into the Child Protection System in the Northern Territory* (Bath Report) concluded, "there are fewer and fewer Aboriginal families able to provide substitute care and more and more children likely to require a placement."[380] These factors appear to account for the decline in use of kinship care and increased use of foster care for Aboriginal children in the Northern Territory. Since 2009–10, the number of Aboriginal children in kinship care in the territory has fallen by 80%. Over the same period, the number of Aboriginal children placed in foster care has increased by 110%.[381]

The factors that prevent placing Indigenous children with kin are compounded by the unique characteristics of the remote Indigenous communities in jurisdictions such as the Northern Territory and Queensland.[382] However, similar obstacles to kinship care are also present in Indigenous communities in south-eastern Australia. The 2012 Cummins Inquiry in Victoria found that "there has been little progress in Victoria in improving the percentage of children placed in accordance with ACPP over recent years."[383] In 2010–11, the proportion of Aboriginal children placed in accordance with the principle was approximately 57%, down from 59.5% three years before. Over the previous decade, the proportion had hit a high of over 65% in 2007–08; but overall the proportion was largely the same in 2010–11 as it was in the early 2000s.[384]

Failure to improve compliance with the ACPP was partly due to demand. Since 2001–02, the total number of Aboriginal children in care in Victoria increased from slightly fewer than 500 to around 900. The Cummins Report attributed the lack of compliance to the inability to recruit sufficient Aboriginal carers to Aboriginal communities featuring high child-to-adult ratios, making it difficult to bring additional children into families. The potential pool of Aboriginal carers was also found to be diminished by the challenges in Aboriginal communities: elevated levels of poverty and disadvantage meant many potential kinship carers were ruled out by personal, social, and financial barriers that compromised their capacity to act as carers.[385] This led Cummins to conclude that due to the "health status of many of the Aboriginal adults and the burden of care giving and social disadvantage that many already carry, it is highly likely that many Aboriginal children will continue to be placed with non-Aboriginal care givers."[386]

Indigenous exceptionalism: "lesser standard of care"

Child protection authorities are clearly struggling to find sufficient numbers of safe and suitable kinship placements, with extended families and other local community members, for many Indigenous children because of the social problems in some Indigenous communities.[387] Yet it should not be assumed on this basis that child welfare concerns always outweigh cultural considerations, and that all of the significant numbers of kinship placements that do occur are actually safe and suitable.

Elevated levels of social dysfunction in disadvantaged Indigenous families and communities mean the systemic problems in Australian child protection – delayed removal of children from inadequate parents and repeated reunion of children with them in the name of family preservation – can have an even more devastating impact on the well-being of Indigenous children. Indigenous and non-Indigenous families and communities with child protection concerns suffer from similar social problems and dysfunction, and Indigenous and non-Indigenous kinship carers face similar health, social, and other challenges that compromise the quality of care for children. However, the impact on Indigenous child welfare is aggravated by Indigenous-specific child welfare policies and practices, which create an additional barrier to secure the best interests of some Indigenous children.

In practice, these policies create an additional layer of Indigenous suffering and disadvantage. This observation especially applies to decisions to place Indigenous children in kinship placements that are sometimes far from safe and suitable, which amounts to affording different treatment to Indigenous children and providing a lesser level of protection to them.

It has been well-documented that because of the ACPP, child protection authorities seek to exhaust potential kinship options, and Indigenous children can be placed into unsafe situations that fail to meet basic standards, in order to maintain contact with culture and preserve identity. Non-Indigenous children would not be placed into care options of this low quality.

Unrealistic decisions to place Indigenous and non-Indigenous children in substandard kinship placements are also driven by systemic factors relating to the cost of and demand for out-of-home care services. However, the ACPP appears to have intensified the problems associated with kinship care for Indigenous children. A culturally appropriate approach to Indigenous child protection means applying double standards to the care and protection of Indigenous children and non-Indigenous children. For example, the Bath Report found that kinship placements for Indigenous children in the Northern Territory had failed to meet basic safety and hygiene standards, and that compliance with the ACPP had justified "Aboriginal children in care receiving a lesser standard of care than non-Aboriginal children".[388]

The same concerns about the lesser standard of care provided to Indigenous children as a consequence of the application of the ACPP have been expressed in the findings of a spate of other recent official reports in other jurisdictions.[389] This includes the Wood Report in NSW, which found that the Aboriginal grandmothers and aunties who provide the bulk of kinship care "tend to have higher rates of poverty and disadvantage and are more likely to be experiencing poorer health than their non-Aboriginal counterparts."[390]

It is difficult to not be sceptical about kinship care when in Victoria the carers of Aboriginal children are (in the words of the Cummins Report) "mostly aged over 50, female and frequently single, and living in poverty with often crowded housing."[391] And it is unclear how routine calls for additional support services will ever be capable of transforming the living conditions of children in kinship care, given the level of entrenched, intergenerational disadvantage in some Aboriginal families and communities that would first need to be overcome.[392] In fact, the focus in the standard policy literature on improving training and support for Indigenous kinship carers is an implicit acknowledgement that, in some cases, complying with the ACPP overrides basic child welfare concerns and placement standards.[393]

A new Stolen Generation?

The growth in the number of Indigenous children taken into care, combined with the inability to place all children in culturally appropriate placements, has led to claims that a "new Stolen Generation" is being created.[394] The parallels drawn with the Stolen Generations are inappropriate: the removal of children is not based on race, but on demonstrable family and community dysfunction. The politically charged assertion that race *is* the issue overlooks the well-founded child safety concerns and assorted obstacles to use of kinship care that drive decisions to remove children from their families and then not place them in accordance with the ACPP. Focusing on race also misses the bigger issue: the real concern is not too much child removal but too little, and not too few kinship placements, but too many inappropriate ones.

The activists and Indigenous community representatives and organisations that make these heated claims need to be held to account for the results of the separatist approach they endorse, which threatens to further encourage child protection authorities to keep abused and neglected children with their parents or to place children in unsuitable kinship placements to maintain connections to Indigenous culture.[395] Both the chairman, Nyunggai Warren Mundine, and the deputy chair, Ngaire Brown, of the Prime Minister's Indigenous Advisory Council have flagged precisely these concerns with current policy, legislation, and practices, which lead to Indigenous children being left in unsafe and damaging situations, in the care of parents who fail to fulfil their parental responsibilities.[396] Bess Price, an Indigenous leader and Northern Territory minister for community services, and the Indigenous academic and commentator Anthony Dillon, have also spoken out about the devastating consequences of placing abused and neglected children in shocking environments with Indigenous kinship carers in accordance with the ACPP.[397]

These warnings about current practices are consistent with long-standing concerns about how part of the national response to the Stolen Generations has been the reluctance of child protection authorities to remove Indigenous children and take them into care for their own protection.[398] This concern was flagged as early as 2000 in a review of out-of-home care services for Aboriginal children in Victoria, which "identified a practice of minimising involvement by statutory child protection services in Victoria in cases where intervention was or is required to avoid significant harm to Aboriginal children."[399] The implication of these well-founded concerns is that despite the over-representation of Indigenous children in the child protection system, child protection authorities are under-responding to the child welfare crisis in Indigenous communities.

Another long-standing concern about the national response to the Stolen Generations has been the inappropriate lengths taken to ensure compliance with the ACPP for Indigenous children taken into care. The 2002 report, *Putting the Pictures Together*, on family violence and child abuse in Aboriginal communities in Western Australia, noted:

Aboriginal communities expressed concern to the Inquiry during consultations that the Aboriginal Child Placement Principles were not appropriate and cited examples where the application of the principles had allegedly resulted in children being placed in situations of risk.[400]

The use of kinship care as the preferred and culturally appropriate placement option may have mitigated concerns about a new Stolen Generation. But in the worst cases, the determination to keep Indigenous children with kin in low-quality placements in dysfunctional communities for the sake of preserving culture and identity have been catastrophic, and have allowed abusers, particularly the perpetrators of child sexual abuse, to continue to abuse children.[401]

In his 2011 book *Aboriginal Self-Determination,* Gary Johns detailed a distressing example from Queensland of the lesser standard of care received by Aboriginal compared to non-Aboriginal children:

> Witness the social worker disciplined for failing to protect a 10-year-old Aboriginal child repeatedly raped at Aurukun in 2005. Her defence was that such children should be reunited and returned to the community for the sake of their "cultural, emotional and spiritual identity."[402]

The social worker had returned the girl to the community from a white foster family because of fears that actions to protect the victim would attract the Stolen Generations label.[403] As Johns concluded, because the ACPP deals with Aboriginal children under a separatist child protection regime, it creates an obvious double standard and is a form of reverse racism with regard to the treatment of Indigenous and non-Indigenous children and families: "the bias in current practices against foster care and the intensely ideological desire to have Aboriginal children stay with their families is causing death and mayhem."[404]

The same concerns about the unintended consequences of the fear of repeating the Stolen Generations lead the respected Indigenous leader Sue Gordon, a retired Children's Court magistrate and co-author of the *Putting the Picture Together* report, to call in 2010 for a national review of the ACPP because Indigenous children placed in the care of relatives were regularly placed at risk. Endorsing the Bath Report's finding that "in some cases the [ACPP] appears to be given primacy over basic child protection considerations", Gordon also argued that "fear of being labeled racist" meant child protection authorities were often reluctant to intervene and remove children suffering neglect and abuse.[405]

Unravelling the conundrum

Despite the well-documented, well-founded, and long-standing concerns about kinship care, anxieties about repeating the history of the Stolen Generations encourage continued efforts to comply with the ACPP. However, worthy sentiments and the good intention not to repeat past mistakes make a bad situation worse when children are left in harmful environments. Adherence to the ACPP even when it compromises child welfare is also a morally dubious exercise in conscience-cleansing on the part of non-Indigenous Australians. The burden of national guilt over the Stolen Generations should not be left to rest on the slender shoulders of children.

The "kinship conundrum" – that the practice of the ACPP to prevent another Stolen Generation will keep open the gaps in outcomes between the most disadvantaged Indigenous Australians and other Australians – needs unravelling if the child protection system is to advance the best interests of Indigenous children.

Other areas of equally well-entrenched Indigenous policy, which have been found not to have served Indigenous people well, have been subjected to extensive national scrutiny and revision in recent times. The rationale for separate provision of health, education, and other services for Indigenous people has been questioned. However, the separatist Indigenous child protection regimes that operate in all jurisdictions have not been subjected to the same degree of scrutiny.

The ACPP and other forms of culturally appropriate child protection practices are not only the result of well-meaning efforts to avoid creating another Stolen Generation. The ACPP needs to be understood as a product of a wider political campaign for Aboriginal rights that emerged in the 1970s, and of the policy settings of the 1970s, that were preoccupied with the pursuit of the goal of Aboriginal self-determination – political, legal, social, and cultural – in all areas of Indigenous policy, including child protection. The association with the Stolen Generation, and the attendant sensitivities and political challenges it poses, have allowed the ACPP to become something of a last bastion for Indigenous separatism: the last, unquestioned area of Indigenous policy still decisively informed by the ideas and objectives of the movement for Aboriginal self-determination.

The real subject for discussion regarding Indigenous child protection should be how political considerations, as distinct from child welfare considerations, account for how the child protection system treats Indigenous children. Lest sentiment continue to get in the way of saving children, it is vital to appreciate that the intention of the ACPP was not simply to prevent a repeat of the Stolen Generations and right the wrongs of past mistreatment, as is commonly assumed.

The common belief that Indigenous children should be placed with kin did not simply develop as a natural response to recognition of the errors of past practices associated with the Stolen Generations.[406] This misconception is powerfully and emotionally fostered by the annual commemoration of National Sorry Day, which is held on 26 May each year. This date is the anniversary of the 1997 tabling in federal parliament of HREOC's *Bringing Them Home* report on the National Inquiry into the Separation of Aboriginal and Torres Strait

Islander Children ("the Stolen Generations Report"), the release of which generated a wave of national sympathy and the demand for a national parliamentary apology. The sentiments evoked by remembering the experiences of members of the Stolen Generations have not only elevated the ACPP beyond scrutiny and questioning, but also rendered alternative policies "unthinkable", including Indigenous adoption from care.

The origins of Aboriginal separatism

The 1997 *Bringing Them Home* report detailed the harmful impact of past child removal practices on Indigenous individuals, families, and communities.[407] The national attention drawn to the stories of victims belonging to the Stolen Generations intensified the commitment to practicing the ACPP, which has been reinvented as a national commitment to avoiding a repeat of the perceived errors of the past, which denied Aboriginal children contact with kin and culture.

This is the popular view of the ACPP. In reality, however, it was developed before the national discussion of past Indigenous child removal practices sparked by *Bringing Them Home*. The focus on ensuring Aboriginal children receive culturally appropriate care placements predates the prominence attained by the Stolen Generations issue in the late 1990s.

The ACPP was first proposed by the Commonwealth Department of Aboriginal Affairs in the late 1970s, and its implementation as national policy embedded in child welfare legislation was agreed to by all states and territories in 1986.[408] The intention was indeed to address the legacy of decades of assimilationist child removal policies. However, the development of the ACPP was also a result of the politicisation of the Stolen Generations issue, which was taken up as an important part of the political agenda of the campaign for Aboriginal rights. The decision to mandate the application of the

ACPP through Australian child welfare laws and officially deal with Aboriginal children under a separatist child protection policy regime reflected the major themes of the Aboriginal self-determination movement that dominated Indigenous politics and policy until the early-2000s.

Aboriginal self-determination was based on the idea that Aboriginal advancement required the separate development of Aboriginal people on their own traditional lands, under their own political, legal, and social organisations, and according to their own cultural and spiritual values.[409] The doctrine was inspired by the national liberation movements that sprung up in Asia, South America, and Africa after the second world war, and won formerly colonised peoples the right to govern themselves.[410] A new age of Aboriginal political consciousness from the late-1960s essentially cast aside the principle that underpinned the successful 1967 constitutional referendum, which saw Aboriginal people included in the Australian census and authorised the Commonwealth to create laws for the benefit of Aboriginal people. The principle that underpinned the referendum – that Aboriginal Australians should have the same rights as other Australian citizens – was superseded by the goal of self-determination and the principle that Aborigines should have separate rights and separate political, legal, and social-service regimes to other Australians, including the special right to recover and retain traditional culture and identity.[411]

As in other postcolonial nationalist movements, Indigenous Australians were thought to require their own political, legal, and social institutions to protect and promote their distinctive culture. The institutional structure that developed chiefly took the form of "Aboriginal-controlled" organisations which were responsible for delivery of culturally appropriate, taxpayer-funded health, education, and other services to Aboriginal communities. This was the beginning of the "Aboriginal industry", largely staffed by a city-based, professional class of Indigenous and non-Indigenous politicians and bureaucrats whose main function was to provide "special" services for the fraction of the Aboriginal population that lived in remote communities.

The granting of land rights (communal ownership of traditional lands) to Aboriginal people created miniature "states" over which Aboriginal organisations exercised quasi-sovereignty. This homeland movement began with the Aboriginal Land Councils responsible for the local government of Aboriginal communities in the 1,200 homeland settlements across Australia which, in theory, allowed Aboriginal people to live traditional hunter and gatherer lifestyles and maintain their cultural and spiritual connection to their ancestral lands. This was the "Coombsian model", named after the chief architect of the separatist policies first implemented by the Whitlam government in the 1970s, Dr H. C. "Nugget" Coombs, the former governor of the Reserve Bank of Australia.

Under this model, it was assumed that for Aboriginal self-determination to have full political and cultural coherence, Aboriginal people, in the homelands at least, not only needed separate local government and property rights, but also needed to live under separate, culture-based laws and have separate, culture-based schooling. The common denominator of Indigenous policy then became the attaining of political, legal, and social institutional autonomy as a means of recovering, maintaining, and preserving traditional culture.[412]

How strong the influence of the doctrine of Aboriginal self-determination was over the formation of Indigenous policy is exemplified by Indigenous child protection policy. The formulation of the ACPP was as much a matter of ending cultural domination and validating the principles that inspired the separatist agenda as of child welfare and avoiding past mistakes and addressing past mistreatment. For Indigenous political movements in postcolonial countries, including the Aboriginal self-determination movement in Australia, the restoration of traditional culture by all means possible, including the care of children, became the definitive political objective. The goal was to reverse the subordinate position and inferior status that colonial invasion and its concomitant oppression of Indigenous society had entailed.[413]

The belief that Indigenous children required culturally appropriate care that came into vogue in the 1970s was an international phenomenon among the "First Nations" in the United States, Canada, New Zealand, and Australia. Under the Aboriginal mission system that operated from the middle of the 19th century until the late 1960s, Aborigines had been subjected to a range of paternalistic controls that sought to suppress traditional culture. Repudiating past child removal practices became a rallying point for political awareness, for when cast in postcolonial terms these practices were presented as the leading edge of policies that had aimed to destroy traditional culture by assimilating Aboriginal populations into the white mainstream, as Aboriginal children who were removed from their families had been encouraged to reject their Aboriginality and cultural heritage.[414]

The way child protection policy was taken up as part of a much wider agenda of Aboriginal self-determination is evident in what can be considered the founding text of the Stolen Generations issue: Peter Read's 1981 report, *The Stolen Generations: The Removal of Aboriginal Children in New South Wales 1883 to 1969*, which was published by the NSW Department of Aboriginal Affairs. The politicisation of the Stolen Generations was typified by Read's claim that past child removal practices had sought to "breed out" the Aboriginal race, and was a "story of attempted genocide" by "White Australia", which sought to assimilate Aboriginal people and eradicate all traces of an Aboriginal culture assumed to be inferior. The theme of "cultural genocide" – which would perpetually feature in advocacy surrounding the Stolen Generations – was a powerful means of raising Aboriginal political awareness and a powerful argument for separatism.[415]

By these means, the memory of assimilationist policies and practices reinforced the centrality of recovering of lost culture to Aboriginal political consciousness and directly informed the logic of the ACPP. It followed that Aboriginal culture and Aboriginal identity were held to be synonymous. And because child removal practices were one of the ways traditional culture had been suppressed and that Aborigines had been assimilated into the mainstream, it was decreed that in the name of self-determination, Aboriginal children must have continuous contact with culture to maintain their unique cultural identity. Thus, in the lexicon of Indigenous affairs, the use of the term "culture" across a range of policy areas has a politicised meaning and is virtually interchangeable with the term "self-determination".

By the early 1980s, the right of Aboriginal people to look after Aboriginal children and sustain Aboriginal culture had become a highly symbolic and crucially important means by which the cause of Aboriginal self-determination was advanced. Recognition of the Aboriginal right to self-determination came to be expressed, in part, by official recognition of this communal right. The political goal and principle of the movement for self-determination – that the advancement of Aboriginal culture required a separate institutional structure – was accepted and authenticated when the states and territories agreed to practice the ACPP in the mid-1980s. State legislation giving effect to the ACPP also gave official recognition and privileged status to Aboriginal organisations granted the right to formal "community consultation" and participation in placement decisions concerning Aboriginal children.[416] Hence, the NSW *Children and Young Persons (Care and Protection) Act*, for example, includes "Aboriginal specific principles" that incorporate the language and intent of Aboriginal separatism. The act (in the words of the 2007 Wood Special Commission of Inquiry into Child Protection Services in NSW) declares that:

Aboriginal people are to participate in the care and protection of their children and young persons "with as much self-determination as is possible" and the Minister may negotiate and agree with Aboriginal people to the implementation of programs and strategies that promote self-determination.[417]

Culturally appropriate

The *Bringing Them Home* report focused attention on past practices by cataloguing the devastating impact that child removals had on the members of the Stolen Generations and their families. Picking up the major political themes of Peter Read's Stolen Generations Report, it also controversially argued that racism had motivated the removal of Aboriginal children from their families and formed part of a genocidal policy of forced assimilation of so-called "half-caste" children into the white community.[418]

In the wake of the divisive debate and controversies generated by the High Court's Mabo decision and the subsequent native title legislation, *Bringing Them Home* upped the political stakes surrounding Indigenous affairs. Its claims about genocide renewed the moral force of the separatist agenda. This reflected the politics of the report's co-author, the HREOC Aboriginal and Torres Strait Islander social justice commissioner, Mick Dodson, who had been a leading figure in Aboriginal politics since the 1970s and a prominent activist for Aboriginal self-determination. The intensely political nature and purpose of the report stemmed from the way that drawing national attention to the Stolen Generations provided a powerful means of re-politicising the issue and advancing the cause of Aboriginal self-determination through discussion of Indigenous child protection policy.

An important feature of *Bringing Them Home*, therefore, was the policy recommendations it made regarding the contemporary over-representation of Aboriginal children in out-of-home care and the need to reduce the number of Aboriginal child removals to prevent a repeat of the policies that had led to the Stolen Generations. The essence of these recommendations was that current child protection practices were as abhorrent as past practices, because it was claimed that decisions to remove Aboriginal children were based on an inherently racist view of Aboriginal culture. *Bringing Them Home* concluded that while the laws and language surrounding child protection had changed, the attitude towards Aboriginal children and families remained "overwhelmingly one of cultural domination and inappropriate and ineffective servicing".[419]

At the heart of these attitudes as described by the report, which were paternalistic at best and racist at worst, was a conflict between Western (that is mainstream Australian) and Aboriginal cultural values regarding children and families. Child protection caseworkers were accused of failing to understand and respect Aboriginal family practices such as lax parental supervision, encouraging children to be independent and self-reliant, and the involvement of extended kin networks in rearing children. Because these practices differed from the Western view of the "normal" nuclear family, "abnormal" Aboriginal customs were incorrectly labelled as neglectful and seen as pathological, dysfunctional, and indicative of problems with the family that raised child protection concerns.[420]

Even at the time, this analysis of "cultural bias" accounting for the over-representation of Aboriginal children in the care system glossed over the reality of social and family dysfunction in some Aboriginal communities.[421] The sort of culturally determined parenting practices described above may have been suitable to the social conditions of the past, but the conditions that gave rise to them no longer existed; these practices no longer function well in the present. The defence of traditional culture, which downplayed its impact on child well-being, minimised the raft of genuine child protection concerns that accounted for the over-representation of Aboriginal children in care, especially the fact that the most common form of maltreatment experienced by Aboriginal children is chronic parental neglect of basic needs, including "adequate food, shelter, clothing, supervision, hygiene or medical attention."[422]

Bringing Them Home was significant in applying principles of Aboriginal self-determination, in relation to child protection, in a culturally relativist manner. It suggested that a different, culturally appropriate, standard should apply in decision-making on behalf of Aboriginal children. The emphasis placed on cultural respect and awareness, and the use of culture to explain the uniqueness of family life in Aboriginal communities, encouraged the use of cultural practices and differences to explain away problems in Aboriginal families, so case workers could avoid being accused of making culturally insensitive or racist judgements. This essentially demanded that the reality of dysfunction be overlooked, and made culture take precedence over child welfare.

While understating child welfare concerns, *Bringing Them Home* further politicised Indigenous child protection and the Stolen Generations issue by applying the standard separatist analysis of the supposed problem and its solution – more Aboriginal self-determination. Culturally appropriate and Aboriginal-controlled child and family welfare services were seen as necessary to overcome the persistence of "cultural domination."[423]

The *Bringing Them Home* analysis has lasting and ongoing implications for Indigenous child protection – the question of "culture" remains pivotal to what is and isn't done to protect Indigenous children. This explanation for the over-representation of Aboriginal children in care has entered the literature and lexicon of Australian child protection, and continues to shape and inspire Indigenous child protection thinking and practice today. Distilling the findings of the body of research into culturally appropriate policy that has grown out of *Bringing Them Home*, the 2007 Wood Report asserted that:

It could be difficult for caseworkers and others, with an understanding that values the nuclear family above other conceptualisations of the "family", to have any insight into the different kind of information that may be required for them to assess the safety of an Aboriginal child, or the appropriateness of the potential options available within the family and community to meet the care and protection needs of the child. ... Caseworkers raised in Anglo-Celtic society may find it difficult to understand and reflect in casework ... the complexity of Aboriginal family and kinship relationship that are important for a child, and for making decisions about where the child should live, if he or she cannot live with parents.[424]

The Wood Report quoted with approval a 2004 Victorian Department of Human Services report, *Protecting Children*, which listed as one of ten "priorities for children's well-being and safety in Victoria" the need to ensure "the system as a whole is inclusive of Indigenous cultures and values."[425] The stress placed on creating an "inclusive" system explicitly made culture (and the underlying politics of Aboriginal self-determination, since Aboriginal control of services was the chief means of achieving inclusiveness) the priority, not child welfare. This priority, along with the separatist rationale for culturally appropriate child protection policy, was also explicitly set out in another report cited by Wood and commissioned by the Secretariat of National Aboriginal and Islander Child Care and the Victorian Department of Human Services, which boldly stated that:

> An *individualistic approach that focuses on the child's needs* without proper consideration of their parent/s' and communities' circumstances has been criticised by Indigenous groups in Canada, New Zealand, and Australia as failing to take into account Indigenous understandings of family and children. [emphasis added][426]

When this culturally appropriate rationale is added to concerns about "stealing" Aboriginal children, "culture" becomes a powerful justification for lack of action by child protection authorities in Aboriginal child welfare cases. It encourages under-responding to the protective needs of Aboriginal children out of fear of being judgemental or culturally insensitive at best, and racist at worst, and can lead to Aboriginal children being left in circumstances from which non-Aboriginal children would be removed.

The policy and practice advice in the standard literature on Indigenous child protection amounts, then, to subjecting Indigenous children to double standards and racism in the name of respecting culture. It is also calculated to raise fears about a new Stolen Generation, to make child protection authorities reluctant to intervene in dysfunctional and dangerous Indigenous families.[427] This is a very powerful deterrent for child protection authorities because of the role that (white) social workers played in past child removal practices. The desire to apologise and make amends for social workers' involvement in the Stolen Generations is a key factor that explains why the profession was so quick to endorse the ACPP and continues to support its practice today.[428]

It appears, however, that the commitment to culturally appropriate child protection practice has been somewhat overwhelmed by events on the ground. This is due to the escalating child welfare crisis in Indigenous communities in recent years, as measured by the increasing number of Indigenous children who have been removed into care. Nevertheless, the same sort of policy advice contained in *Bringing Them Home* is being redeployed to explain the worsening over-representation of Indigenous children in care and to promote non-intervention in Indigenous family and community dysfunction. This is evident not only in official literature such as the Wood Report and in the recommendations of similar recent public inquiries into child protection, but also in other opinion-shaping commentary and analysis. Writing in *The Guardian* in March 2014, the Australian filmmaker and activist John Pilger accused Australian child protection authorities of perpetrating a repeat of the "infamous Stolen Generation of the last century." Drawing attention to the fact that today, the number of Aboriginal children in care is five times what it was in the mid-1990s, Pilger argued that "assimilation remains Australian government policy in all but name", and was based on an "official attitude" in Australia that regarded Aboriginal people as "morally deficient".[429]

The explosive claims that racist policy and genocidal intent are behind the over-representation of Indigenous children in care also feature in commentary on Indigenous child protection by Paddy Gibson, a senior researcher at Jumbunna Indigenous House of Learning at the University of Technology, Sydney. Based on the fact that the number of Indigenous children currently in care is greater than at any time during the Stolen Generations period, Gibson endorses the view that this represents a "new Stolen Generation", driven by a return to what is essentially the assimilation policy of earlier eras.[430] Gibson has acknowledged that child removals are a consequence of the reality that many Aboriginal communities "suffer developing world living conditions". His analysis could be viewed as updating the *Bringing Them Home* account of "paternalistic attitudes" framing Aboriginal culture itself as a child welfare problem, while (contradictorily) calling for greater government investment in "community-development". A code for Aboriginal-controlled social services, and a call to repeat and extend the failed policies of Aboriginal self-determination.[431]

According to Gibson, "the triumphant politics of assimilation have exacerbated the drive to remove Aboriginal children".[432] This appears to claim that growth in Indigenous child removals is a result of the policy shift in recent times away from the separatist agenda and towards mainstreaming of health, education, and other services for Indigenous communities. Politicised claims about racism driving removals overlook the reality that today, child protection policy is principally driven by the opposite of assimilation, due to the commitment to the ACPP. Moreover, it aggravates the way that Aboriginal politics, in the guise of respecting culture, downplays the genuine child welfare concerns that exist in Indigenous communities.[433]

Untouched by the revolution

Culturally appropriate child protection policies are a legacy of the Aboriginal self-determination movement in vogue in the 1970s. Over the following decades, the dream of self-determination has turned into a nightmare. The dire social conditions among many Aboriginal people, especially those who live in the homelands, exposes the dream that Aborigines would live in ancient ways and enjoy culturally-rich lives on their traditional lands as a fantasy. A return to hunting and gathering had never been realistic, and geographic isolation from mainstream economic opportunities meant these communities could only be sustained by government transfer payments and other public funding for governance and social services. Homeland communities became bywords for near-universal welfare dependence, which initiated the downward spiral into personal, family, and social dysfunction associated with a slew of related social problems including alcohol and drug abuse, gambling, domestic and communal violence, and the maltreatment and sexual abuse of women and children. Living on traditional lands did not mean living traditional lives. If traditional culture survived the maelstrom, its practice has been found to be often intermittent at best, and it is frequently distorted into a supposedly customary sanction for violence and abuse against women and children.[434]

Much has changed in Indigenous policy since the 1970s. Especially over the last decade and a half, commentators, experts, the media, and policymakers across the political spectrum have recognised the dismal truth that the goal of Aboriginal self-determination has not advanced the welfare of many Indigenous Australians. This re-evaluation of the post-1970s period in Indigenous affairs has stimulated a revolution in Indigenous policy. Since the early 2000s, the separatist policies that had dominated Indigenous affairs have been marginalised, at least at the federal level. They have been recognised as failed experiments, and superseded by the policies and objective of "mainstreaming" health, education, and other services in Indigenous communities. The aim is to bring Indigenous people into full engagement with educational and employment opportunities. This policy shift away from the self-determination model was definitively signalled by two pivotal events: the Howard government's abolition in 2005 of the peak Aboriginal-controlled organisation, the Aboriginal and Torres Strait Islander Commission, and the same government's Northern Territory Emergency Intervention into Homeland Communities in 2007 (which the Rudd and Gillard Labor governments continued).

Yet at the state level, child protection policy has remained untouched by the revolution. Relatively little has changed because policies such as the ACPP, and separatist thinking that is no longer accepted in other areas of Indigenous policy, remain influential. This is partly because health, education, and employment are areas of both federal and state government responsibility. The overlap has generated much greater scrutiny of these policy areas at the national level than has hitherto been the case for Indigenous child protection, which has largely remained a state political issue and responsibility even though the national implications ought to be obvious.

Culturally appropriate Indigenous child protection policies mean that we are practicing a form of 1970s-style separatism that is now widely acknowledged, in other areas of Indigenous policy, to be the chief cause of the gap between the social and economic outcomes for disadvantaged Indigenous people and other Australians. Nevertheless, the ACPP, or rather the Indigenous policy thinking of the 1970s, continues to be applied to drive process and evaluate outcomes in Indigenous child protection policy, even though it advances the outdated political objective of Aboriginal self-determination at the expense of Indigenous child welfare. Indigenous politics, in combination with concerns about preventing a repeat of the Stolen Generations, distorts Indigenous child protection policy. This political distortion of priorities means that on-the-ground realities are frequently overlooked or obscured. The limited debate that occurs about the failure to comply with the ACPP is therefore insufficiently aware of the reality that kinship care is harmful to some (perhaps many) Indigenous children and that increasing its use is impossible to do safely. Instead of accepting and dealing with the increasing difficulty of reconciling the commitment to maintaining contact with kin and culture with child welfare, in the context of the worsening child welfare crisis in Indigenous communities, the debate is dominated by restatements of the political positions assumed in the 1970s and 1990s. This includes the cultural relativism that evidently dominates the standard literature informing culturally appropriate Indigenous child protection practice. This literature encourages caseworkers to respect cultural differences between mainstream and Indigenous family practices, such as lack of proper parental care and inadequate parental supervision in Indigenous families. Such respect comes at the price of underestimating the threat to child welfare when children are left in unsafe environments or placed in substandard kinship care.

The findings and recommendations of recent official inquiries into child protection in Victoria and Queensland demonstrate how the politics of Indigenous child protection distort perceptions and debate. The Cummins Report in Victoria lamented that despite recognition of the traumatic experiences of the Stolen Generations, the number of Aboriginal children in care remained "unacceptably high".[435] While it was accepted that over-representation in care reflected the entrenched disadvantage and dysfunction in many Aboriginal families, the Cummins Report endorsed taking a "holistic view" of the needs of Aboriginal communities and concluded that "outcomes for vulnerable Aboriginal children and families will only improve once practical gains in Aboriginal self-determination about children and families are achieved."[436]

The Cummins Report's recommendations included advising that "culturally competent approaches to family and statutory child protection services for Aboriginal children and young people should be expanded."[437] It also recommended delegating full responsibility for the provision of out-of-home care for Aboriginal children to Aboriginal communities, on the basis that "such a plan will enhance self-determination and provide a practical means for strengthening the cultural links for vulnerable Aboriginal children."[438]

Prioritising culture and self-determination satisfied the political principle of Aboriginal self-determination – and the interests of Aboriginal-controlled organisations that stood to benefit by way of taxpayer funding for culturally appropriate services. It also alleviated community anxieties about the potential for current child removal practices to repeat the history of the Stolen Generations. But the Cummins Report paid only passing attention to the best interests of Aboriginal children, and was silent about the impact on child welfare of culturally appropriate child protection practices. This flew in the face of the major reservations about kinship care that had been flagged by no less than the peak Aboriginal out-of-home care body, the Victorian Aboriginal Child Care Agency (VACCA):

> ... it was never the intent of the ACPP to place children with members of their family or community who presented a danger to them. If we do not protect Aboriginal children from abuse, the legacy will be a new generation of adults/parents who view abuse as normative rather than unacceptable and harmful.[439]

The 2013 Queensland Carmody Report appears at a glance to have taken a different approach to the Cummins Report. The Carmody Report implicitly acknowledged that culturally appropriate policy and practice were compromising child welfare when it stated that "efforts to reduce over-representation should not result in a different standard of protection being afforded Aboriginal and Torres Strait Islander children than that afforded non-Indigenous children."[440] Yet rather than take this insight through to its logical conclusion – that different standards should not apply to Indigenous children – the Carmody Report emulated the Cummins Report by focusing on the alleged need for an even more culturally appropriate child protection regime.

The Carmody Report began with endorsing the view that, even given the social dysfunction in Indigenous communities, the over-representation of Indigenous children was attributable to "misperceptions about child-rearing practices in Aboriginal families … lead[ing] to incorrect assumptions about children's protective needs in some circumstances."[441] This analysis of the supposed problem led on directly to the major recommendation: because "keeping children out of the system is made more difficult by departmental officers having a poor understanding of Aboriginal and Torres Strait Islander cultural and family practices", Carmody recommended that Aboriginal-controlled organisations have a "more meaningful role in the delivery of statutory child protection practice",[442] as per the self-determination principles of the *Child Protection Act 1999*. The report envisaged not just greater consultation about the care and protection of Indigenous children, but a delegation of "responsibility for statutory practice over time" to Aboriginal-controlled agencies that were "familiar with local circumstances and have the requisite cultural competence."[443]

The Carmody Report noted that the proportion of Indigenous children in care who were placed in accordance with the ACPP was just over 50%, down from 64% in 2006. It also noted competing views on kinship care, where some stakeholders felt the ACPP was not given due importance in making decisions about placements for Indigenous children while others felt it was given too much weight. At face value, the Carmody Report endorsed the principle that "the child's overall best interests should always be paramount."[444] Yet the message sent on the key issue – whether child welfare or culture should take precedence in making decisions about kinship placements – was mixed at best. The Carmody Report not only recommended that Aboriginal-controlled organisations have input into identification and assessment of potential care, but it also stressed that "all reasonable efforts should be made to exhaust potential kinship carers for children".[445]

"Reasonable efforts" amounted to recommending a culturally appropriate approach that gave priority to compliance with the ACPP above considerations of child welfare. Carmody recommended the use of a special assessment tool for Indigenous carers that employed "a conversational 'yarning' style to assess key areas of carer competency, and visual cards to identify competency in each of the core areas … enabling potential kinship carers to participate fully in the assessment process." The justification for employing a simplified, less rigorous form of assessment was not just to overcome the evident illiteracy of potential kinship carers. There was also the need to "make the process less confronting" because:

> some adults can be reluctant to seek approval as kinship carers because they find the assessment process intimidating. Many have reported feeling that their own ability to care for their children has been put under the spotlight during the process.[446]

The emphasis the Carmody Report appeared to place on children's best interests was dubious; its highly questionable recommendations can actually be read as an official warrant to afford Indigenous children a lesser standard of protection.

The politics of suffering

That culturally appropriate child protection may mean a lesser standard of care for Indigenous children makes the ACPP an example of what the anthropologist Peter Sutton has termed the "politics of suffering". Based on decades of professional observation of Aboriginal politics in Aboriginal communities, Sutton's analysis of the root error of Indigenous policy is that the political objective of self-determination – including the right to recover and retain culture as the source of Aboriginal identity – has too often taken precedence over basic considerations of human welfare, particularly the well-being of children.[447]

Having worked since the 1970s in the Cape York Peninsula, where he witnessed first-hand the decline in living conditions in the homeland community of Aurukun, Sutton reassessed the political project of Aboriginal self-determination and concluded in his 2009 book, *The Politics of Suffering*, that Indigenous policy has been marred by a profound confusion of means and ends. The priority given to self-determination, combined with the influence of cultural relativism – defined as a reluctance to criticise traditional cultural practices by judging them against modern or mainstream values – meant that the failure of the separatist agenda, measured by the social dysfunction in Aboriginal communities, did not register either politically or in terms of policy for far too long.

Worse, and of greater consequence, was the way the resulting suffering in Aboriginal communities was further politicised and practical problems – health, safety, and child welfare – were perpetually reduced to the standard political claim that Aboriginal problems required empowering Aborigines to deliver Aboriginal solutions. The solution perpetually proposed for the problem caused by the separatist agenda (at least until the early 2000s) was for more of the same: more self-determination through Aboriginal-controlled, culturally appropriate agencies. Pulling no punches, Sutton asserted that the main beneficiaries of the politicisation of Aboriginal suffering were the politicians, bureaucrats, and service providers employed at taxpayers' expense in various arms of the Aboriginal industry.[448]

Like other reassessments of the era of self-determination, including those of Noel Pearson, Helen Hughes, and Gary Johns, Sutton's faced up to the fact that the seeds of social deterioration in Aboriginal communities were planted by the separatist policies implemented in the 1970s. However, Sutton's analysis went further, and examined the "interplay" between policy and culture. The massive policy failures of the post-1970 period, in his view, had been compounded by the interaction with cultural factors – by the legacy of Aboriginal traditions, practices, and habits accumulated over time and passed down through the generations, particularly concerning the raising of children.

The problems in Aurukun and other similar homeland communities could not be blamed on colonial oppression, lack of self-determination and the suppression of Aboriginal culture, Sutton argued, because in these communities with the worst problems, Aboriginal people had continued to live closest to a traditional manner and on their traditional lands. "Community dysfunction", as Sutton put it, "[was] at its greatest in those places where history and the colonisation process had been the most recent, and therefore the kindest."[449] In these communities, in fact, the problems caused by separatist policy had been compounded by failure to integrate with the modern, mainstream cultural norms of First World, Australian society.

Sutton's diagnosis of culture as a problem and cause of suffering set the established paradigm of Indigenous policy and politics on its head. Attributing Aboriginal disadvantage to the significant role played by traditional culture means that Indigenous policy and politics' overemphasis on maintaining traditional culture in the name of self-determination has been misguided, overlooked the human costs, and has been positively harmful to some Aboriginal people. It shows that some aspects of Aboriginal culture are a means of perpetuating, not relieving, Aboriginal disadvantage, because they perpetuate traditional practices that cause or contribute to contemporary suffering, especially among Aboriginal women and children.

Sutton maintained, for example, that high levels of interpersonal violence in some Aboriginal communities reflect traits deeply embedded in traditional culture. The widespread violence endured by Aboriginal women and children was certainly exacerbated by social dysfunction in these Aboriginal communities, which had stemmed from welfare dependence and chronic alcohol abuse. But Sutton's view is that such violence will not be addressed without addressing the violent way of resolving conflict that Aboriginal men are socialised into from early childhood. For example, harmful traditional practices include the "deliberate infliction of pain on babies" as a means of encouraging the seeking of physical "payback", and a "reluctance to attempt to control the anger of children, especially boys against women, and a reluctance to control physical fighting among children."[450]

It followed that these and other harmful aspects of Aboriginal culture that had outlived their usefulness – including hygiene and sanitation habits suited to a hunter-gatherer lifestyle but unsuitable for sedentary settlement – had to be modernised by integration with the mainstream if Aboriginal well-being is to be advanced. Again refusing to pull punches, Sutton declared that:

> Culturally transmitted behaviour and attitudes are at the centre of the huge differences between Indigenous and non-Indigenous health outcomes ... If people want a typically modern health profile they need to adopt a typically modern set of health practices.[451]

Sutton thus counselled against the simplistic cultural relativism that had plagued Indigenous policy: all that could be called customary was not good just because it was traditional, as this risked overlooking the negative consequences of those practices.[452] His own politically incorrect assessment of the welfare deficits attributable to Aboriginal culture extended to blunt criticism of neglectful Aboriginal parenting practices, which he described as a "customary permissiveness in the raising of children that at times includes a casualness about their health."[453]

This is to say that culturally embedded permissive Aboriginal parenting practices are relevant to the neglect of children's most fundamental needs, and play an important role in accounting for common child welfare problems, such as the chronic malnourishment of underweight younger children in some Aboriginal communities. This directly contradicts the often expressed notion, following the doctrine of self-determination, that "engaging in traditional cultural practices and reclaiming a sense of cultural identity is the key to alleviating Aboriginal disadvantage".[454] This is also to say that Aboriginal parental neglect, however culturally determined it is, is anything but benign with regards to the care of children.

It may not be politically correct to discuss how culture might be maladapted and have negative welfare effects. But nor is it racist to do so. Quite clearly, the intersection of Indigenous culture and politics, as it relates to child welfare, parenting, and family life in Indigenous communities, is a subject that must be openly discussed if child protection policy is to advance the best interests of Indigenous children.

Don't lose another generation: depoliticising Indigenous child protection

To end the suffering of Indigenous children, the politics must be taken out of Indigenous child protection. Like Indigenous health and education policy, child protection policy needs to be depoliticised to correct the malignant effects of treating some Indigenous Australians differently to other Australians. We should no longer tolerate continued sacrifice of the welfare of individual Indigenous

Australians, particularly women and children, in pursuit of a political dream of self-determination that has long gone sour.

Forms of separatism have a long history in Indigenous policy, stretching from the formation of the Aboriginal missions in the 19th century and extending through to the ascendancy of Aboriginal self-determination in the 1970s. What unites these otherwise different social experiments is that all were based on the notion that Aborigines needed "special treatment" and to be protected from the mainstream. As Helen Hughes described the similarities in her landmark 2007 expose on the dire social conditions of the homeland communities, *Lands of Shame*:

> Aborigines and Torres Strait Islanders have been discriminated against by being treated differently for more than 200 years. It is not true that various policies have been tried and have failed. Policies have always been discriminatory, treating Aborigines and Torres Strait Islanders differently from other Australians. Sadly the most damaging discrimination in Australia's history has been the exceptionalism of the last 30 years that was intended to make up for past mistreatment. It has widened the gap between Indigenous and mainstream Australians in critical respects.[455]

Today we are conducting a different version of the same separatist experiment, in the form of kinship care and other forms of culturally appropriate child protection policy and practice for Indigenous children, which is making it more difficult to close the gaps between disadvantaged Indigenous people and other Australians.

After two centuries of failed separatist experiments, the aim of Indigenous policy in the 21st century should be to end special treatment and give all Indigenous Australians the same opportunities as other Australians, regardless of race. Yet while much has changed in Indigenous policy in recent years, Indigenous child protection policy is stuck in the 1970s. The ACPP pursues the largely discredited separatist agenda of Aboriginal self-determination, and struggles under the weight of its internal contradictions: the priority it gives to culturally appropriate care cannot be reconciled with a commitment to child safety.

The trend that sees increasing numbers of Indigenous children unable to be placed in kinship care should be welcomed and encouraged as reflecting a belated and overdue recognition of the basic principle that the welfare of Indigenous children cannot be compromised. We also need to accept this new reality because the demographic factors that have led to an oversupply of children and undersupply of kin carers will intensify in coming decades. The last generation of functional, mission-educated grandmothers and aunts who have performed the bulk of kinship care is dying out, and will not be replaced in the same numbers by the next generation – whose capabilities have been impaired by Indigenous communities' forty-year downward spiral into dysfunction. This means there is simply no option but to pursue alternatives to the ACPP and kinship care.

Despite the sentiments and sensitivities, we have to start to thinking the "unthinkable" about Indigenous child protection, because the status quo is unviable. Given the existing shortage of Indigenous carers and the resulting inability to place approximately half of all Indigenous children in kinship care, failure to implement alternatives to the ACPP – such as a non-discriminatory adoption policy that secures a sufficient supply of safe and stable homes for Indigenous children – will have a negative impact on child welfare. If adoption for Indigenous children were restricted only to Indigenous families, unavailability of suitable Indigenous adoptive families would mean that Indigenous and non-Indigenous children continued to receive separate and unequal treatment.

If the status quo persists, the inability to comply with the ACPP due to demography and dysfunction will be liable to encourage child protection authorities to under-respond and leave children in abusive and neglectful homes. Indigenous children will also be at greater risk of continuing to be churned through foster care in pursuit of family reunification, and will experience the damaging effects of instability combined with prolonged exposure to abuse and neglect. The danger is that efforts to prevent a repeat of the Stolen Generations will mean that another generation of Indigenous children may be lost. The developmental, educational, and employment "gaps" that result from these children's exposure to neglect, abuse, and instability will leave them trapped in disadvantaged circumstances and communities for life.

To avoid the unpalatable consequences of persisting with a discriminatory policy, more Indigenous children, as well as non-Indigenous children, should be freed to be adopted from care. This means the mainstreaming revolution should be extended to Indigenous child protection, and Indigenous and non-Indigenous children should be treated the same. But if the non-discriminatory use of adoption for child protection purposes, for all children, is to gain acceptance, and if the ultimate taboo on adoption of Indigenous children is to be lifted, concerns that this would amount to stealing children all over again will need to be allayed. Making Indigenous adoption from care a feasible policy will require finding new ways of reconciling the promotion of child welfare via adoption with legitimate concerns about the need to foster the culture and identity of adoptive children.

The path to reconciling Indigenous adoption with Indigenous cultural identity starts with recognising that the culturally appropriate framework currently applied to Indigenous child protection is more than just a hangover from the Aboriginal politics of the 1970s. It is also based on an outdated understanding of the relationship between traditional culture and the formation of Indigenous identity, and is no longer consistent with contemporary understandings and definitions of modern Aboriginality in 21st-century Australia. The implications of the changing nature of Indigenous identity for Indigenous child protection and adoption are considered in the next and final chapter.

7

Taboo no more: normalising "open" adoption from care

Adoption an option

The debate is slowly changing, and discussing adoption and its benefits is becoming less controversial. Support for adoption from care is gradually emerging and increasing in response to mounting concerns about the parlous state of child protection in Australia. That support is being driven by the evidence-based debate that has developed in recent years concerning the systemic flaws in state and territory child protection systems. The awareness that current practice is bad for children, and that what is being done in the name of avoiding past mistakes is harmful and damaging, is slowly creating a cultural shift in attitudes towards the principle and practice of adoption from care.

One measure of the growing support for adoption, and of the impact of sustained criticism of the child protection status quo, is that adoption has begun to feature in the recommendations of official inquiries. This has not encompassed a wholesale identification of the systemic flaws associated with family preservation, but it still represents significant progress. Having recognised the large number of children "drifting" in and out of care, the Queensland Carmody Inquiry suggested that rather than "unrealistically" pursuing reunification at all costs and churning children through multiple entries into care, multiple foster placements, and multiple failed reunions, alternatives to family preservation need to be pursued, given how crucial stability and permanence are to child welfare and development. The inquiry recommended that child protection caseworkers should be directed to "routinely consider and pursue adoption", especially for younger children, when the family circumstances suggest the chances of successful reunification are slim.[456] Similarly, the 2011 Cummins Inquiry in Victoria recommended that barriers to adoption of children from out-of-home care should be identified and eliminated.[457]

The chief judge of the Federal Circuit Court, John Pascoe, and the chief justice of the Family Court, Diana Bryant, have both also expressed support for greater use of adoption for some children in foster and other forms of care. "Let's have a look at adoption because there are so many children in care", Chief Judge Pascoe told *The Australian* in August 2014. "Maybe some of them could be adopted and would be better off being adopted." Chief Justice Bryant contrasted the local situation with the UK:

> We've taken the view in Australia that adoption of children who have parents is a last resort and that children remaining in care is preferable. In the UK, they've had a very different approach and with the courts' permission they've allowed adoptions against the objections of parents, where children have been in care for some time. They're starting to change their view a bit and perhaps we've been too far at the other end of the spectrum.[458]

The first national commissioner for children was appointed to the Australian Human Rights Commission in 2013. Since her appointment, Megan Mitchell has generally stuck to the orthodox line, proclaiming that the "national shame" that is the number of children in care indicates "we're not doing enough, early enough" to help dysfunctional families.[459] But recently, the commissioner has supplemented her calls for more of the same failed approach, suggesting that "on the other hand we need to look at how we might be able to place more children in permanent alternatives like adoption or long-term guardianship with another family." Ms Mitchell has argued that when adoption is "clearly in a child's best interest ... we should be trying to pursue it", because:

> Unfortunately in Australia we've had a bit of a history of long-term foster care and that really isn't an ideal situation ... by moving about that system and not having that stable long-term care arrangement they [children] are more subject to abuse and neglect and other forms of damage that can occur for them ... For children to live a normal life they need to stay with the same family, form strong attachments and bonds with that family, be able to stay at the same school, form friendship groups, go to the local recreational and sporting clubs. These are the things that provide stability and belonging in a child's life.

The commissioner's powerful advocacy, and telling description of the benefits of adoption for children, has even forced those in the sector with a vested interest in the status quo to concede ground. "There's no doubt that we need to create better stability and permanence there for children who are removed", said the CEO of Berry Street, one of the largest family support and out-of-home care services in Victoria, who has conceded that "adoption is one of the options for some of the children."[460]

What once was taboo is clearly gaining greater acceptance. A tipping point in the debate about child protection policy may have been reached with the release in April 2015 of the scathing report of the inquest into the death of Chloe Valentine. South Australian coroner Mark Johns found the way Families SA had taken the "path of least resistance"[461] proved the state's child protection system was "broken and fundamentally flawed".[462] The coroner's report broke the usual mould of official inquiries because in calling for "nothing less than a massive overhaul of Families SA",[463] Mr Johns recommended changes that went far beyond reinventing the existing failed approach. Zeroing in on the department's "culture and training of its staff"[464] and the need for fundamental change, the coroner recommended that "adoption should have a place in the alternative placement options in the child protection system."[465]

Citing extensively from my research, the coroner noted that the "criticisms of the child protection system in Australia" that had been detailed (and which are restated in this book) "were borne out by the evidence" and "resonates very strongly when one considers the history of Chloe Valentine". This led Johns to "the very firm opinion that permanent removal to adoptive parents should have a place in the child protection system". The systemic flaws identified in my work and borne out by the evidence in the Chloe Valentine case included:

- child protection agencies are preoccupied with family preservation as the primary goal and fail to take appropriate action to protect vulnerable children with well-founded and ongoing safety concerns
- troubled parents receive a range of support services and virtually limitless opportunities to address their problems, with child removal only occurring as a last resort
- too many children are left in dangerous situations due to the current emphasis on family preservation and the misguided bias towards keeping demonstrably abusive and neglectful families together
- the pendulum has swung too far in favour of protecting the "rights" of dysfunctional biological parents at the expense of the best interests of children
- child protection is plagued by a permissive culture of tolerating parental drug abuse and downplaying the attendant risks to drug abusers' children
- proposals to invest more time and effort into family support services ignore the damage done to children by the relentless pursuit of efforts to support families

- adoption is a taboo subject in the child protection world and child protection agencies have a culture of resistance to adoption.[466]

The significance of the coroner's report and recommendations with regard to shattering the adoption taboo cannot be exaggerated. When we hear the name Ebony, we think "starved girl". When we hear the name Dean, we think "suitcase". When we heard the name Chloe, we used to think "motorbike". Now we will think "adoption" – as the way to rescue and save children like Chloe, Dean, and Ebony.

While the coroner was adamant that adoption should play a greatly expanded role in child protection, he did "not purport to be in [a] position to offer a settled model of what the role of adoption in the child protection system should look like."[467] However, guidance for other jurisdictions on a suitable model for adoption from care has been provided by the real policy breakthrough that has occurred in NSW. At the time of the Wood Report, the minister in charge of DoCS issued the standard clichés about intervening in families "only as last resort".[468] Less than four years later, NSW policymakers had embraced the word "adoption" and the language of permanency, stability and belonging in a "home for life."[469]

In 2013, the NSW Coalition government under the leadership of former premier Barry O'Farrell legislated a sweeping reform program designed to address the systemic problems plaguing the child protection system, significantly reducing the number of children languishing in care by significantly increasing the number of children who are adopted. This chiefly involved implementing important changes to child protection laws, policy, and practice. The changes were carefully designed to ensure adoption is a viable and well-used pathway to securing a permanent alternative family for children who have little prospect of being able to live safely with their birth parents. New rules were laid down regarding timely, realistic decision-making about permanency for children in care.

Under the new permanency planning regime, it is mandatory for a decision to be made about whether restoration to the parents is feasible within six months of entering care for children under two years of age and within 12 months of entering care for children aged two years and older. Once it is determined a child cannot safely go home, an application is to be made in the Supreme Court for an order to legally free them for open adoption by a new family.[470]

That the legislative amendments – which were opposed by the Labor Party – managed to pass both houses of the NSW parliament is a testament to the political skills and commitment of Pru Goward, the former minister for family and community services, and the architect and champion of the reforms. Goward managed to achieve what might have been considered the impossible: making significant and controversial changes to child protection practice in the state without courting political disaster, and despite the usual claims from opponents about a new Stolen Generation.[471] Her success in the portfolio led to promotion within the government.

Similar to the NSW reforms, new laws passed the Victorian parliament in September 2014, introducing "permanent care orders" and centred around enforcing timely and realistic decision-making to achieve stability for children. Another main feature of this legislation is strict timelines. Parents will have an initial 12 months to resolve issues so they can resume care of their child. At the end of this period, an additional 12 months will be provided if reunification is likely to be achieved in the 12 months, or permanent alternative care will be sought. Permanent carers become the legal parents of children who remain in care until adulthood, as a means of limiting further disruptions by either parents or the department. This is designed to swing the pendulum back from family preservation by curtailing parental rights to the extent that children are all but adopted, except in name. Nevertheless, the Victorian reforms took the line of least resistance with regards to achieving greater permanency for children, and dodged the politically and culturally contentious issues around adoption despite its demonstrated benefits for children compared to long-term foster care.[472]

National leadership and national targets

Despite positive policy developments and shifts in attitudes, the Victorian government's reluctance to embrace adoption indicates we still have a long way to go to make it the norm when it is unrealistic for children to go home. The biggest challenge is to bring about cultural change at the departmental level in state and territory child protection authorities. Otherwise, adoption laws will prove to be dead letters. Clear signals need to be sent to social workers, and strong political leadership is needed from responsible ministers – armed with the facts about the causes and consequences of the child protection crisis – to ensure that "family preservation at all costs" and endlessly trying to fix unfixable families is superseded by the principle of early statutory removal and adoption. However, the ideological and institutional investment in family preservation remains a formidable obstacle. There is a role for national leadership by the federal government in overcoming these obstacles and the lack of effective policy response in most jurisdictions to the ever-worsening child protection crisis.

The gross disparity between the high number of children in care and the low number of local adoptions has led to child protection gaining overdue attention from the federal government. In December 2013, the Abbott government announced it would take action to make it easier for Australian parents to adopt children locally and from overseas. Acknowledging the taboo that exists on adoption, Prime Minister Tony Abbott announced his government was committed to taking adoption out of the "too-hard basket" and streamlining the adoption process.[473] A new service, Intercountry Adoption Australia, was announced in January 2015, and is intended to remove red tape and help parents negotiate the adoption process with foreign governments. Action on overseas adoptions was rightfully acknowledged as a brave move into what had formerly been a policy no-go zone for federal governments, and occurred in the face of warnings by anti-adoption advocates about the dangers of removing children from their cultures.[474]

Yet action on overseas adoption contrasts with no movement by the federal government on local adoption, which appears to have remained firmly in the politically too-hard basket. The difference with overseas adoption may be partly due to the effective advocacy of the overseas adoption cause. This cause has been championed by the Adopt Change organisation (formerly National Adoption Awareness Week), led by the high-profile pro-adoption campaigner, actor Deborra-lee Furness. The successful advocacy for overseas adoptions offers proof that politicians prefer to lead on the contentious issue of adoption when public opinion has been shaped by others and they believe the community is prepared to support a pro-adoption policy direction.

Similar advocacy for national leadership on local adoption has focused on two proposed initiatives.[475] The first concerns emulating the way the adoption rate has been lifted in the US by the operation of the Clinton administration's *Adoption and Safe Families Act (1997)*, which rewards states that increase the number of adoptions from care with additional federal government funding that must be invested back into the state's child protection system.[476] A similar national adoption incentive payment scheme in Australia should be considered by the federal government as an enhanced means of distributing existing Commonwealth funding for community services to states and territories.

The second proposed initiative is the declaration by the federal government of annual national adoption targets, the purpose of which would be to encourage other jurisdictions to follow NSW's pro-adoption lead and to make state and territory child protection authorities more accountable for their performance. National adoption targets would enable the federal government to send a clear signal to all states and territories and provide national policy oversight and direction about the need for greater use of adoption, with the overall objective being to boost the number of local adoptions from care to the level of more adoption-friendly countries, such the US.

The call for national adoption targets has been endorsed by Barnardos Australia, one of the few children's charities that still operates an adoption program in Australia. Barnardos Centre for Excellence in Open Adoption has argued the federal government should insert a target for open adoption into the national standards for out-of-home care.[477] Critics argue that targets are arbitrary and, rightly, that each adoption has to be based on the circumstances of each and every child. No one suggests otherwise, and, of course, targets would be "soft" and not mandatory, let alone arbitrary.

NSW Supreme Court Justice Paul Brereton, who handles most adoption cases in the state, strongly supports the use of adoption as a superior means of providing security and stability for children because it provides a family name and family for life beyond the age of 18. But he also argues that each case needs to be decided on its facts and targets would not "help anyone".[478] It is telling, however, that one judge is able to deal with all adoptions in NSW each year when more than 18,000 children are in care.

The purpose of national adoption targets would simply be to highlight the disparity in use of adoption in Australia compared to overseas due to entrenched anti-adoption attitudes in Australian child protection authorities. Targets are simply a means of helping overcome the ideological and institutional obstacles in the path of greater use of adoption. The federal government has no direct authority over local adoption policy, which, together with child protection, is a state and territory responsibility. But national involvement in child protection policy would be consistent with national initiatives in other areas involving significant state and territory government policy failures, such as education, health, and Indigenous policy.

Former Western Australian treasurer and attorney-general Christian Porter, now federal member for Pearce and Minister for Social Services, has recognised the key to the NSW adoption reforms is that they address the problems of "drift", instability, and overemphasis on family preservation and reunification by establishing mandatory timeframes for evidence-based decisions about permanency and the active pursuit of adoption. As Porter has also characterised their purpose, the NSW reform legislation aims to set out the principles "that will guide internal departmental decision making", with the ultimate aim of achieving "a practical change in the operation of Departmental policy." Porter makes an acute assessment of the considerable powers of interpretation and implementation wielded by the departments, which remain highly relevant to the success or failure of the NSW reforms:

> Significant discretion resides with the relevant staff of the bureaucracies, who make critical decisions, such as whether and when to pursue certain cases or make certain applications under the legislation governing the removal of children to care or adoption. This being so, it is often the case that even subtle differences in emphasis or internal culture in relevant decision-making bureaucracies are likewise liable to have a very significant effect on actual outcomes.[479]

Here lies a potential benefit of national adoption targets and adoption incentive payment schemes in overcoming the pro-family preservation and anti-adoption internal culture in child protection authorities. We need to remember that in bureaucratic systems (such as state and territory child protection authorities), objectives that are measured and rewarded are those most likely to be achieved. It is also important to understand that social workers remain traumatised by the profession's involvement in past adoption practices, including forced adoption and the Stolen Generations. Only 12 departmental officers staff the division responsible for managing adoptions from care in NSW – an unofficial "go-slow" policy that demonstrates the continued ability of the bureaucracy to determine its own priorities.[480] National adoption targets and incentive payments would help circumvent the anti-adoption cultural and political resistance and facilitate much-needed ideological and institutional change in child protection authorities by providing clear political direction. Responsibility for reviving the use of adoption would be rightly and definitively assumed by the politicians, both federal and state, who are ultimately in charge of the system.

National adoption targets would also keep the pressure on and help overcome the resistance of the major stakeholders, especially the NGO lobby. The NSW Association of Children's Welfare Agencies (ACWA) maintains that although the NSW government's *Safe Home for Life* pro-adoption reform agenda is designed to "make adoption easier", the NSW child welfare legislation (as in all jurisdictions) has retained a preferred placement hierarchy that nominally makes children remaining with and being reunified with parents the first priority. According to the ACWA:

> What this means in real terms is a push to keep families together through educating and assisting parents struggling with their own issues to make the changes they need to make in order to keep their children. Supporting families to create safe and caring environments is the key to keeping children safe, enabling them to grow and reach their potential. [481]

This interpretation suggests that adoption will only occur in exceptional cases, when all efforts to keep families together have been exhausted. This suggests that the family preservation orthodoxy is not dead yet, and there are influential forces determined to keep it alive.

The UK experience: hope for change

Despite the significant cultural and political obstacles, change is possible with the right political commitment and leadership. This is the lesson of recent events in the UK, which have led to a significant increase in adoptions from care. Under the Cameron government, adoption has been embraced as one important means of dealing with Britain's "broken society" and addressing the squalor, violence, chaos, and dysfunction that characterises the worst underclass families.

In the four years since 2010, the number of adoptions from care in England has increased by 58%. In the year to the end of March 2014, 5,050 adoptions had been completed, the highest level on record.[482] The rising number of adoptions is attributable to the Adoption Action Plan implemented by the Cameron government, which aimed to remove the red tape and other barriers preventing the local council authorities responsible for child protection services from achieving more, and more timely, adoptions. The adoption reforms and their impact have been a triumph for their architect and champion, former education secretary Michael Gove, who successfully took up the political and cultural challenge of reframing the public debate about adoption.

In a number of speeches and newspaper articles, Gove cogently and passionately marshalled the evidence that refuted the orthodox "preoccupation with rights of biological parents", which he argued exposed children to "appalling neglect and criminal mistreatment".[483] On the back of a spate of horrific deaths of known children and various reports and inquiries into the failures of child protection services, Gove argued the real problem with the child protection system was not that too many children were in care, but that "far too many children [are] spending too long in homes where they are not receiving the care they need." Citing the "strong evidence that, in recent years, there has been too much reluctance to remove a child from circumstances of consistent and outright abuse and neglect",

Gove asserted that the poor outcomes achieved by children in care who failed in school, became unemployed, ended up in prison, and suffered mental illness, were not due to having been removed from their families, as was the common claim, but "were a consequence of what had happened to them before they were taken into care."

While understanding why social workers might wish to do everything to keep families together, Gove demanded that "optimism bias" and "the hope that things will improve" be set aside, and be replaced by the "instincts to intervene and rescue". Recognising "just how much damage is done to a child every day it spends in a home where there is no security, safety and certainty of affection", Gove insisted that "for some of the most vulnerable children, the sooner they are taken into care, the better." Citing the evidence that showed "maltreated children who remained in care did better than those who were sent home to their families", Gove argued the vicious cycle of instability and repeat abuse and neglect must stop by making sure fast and decisive intervention occurred to ensure children are "removed to a place of greater safety."

Recognising that sometimes this would be mean long-term fostering, Gove also cited the evidence that showed adoptions were most likely to last and had less disruption than foster placements. He insisted that achieving the goal of providing more children with safe and permanent homes meant there must be more adoptions "because adoption provides what abused and neglected children need most – stability, certainty, security, love." [484] Attacking the "wrong values" of the current system, Gove, despite his awareness of the sensitivities, pulled no punches in his advocacy for adoption:

> I know there will be some who will accuse us of baby-snatching. But when you read, as I have, of what the amoral residents of the most broken parts of Britain do to their children then no one with a conscience would want us to do

anything other than snatch these innocents away from this suffering.[485]

To reverse the 17% decline in adoptions that had occurred over the previous decade, and which had led to the lowest number of children adopted in England in 2011 since 2001, the Cameron government, under Gove's direction, introduced a range of new initiatives. To address significant regional variations in rates of adoption from care, national performance tables were published to encourage best practice across all local authorities and speed up the adoption process. The average time between a child entering care and being adopted was found to be two and half years, a lag attributed to administrative inertia linked to bloated and unnecessarily complex assessment processes. New, streamlined assessment guidelines issued to local authorities in 2011 targeted the way social workers' ideological hostility to adoption was expressed through "ridiculous" bureaucratic hurdles involving lengthy form-filling-out requirements, which allowed a plethora of reasons to be found to reject potential adoptive parents. The new rules prevented local authorities from rejecting applications to adopt based on trivial and irrelevant "tick-box" factors, such as smoking or being overweight, or the number of pets in the home, which were unlikely to compromise capacity to be a loving parent.

The revised assessment criteria also prohibited potential adopters from being turned away due to race or social background. Previously, adoptions could be either delayed or prevented by an unrealistic quest, which Gove described as "politically correct", to match children with the "perfect family" that matched their racial, religious, class, cultural, and linguistic backgrounds. Concerns about the potentially negative psychological effects of separation from birth families and cultural heritage on identity and sense of self had led to black children waiting 50% longer to be adopted than children from other ethnic groups, and to a black child being three times less likely to be adopted than a white child.[486]

Gove's personal circumstances made him uniquely placed to address this most controversial aspect of the adoption question. Born to an unwed mother in 1967, he had entered care and was adopted aged four months. His parents had also adopted his sister as a baby, who was then found to be profoundly deaf. He admitted that his own experience of being "given the stability, security, and love which allowed me to enjoy limitless opportunities", naturally coloured his attitudes to adoption.[487] But this also gave him the authority to powerfully address the identity issue. While he recognised that an "ethnic match between adopters and child can be a bonus", his view remained that it was "outrageous to deny a child the chance of adoption because of a misguided belief that race is more important than any other factor."[488] This view was not only founded on the injustice of denying vulnerable children the benefits of a safe and permanent family for life. It was also informed by his acute awareness of the "amazing opportunities" adoption had given him and his sister, which had transformed their lives and had transcended "carrying a legacy of pain, loss and uncertainty into adult life", even though his father and mother "had nothing in common with the woman who gave birth to me".[489]

The most significant symbol of how central adoption has become to the debate about child protection in Britain is the support and backing Gove's reforms have received from the prime minister. In a major speech delivered in August 2014, which outlined the government's approach to a variety of aspects of family policy, David Cameron reaffirmed the government's commitment to "help more children in care find a loving family through adoption." Highlighting the way Gove's new rules, including the sweeping away of "ridiculous" restrictions on "placing black children with white families", had led to "staggering" increases in the number and speed of adoptions, the prime minister declared that "we're not stopping there". Expressing his determination "to do everything we can to unleash this adoption revolution in our country" and ensure more children found a loving family, especially disabled and other "hard to adopt" children, Cameron announced the creation of "a new national Adoption Support Fund" to pay for remedial and other services for children with special needs. The aim was to reassure adoptive parents that they could "count on good support – not just in the early days, but years down the line if needed."[490]

The success of what Gove called his "crusade" shows the greater use of adoption from care can be made a major political and policy issue. The UK experience suggests it is feasible for politicians, with the facts at hand and the right arguments in mind, to successfully advance a pro-adoption reform agenda and not be dissuaded by cultural sensitivities from taking up and staying on that course. It also suggests well-designed reforms that target real problems and obstacles in the system can achieve significant improvements in adoption rates.

In Australia, we await the arrival of a prime minister willing and able to speak of their determination to unleash the adoption revolution, who takes credit for staggering increases in adoptions, and who takes responsibility for children being adopted on a colour-blind basis. That day must come if more Australian parents are to have the chance to adopt and more Australian children are to have the chance to be adopted.

Driving cultural change

The seeds of a "national approach" to adoption reform in Australia were planted by the Senate Community Affairs References Committee report, *Out of Home Care*, of August 2015. The minority report by Coalition senators Zed Seselja and Joanna Lindgren called for national leadership to end the "bias against adoption" in favour of a "'child-first' approach to decision making and policy development". The Federal government was urged to push the states and territories, through the deliberations of the Council of Australian Governments, to embrace "the NSW model so that more children under long-term care have the opportunity for adoption and permanency."[491]

While federal government action on adoption is important, it is no panacea. Neither national adoption targets, national adoption incentive payments, nor a UK-style national adoption support fund are substitutes for state-based reform of child protection policy and practice. A much stricter statutory child protection regime is obviously crucial, and politicians will have to mandate a new direction that will drive cultural change and overcome entrenched anti-adoption attitudes.

Dysfunctional parents should have an opportunity to access support services that help them address their problems when they first come under child protection scrutiny. This is precisely what permanency planning laws are designed to achieve, but with time limits applied to ensure that unsuccessful early interventions are not endlessly prolonged. Sound practice, in the best interests of children, must be that parents' first chance to get their acts together is also their last. Dysfunctional parents must have full knowledge of the looming consequences if they do not shape up – the permanent removal of children and severance of parental rights.

Requiring caseworkers to insist on timely and substantial commitment to and achievement of behavioural change, and ensuring that attempts to rehabilitate the family and reunite children with parents are not endless, is neither harsh nor unreasonable. It is unreasonable to prioritise the needs of bad or inadequate parents over the needs of their children. It is unreasonable to ignore how last-resort removal and unstable living arrangements compromise the crucial early years of childhood. It is unreasonable to underestimate the extent of parental problems and the risks they pose to children. It is also unreasonable to insist that parents consent to severing parental rights. Whatever else can be said of them, they remain parents and will not wish to voluntarily sign away their children. This is why the state will need to step in and take action to dispense with parental consent – where needed – if more adoptions from care are to occur.

Restoring foster care to what it can and should be for many children – a natural pathway to adoption – also requires realistic assessment of the circumstances in which adoption is most likely to occur and what is best for children. The last resort of opponents of any move towards greater use of adoption is to point to the large numbers of high-needs children in care and claim that adoption is clearly not a suitable option for many "unadoptable" children.

A severely troubled 12-year-old who has been let down by the system is, of course, more likely to end up in institutional care than be adopted. The greater the parental abuse and neglect endured, and the more unstable the care history, the more severe will children's problems be and the greater the chance of adoptions either not occurring or breaking down.

Earlier removal, when children are younger and less damaged, combined with realistic assessments of the likelihood of successful family reunions, will reduce harmful delays, help recruit and reassure adoptive parents, and increase the chances of children finding good and stable adoptive homes. A pool of prospective adoptive parents can be recruited simply by implementing reforms that make local adoption from care a realistic and desirable prospect. This should include the use of "concurrent planning", where children are placed with potential adoptive families when they enter foster care and before a plan for adoption has been agreed. Recruited parents will have to be committed to helping children overcome the difficulties that many children with suboptimal backgrounds will face. Fortunately, the right people will be self-selecting, as this kind of commitment is implied in their decision to adopt from care.

Making adoption the rule rather than the rarest exception will require a concerted political effort. Policymakers can facilitate more local adoptions by undertaking a range of other measures. This includes education of the judiciary about parental incapacity, child development, and risks to children, particularly in cumulative harm cases involving irreversible development deficits caused by chronic neglect of children's physical, emotional, and psychological needs. It also includes promoting awareness that forced adoptions will be open and that opportunities for ongoing contact with birth families will mean that a well-adjusted child will have a better chance of re-establishing a meaningful relationship with dysfunctional biological parents.

There will also be a need for extension of temporary care allowances to adoptive parents, plus needs-based ongoing financial support for families adopting sibling groups and children with high needs. Similarly, there will be a need for guaranteed access to pre- and post-adoption support services (including respite care) to reduce breakdowns and assist with children's integration into their new, functional families. This means there also will need to be an understanding that while adoption won't be cost-free, it will deploy funding in the children's best interests rather than wasting it on failed policies. Adoption will also be less costly than long-term care costs, especially those of much more expensive residential facilities.

There are, then, compelling and interrelated economic as well as child safety reasons to put greater use of adoption from care on the agenda of state and territory governments. Adoption shifts the bulk cost of raising children off government budgets. It is the only affordable way to provide stable homes for all the children in Australia who cannot live safely with biological parents.

Greater transparency in the child protection system is also required to enable the move towards adoption, starting with more meaningful national data. This should encompass, as a means of driving profound policy and practice change, the publication of annual data on the number of children in care, how long they have been there, and the number of children available for adoption. This would help promote recruitment of adoptive families, and disprove the claim that Australians don't want to adopt locally. Currently, few prospective adoptive parents even enquire about local adoption because the chances of success are so low. These families are instead forced to pursue what prove to be expensive and drawn-out adoptions from overseas, or invasive, expensive, repeated, and often heartbreakingly unsuccessful IVF procedures, despite the thousands of local candidates for adoption living in care.

Indigenous exceptionalism redux?

There is much to recommend in the pro-adoption policy developments in NSW, and much for other states and territories to emulate. By challenging the adoption taboo, the NSW government showed courage in taking considerable political risks. Perhaps wisely, it exercised caution with respect to Indigenous children in care. Despite the range of benefits for children associated with adoption, the government "acknowledged, however, that adoption is not considered a culturally accepted practice for Aboriginal children". On this basis, the policy in NSW will be that "decisions on providing such stability, security, and certainty for Aboriginal children in OOHC will only be made in accordance with the Aboriginal Placement Principles".[492] This will also entail persisting with "Aboriginal-controlled" foster and kinship care services, under the remit of the peak Aboriginal out-of-home care body – the Aboriginal Child, Family and Community Care State Secretariat (AbSec) – to ensure care and support for Aboriginal children and their carers is "culturally appropriate".[493]

Clearly, the Stolen Generations continue to cast a long shadow over Indigenous child protection policy. However, the NSW policy of persisting with the ACPP is in danger of being mugged by reality. In December 2014, the NSW Labor deputy opposition leader and former child protection minister, Linda Burney, argued that Indigenous children were "just not willy nilly placed in any Aboriginal family."[494] Yet in July 2015, the chair of AbSec told the Royal Commission into Institutional Responses to Child Sexual Abuse that child protection authorities too often went with "expedient" options when placing Indigenous children in care:

> You want kids to go to family but they have to be safe. Quite often family (options) sits in front of safety. Just because you put your hand up to say you are kin does not mean you are a suitable candidate to care for children. Kids need to be in their community and need to be raised there but they need to be raised by people who can do that.[495]

Other Indigenous and non-Indigenous witnesses also stated that kinship care placements received inadequate scrutiny, and that children were exposed to the sale of drugs and were abused by community members meant to protect them. The co-chair of the National Stolen Generations Alliance even suggested the problems were so bad that reconciling child welfare and the development of culture "may mean, heaven forbid, that we revert back to the missions. We take our kids out of care or the care that they are not getting … and put them back on the missions but with their parents, their carers, so we're learning that culture and belonging." [496]

What evidence before the Royal Commission starkly illustrated was the way the nation's efforts to address the specific legacy of the Stolen Generation via the ACPP threaten to undermine the overarching practical objective of reconciliation, which is to eradicate the shameful disadvantages, abject poverty, and lack of opportunity that too many Indigenous Australians, particularly children, have long continued to suffer. The continued use of kinship care for reasons of culture and identity threatens to deny another lost generation of Indigenous children, especially those who live in the most disadvantaged remote communities, the chance to enjoy the full freedoms, benefits and opportunities of Australian citizenship enjoyed by other Indigenous and non-Indigenous Australians.

All Australians of good will endorse the aims of reconciliation. But to achieve it, we need to undertake the difficult task of revising well-intentioned separatist policies that have caused suffering. The revolution in Indigenous affairs of the last decade and half or so has addressed other Indigenous policy failures by marginalising the separatist agenda in favour of mainstreaming Indigenous services. There is no escaping the realisation that continuing priority given to "culture" at the expense of child welfare in Indigenous child protection is inconsistent with the shift away from separatism towards mainstreaming Indigenous policy as the way to close the gap between the most disadvantaged Indigenous Australians and other Australians.

To apply the same mainstreaming approach to revising separatist Indigenous child protection policies definitely does not imply that questions of culture and identity are irrelevant and should be overlooked. On the contrary, the challenge is to find new ways of reconciling cultural and child welfare considerations. The starting point is to realise that the priority given to compliance with the ACPP, based on the idea that retention of culture is the source of Aboriginal identity, is outdated compared to modern definitions of Aboriginality that have developed in line with the changing character of the Indigenous population.

Reconciling modern Aboriginal identity and child welfare

The number of Australians who are identifying as Indigenous is growing rapidly. The latest Australian census recorded a remarkable 21% increase in the numbers of Indigenous Australians. In 2006, 455,028 people identified as Indigenous; by 2011, the number had increased to 548,400,[497] and "the changes appear to have been driven by changes in self-identification in urban areas."[498] The most rapidly growing part of the Aboriginal population lives in urban areas. In 2011, 35% of Indigenous people in Australia lived in major cities, up from 31% in 2006. The inner regional population held steady (22%), while the proportion living in outer regional (22%) and remote or very remote areas (21%) fell by 2% and 3% respectively.[499] The highest regional increases in the Indigenous population between 2006 and 2011 occurred in south-eastern Australia, mostly in the major urban regions – the ACT (44%), Victoria excluding Melbourne (41%), Melbourne (41%), Brisbane (40%), Adelaide (38%), and Sydney-Wollongong (37%).[500] The growth in the Indigenous population suggests that the modern definition of Aboriginality increasingly makes it an ethnic identity based on self-identification, contemporary recognition, and family history and descent from an Aboriginal ancestor.[501] The official three-part definition of Aboriginal identity used by the Commonwealth for legal and administrative purposes is based on (1) ancestry, (2) self-identification, and (3) acceptance by the Indigenous community in which they live.[502]

This modern definition of Aboriginality is a product of high rates of Indigenous intermarriage: in 2006, 52% of Indigenous men and 55% of Indigenous women were partnered (married or lived with) a non-Indigenous spouse, with rates of intermarriage highest in capital cities in south-eastern Australia.[503] The overall proportion of mixed couples (one Indigenous and one non-Indigenous partner or spouse) as a proportion of all Indigenous couples (where at least one partner is Indigenous) was 71.5%.[504] This is also significant in accounting for the growth in the Indigenous population, because the Australian Bureau of Statistics and other government organisations "commonly treat all children of intermarriage as Indigenous Australians."[505]

Modern Aboriginal identity is also a product of and reflects the overall distribution of the Indigenous population, or, more accurately, is a product of and reflects the social status of the approximately three quarters of all Indigenous Australians who reside in major cities and regional towns.[506] Those within this group of urban Indigenous Australians are thoroughly integrated into mainstream society to the point that in relation to education, employment, housing, and other social welfare indicators, they are similar to their non-Indigenous peers – without this "resulting in a diminution of Indigenous identification."[507]

These statistics, and the changing character of the Aboriginal population that they illustrate, are significant in two interrelated ways concerning the "construction of Aboriginal identity."[508] First, they indicate that modern Aboriginal identity is no longer based on biological racial identity or on being culturally Aboriginal in the traditional sense, as in having continuous contact with Aboriginal culture and traditional lands. Without this contact, a person can still identify as Aboriginal based on pride in one's background. As Sara Hudson has argued, this is similar to the way identity is generated through connection to ancestry, traditions, and culture among other ethnic groups in multicultural societies.[509]

Second, the factors that make a person successful in mainstream society – principally education and employment – do not make a person less Aboriginal, because modern Aboriginal identity is different to race and culture. This means the debate about identity can move beyond the fraught and politically charged controversy over the meaning of integration into the mainstream. In the past, integration has tended to be portrayed as synonymous with the assimilationist, paternalist, and culturally genocidal policies of earlier eras, to promote the political cause of self-determination. Understanding that integration is compatible with modern Aboriginal identity means the long-standing objections to mainstreaming Indigenous child protection policy – including the supposed risk of creating of "a new Stolen Generation"

– have lost their validity on the basis of preserving Aboriginal identity. It is clearly now possible for the majority of Indigenous Australians to fully integrate with mainstream Australian society while preserving their Aboriginal status and identity.[510]

As the work of Gary Johns, Peter Sutton, and Helen Hughes and Mark Hughes have all suggested, the link between traditional culture and identity now has far less coherence as a source of Aboriginality due to the realities of contemporary Australia, the changing character of the Indigenous population, and the claiming of Aboriginal identity by those with virtually no contact with traditional culture. No matter how distant or non-existent the connection with culture, Aboriginal identity is recognised and accepted by both Indigenous and non-Indigenous communities. Just as importantly, integration with the mainstream is no barrier to modern Aboriginal identity, belonging, and recognition.

The idea that Aboriginality depended on continuous contact with traditional culture made more sense in the 1970s as political strategy, as a way of advancing the political objective of self-determination, but the separatist agenda has now been discredited and superseded. The idea that the advancement of Indigenous people lies in mainstreaming Indigenous policy is largely accepted with respect to education, health, employment, and economic development. Yet the same shift in thinking and practice has not occurred in relation to Indigenous child protection policy. The rationale for the ACPP remains the outdated and superseded understanding of the relationship between Indigenous culture and Indigenous identity, based on the belief that children must be placed with kin to have continuous contact with traditional culture and maintain their Aboriginality. The ACPP is a hangover from a different age of separatist Indigenous policy. Recognising how outdated this last bastion of self-determination has become opens the way forward to reforming current policy and practice in the best interests of Indigenous children.

The last frontier of the mainstreaming revolution

It is time to stop thinking of Indigenous adoption from care as unthinkable and as "stealing" children again. Action to extend the mainstreaming revolution to Indigenous child protection and end all forms of Indigenous exceptionalism and "special treatment" is well overdue.

Under a mainstreamed Indigenous child protection regime, Indigenous and non-Indigenous children would be treated the same. Open adoption would be used on a non-discriminatory basis to provide Indigenous children who cannot live safely with their parents or kin with safe and nurturing families. The obvious place to start the revision of current policy and practice is to revisit the NSW adoption reform legislation to include rather than exclude Indigenous children.

If adoption is a culturally unacceptable practice for Aboriginal communities, and Aboriginal children must therefore endure upbringings that compromise their futures and perpetuate the cycle of disadvantage, then perhaps this aspect of Aboriginal culture has outlived its usefulness. Perhaps we should also see the cultural taboo on Indigenous adoption for what it plainly is: another example of Indigenous politics getting in the way of the care and protection of children. Culture should be given due importance, but not at the price of endangering child welfare. This principle ought not to be controversial in a country such as Australia. In functional societies, adults are responsible for passing on cultural knowledge to the next generation; culture is not something that children should suffer to acquire – that is a perverse inversion of the proper social order and the generational compact between young and old. This means culture should have to follow Indigenous children to safety, not that children's safety should be compromised for culture's sake.

It follows that cultural considerations need not pose an

impenetrable obstacle to mainstreaming of child protection policy and Indigenous adoption. Maintaining a child's cultural identity is now a standard expectation for overseas adoptions: adoptive parents must acknowledge that children are not blank slates and must say how they will ensure contact with the child's birth culture, such as by involvement in traditional cultural and community activities, maintaining links with natural parents and extended families, or by travel to the child's birth country. Integrated Aborigines living in mainstream Australia are also finding ways to ensure that they and their children foster their identity through contact with culture.[511] Moreover, "cultural support plans", which are designed to ensure the large minority of Indigenous children who are currently unable to be placed with kin can connect with culture, are already a standard part of child protection practice.[512]

In a revamped, non-discriminatory Indigenous child protection system, the Aboriginal industry could play a constructive role in reconciling considerations of culture with considerations of child welfare through the delivery of formalised, professionalised, and funded cultural support programs as a key part of the provision of culturally appropriate adoption and permanent care services for Indigenous children and their families.[513] Here too, as with other aspects of child protection reform, national leadership and policy development by the federal government, parallel to that provided in the areas of Indigenous health, education, and employment, will also be needed. This leadership would help hasten political acceptance of mainstreaming and spur state governments into modernising Indigenous child protection policy as a vital, nationally important means of closing the gap in outcomes between disadvantaged Indigenous Australians and the rest of the population. High-level Indigenous leadership will also undoubtedly be needed to smooth the way for government action on the issue of Indigenous adoption.

The right to escape and the right to return to country

Despite the high stakes regarding the welfare of Indigenous Australians, some will still say that mainstreaming Indigenous child protection remains unthinkable. But who says so, and why do they say it? It is unthinkable for many in the Aboriginal industry because changes to Indigenous child protection would chiefly involve the recognition of the unsuitability of kinship care and likely removal of more children from the homelands. A major potential implication is that removing children would bring the long-term future of the homeland communities into question, which would have funding implications for the myriad Aboriginal-controlled organisations that provide services in those communities, and for the largely city-based, well-educated, well-off, and integrated Indigenous elite who staff these organisations.

It is ironic that these elites stand to benefit from denying the most disadvantaged and vulnerable Indigenous children the opportunity to enjoy all the benefits and opportunities of Australian life that they and their children enjoy. It is doubly ironic that this would be done in the name of preserving contact with kin and culture, based on a definition of Indigenous identity that these elites deem irrelevant with respect to their own and their children's identity.[514]

The real concern driving objections to mainstreaming Indigenous child protection is that this would make it harder to sustain the residual political justification for the institutional legacy of the era of Aboriginal self-determination. In the long run, this would threaten the future of much of the Aboriginal industry, which would lose both its reason for existence and its rationale for its call on public funding. The continued practice of the ACPP therefore means that Indigenous politics still take priority over the welfare of Indigenous children. This makes Indigenous child protection the most pressing instance the nation faces today of the persistence of the politics of suffering.

The focus of reform in this area should be how best to normalise the experiences of all Indigenous people in this country. The ACPP and other culturally appropriate child protection policies stand among the various separatist social experiments that Indigenous Australians have been subjected to for two centuries, from the missions to the homelands movement. In the wake of the Stolen Generations, it is easy to appreciate why the issue of moving away from these policies is so sensitive. We should also acknowledge the efforts of Indigenous leaders, such as Warren Mundine, Noel Pearson, and others, to promote economic development and social norms in Indigenous communities, and hope that these efforts succeed. But we also need to face up to the reality that these efforts are also experiments in social re-engineering, the success or failure of which is far from certain.

Because of that uncertainty, we should deal with what we know to be true, which is that there are many people in Indigenous communities who are incapable of functioning in mainstream society.[515] They are literally trapped, and denied the choice of leaving. If we keep doing what we are doing in Indigenous child protection, future generations may also be denied the chance to escape, because compliance with the ACPP will keep open the gap in outcomes with mainstream Australia, and keep them trapped in dysfunction.

Adopted Indigenous children, however, would not only get the chance to escape. They would also have the opportunity to return to homeland communities as functional adults if the social experiments of Mundine, Pearson, and others succeed and there is a life worth living there. In this, above all, Indigenous adoption would mean that we no longer would have to endure the existing, intolerable, and fundamentally un-Australian situation that persisting with the last bastion of Aboriginal separatism will otherwise entail. Embracing Indigenous adoption as the path to true reconciliation will mean that the most disadvantaged Australians will no longer be left to suffer as the last, helpless victims of the failed political ideology of self-determination.

Acknowledgements

My formal qualifications are in history. I was trained to understand worlds that are not my own and to make them explicable to others. Thank you to all those with first-hand experience who have complimented me on the accuracy of my account of Australia's child protection disaster. Such praise has been worth the professional lifetime in the making.

This book would not exist but for The Centre for Independent Studies (CIS). If my research had relied on the backing of institutional players in the sector, it would never have been able to progress and take the direction it did. Think tanks can play a vital role in a vibrant civil society. The willingness of like-minded people to join together and inform fellow citizens about public policy issues is an invaluable democratic resource – a resource that has given me the chance to formulate the ideas expressed in this book. My thanks, credit, and gratitude go to the Centre's executive director, Greg Lindsay, and to all the staff, members, and supporters of the CIS.

On behalf of all at the CIS, I would like to acknowledge the Thyne Reid Foundation for its generous support of my position as a research fellow in the Social Foundations Program. Thank you for granting me the time and opportunity to study, think, and write about subjects as sensitive and crucial as child protection and adoption.

Ellis Wayland and Christopher Miller of SOS Children's Villages Australia have also provided moral and material support for which I am grateful.

Professor Christopher Goddard of Child Abuse Prevention Research Australia (CAPRA) at Monash University read and commented on the research reports this book is based on, and provided many valuable suggestions that improved them. Professor Goddard's advice has been irreplaceable, and his passionate commitment to exposing and fixing the flaws in Australian child protection systems was infectious.

John Hirst has been a mentor for almost 20 years. The single most important intellectual experience of my life was the opportunity to work with John as a research assistant for his 2005 *Quarterly Essay* on family law in Australia. It was an education in how cogent research and writing can yield compelling analysis of complicated issues. I am extremely lucky not only to have had the opportunity to learn from John but to have had him in my corner and been able to seek his counsel on this project and many other subjects.

Many of my current and former colleagues at The Centre for Independent Studies read, discussed, and encouraged my child protection research. Thanks to Professor Peter Saunders, the late Professor Helen Hughes, Jennifer Buckingham, Barry Maley, Jessica Brown, Sara Hudson, Alex Philipatos, and Peter Kurti. Jennifer Buckingham and Peter Kurti also read the entire manuscript of this book and helped shape a much-improved final version. Acting research manager Simon Cowan helped smooth out the various internal processes associated with the production of this book. Many thanks.

Thanks as well to Mangai Pitchai, the CIS's former editor, who worked on all but one of my research reports on child protection policy. Thanks to Karla Pincott for editing my report on kinship care, for general editorial advice, and for helping conceive the cover design. Thanks also to Leonie Phillips, formerly of the CIS and now a director of public-relations firm Thought Broker, who taught me so much about her area of expertise – the clear and effective communication of complex ideas.

I would also like to thank the interns who compiled the data and graphs that appear throughout this book. Matthew Stockton, Christian

Stojanovski, Blaise Joseph, and Aloka Kumarage all provided much-appreciated assistance and work of a consistently high standard.

Thank you also to Jim Beatty for his advice on the manuscript.

Anthony Dillon, Nigel Parbury, and Kerryn Pholi read my work on Indigenous child protection and generously shared their knowledge and insights.

The responsibility for this book is solely my own.

I would also like to acknowledge Rebecca Weisser, former opinion page editor of *The Australian*, who unfailingly published my op-eds on child protection issues and gave me opportunities to publicise my work and influence public debate.

Thanks also to the growing band of politicians and other public officials who have taken heed of my work and its message.

Ben Hourigan has done an outstanding editing job, and provided the fresh eyes and perceptive pen that I needed. Thanks as well to Anthony Cappello and all at Connor Court Publishing. Anthony has filled what used to be a yawning gap in the intellectual life of the nation for us on the centre-right. Connor Court's success has shown that "conservatives" not only read books, they also write them.

A big thank you to Deborra-lee Furness for agreeing to write the foreword. Deborra-lee's enduring commitment to the cause of adoption reform in Australia is measured by the excellent advocacy work of Adopt Change. Thank you to Kerry Chikarovski for introducing me to the organisation. It has been a pleasure to get to know chief executive Jane Hunt and former chairman and now non-executive director John O'Neill, and to witness the impact Adopt Change is having on attitudes to adoption in this country.

APPENDIX. COUNTING THE COST OF THE CRISIS

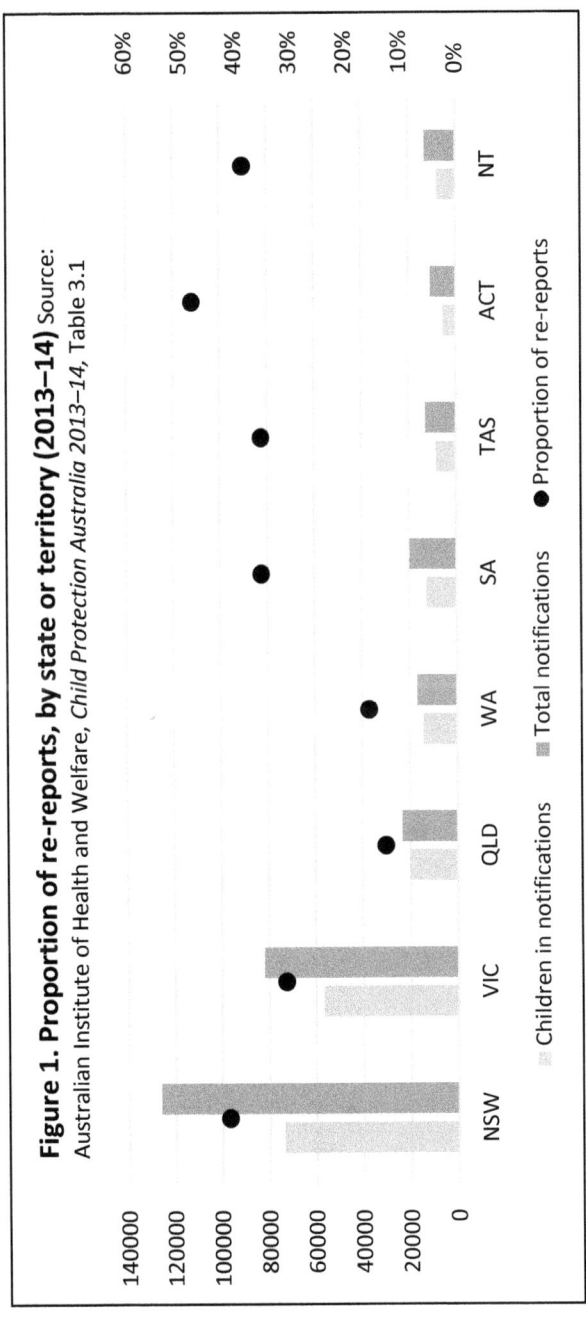

Figure 1. Proportion of re-reports, by state or territory (2013–14) Source: Australian Institute of Health and Welfare, *Child Protection Australia 2013–14*, Table 3.1

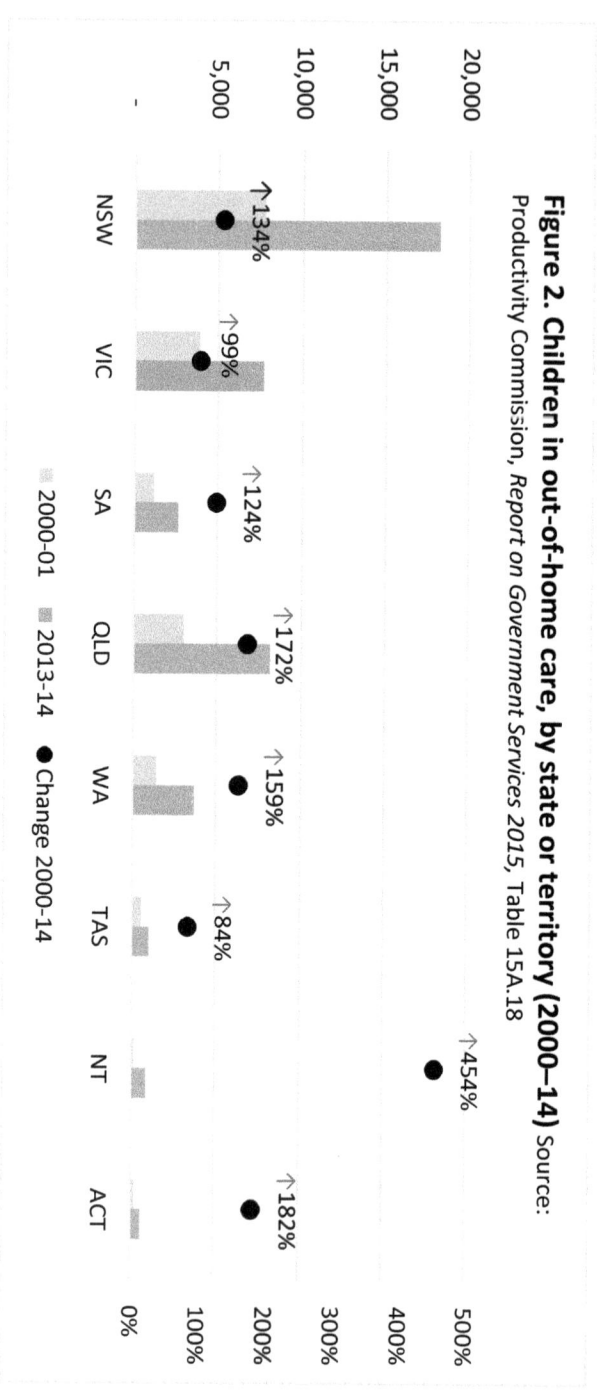

Figure 2. Children in out-of-home care, by state or territory (2000–14) Source: Productivity Commission, *Report on Government Services 2015*, Table 15A.18

Why Adoption Will Rescue Australia's Underclass Children 245

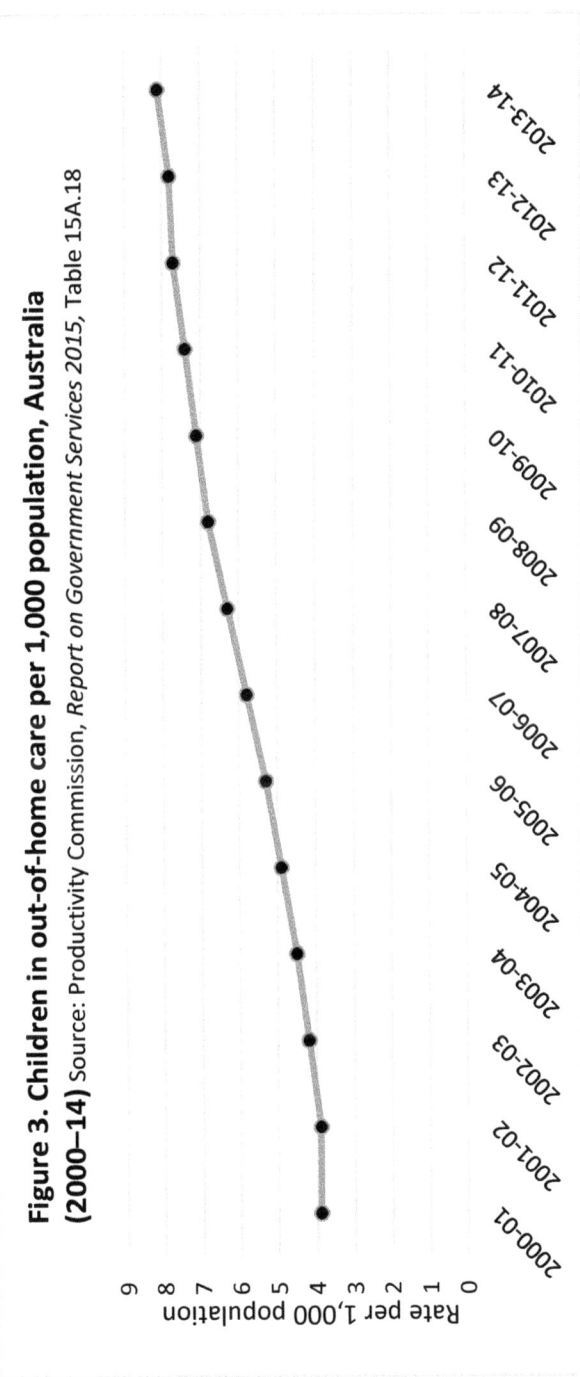

Figure 3. Children in out-of-home care per 1,000 population, Australia (2000–14) Source: Productivity Commission, *Report on Government Services 2015*, Table 15A.18

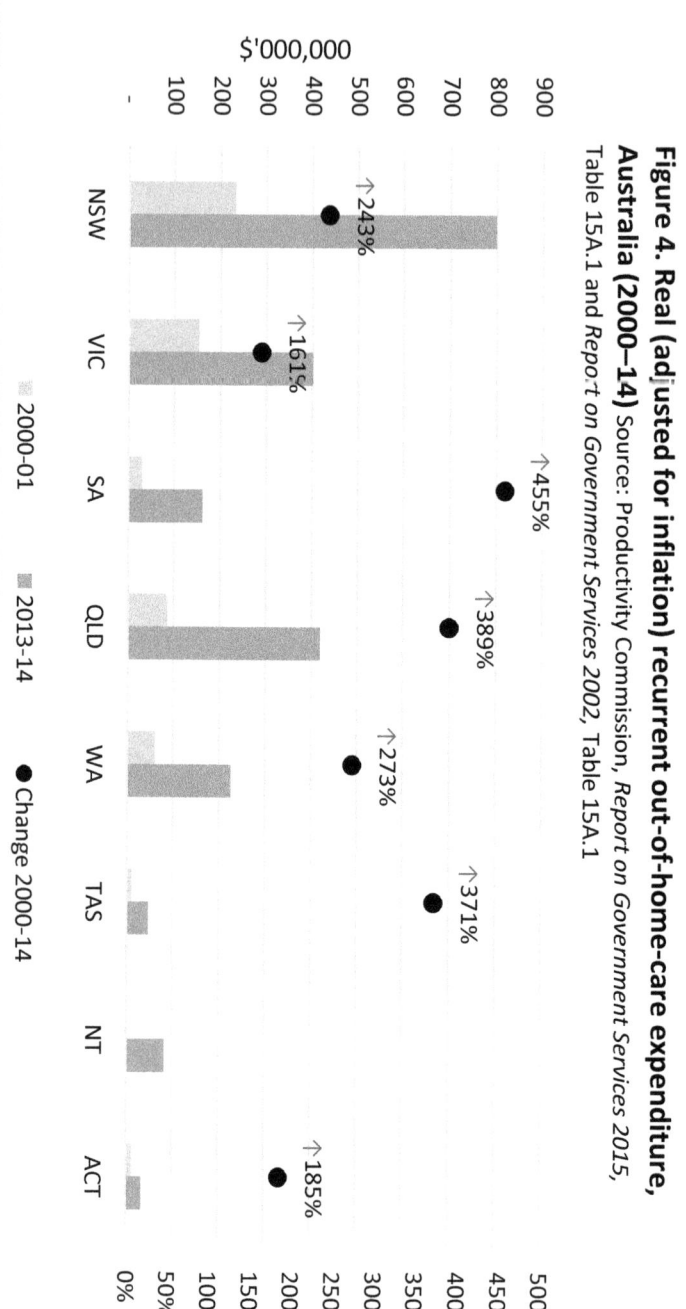

Figure 4. Real (adjusted for inflation) recurrent out-of-home-care expenditure, Australia (2000–14) Source: Productivity Commission, *Report on Government Services 2015*, Table 15A.1 and *Report on Government Services 2002*, Table 15A.1

Why Adoption Will Rescue Australia's Underclass Children 247

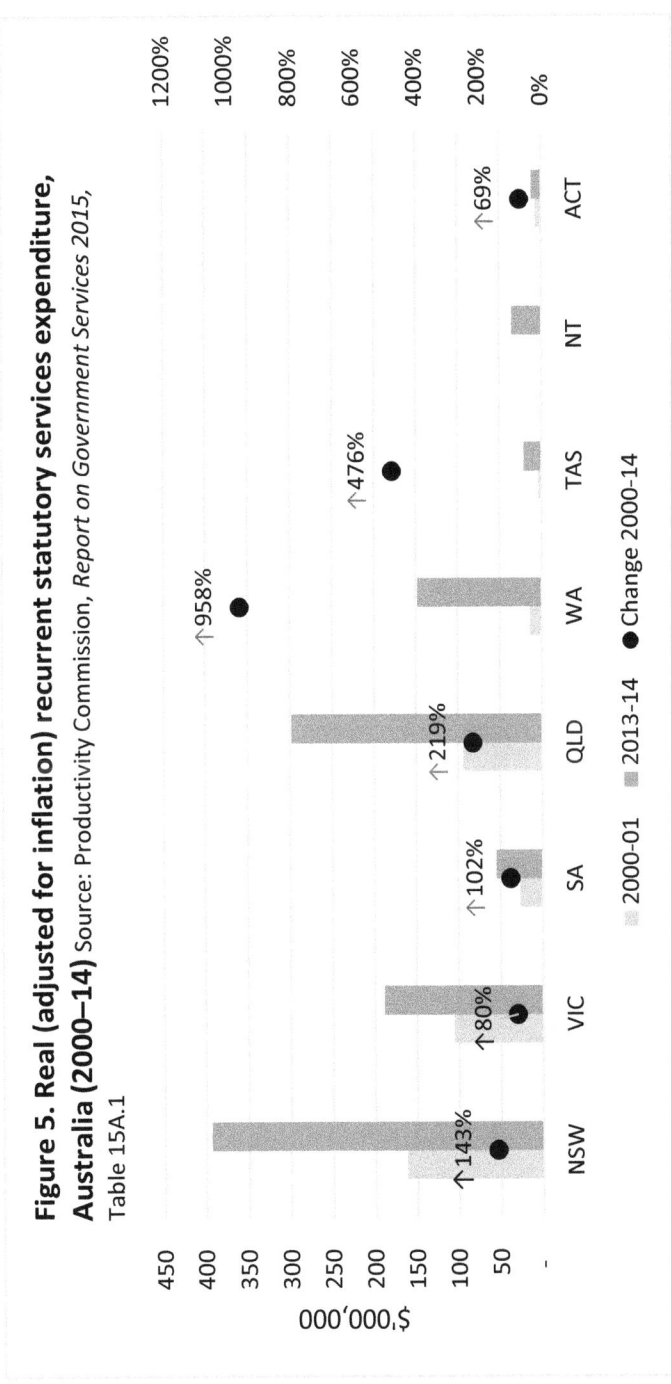

Figure 5. Real (adjusted for inflation) recurrent statutory services expenditure, Australia (2000–14) Source: Productivity Commission, *Report on Government Services 2015*, Table 15A.1

248   The Madness of Australian Child Protection

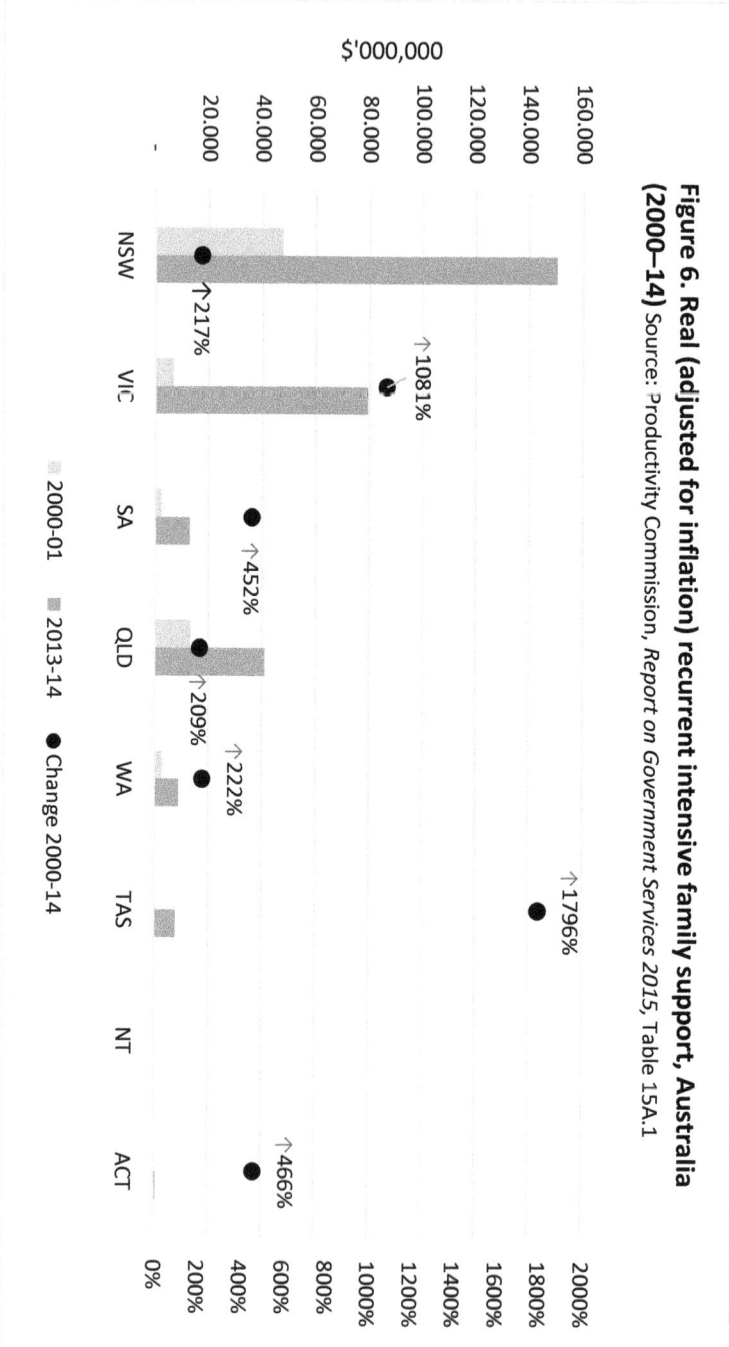

Figure 6. Real (adjusted for inflation) recurrent intensive family support, Australia (2000–14) Source: Productivity Commission, *Report on Government Services 2015*, Table 15A.1

Why Adoption Will Rescue Australia's Underclass Children 249

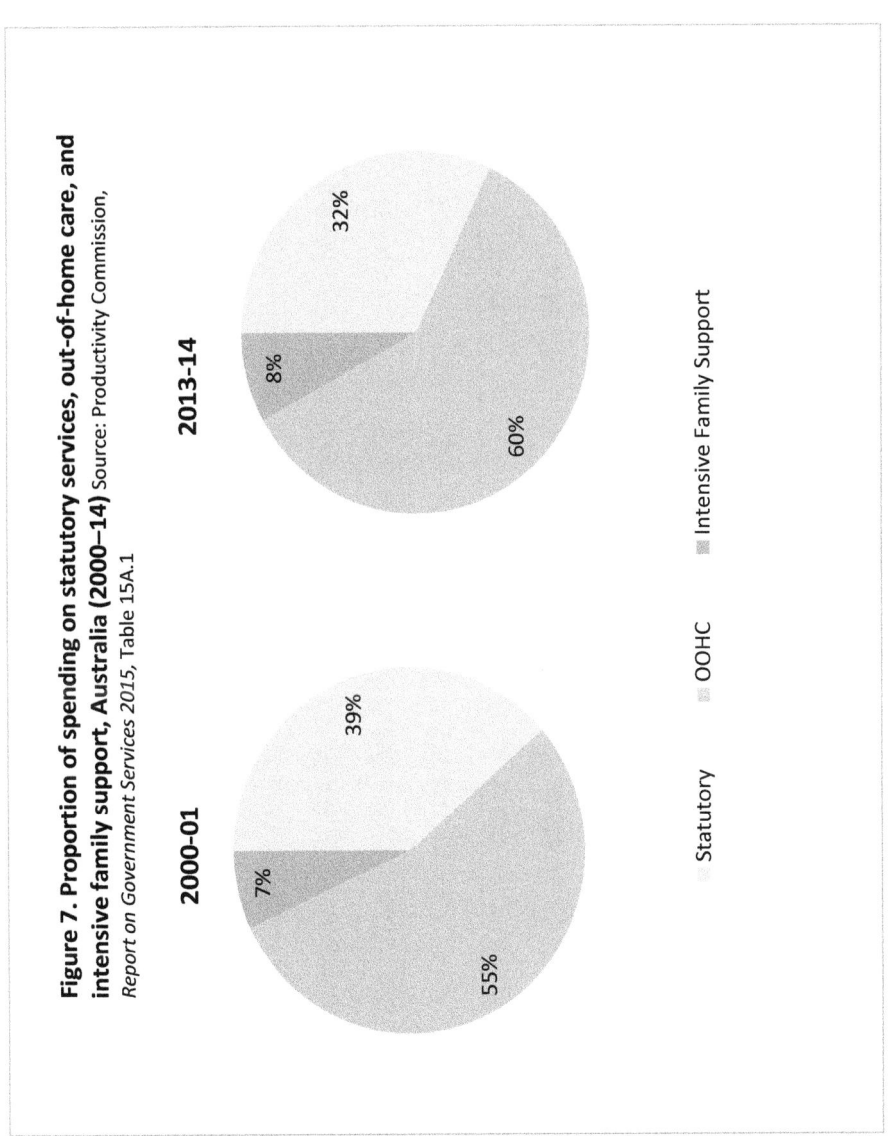

Figure 7. Proportion of spending on statutory services, out-of-home care, and intensive family support, Australia (2000–14) Source: Productivity Commission, *Report on Government Services 2015*, Table 15A.1

250   The Madness of Australian Child Protection

Figure 8. Proportion of spending on statutory services, out-of-home care, and combined intensive family preservation and family support, Australia (2013–14)

Source: Productivity Commission, Report on Government Services 2015, Table 15A.1

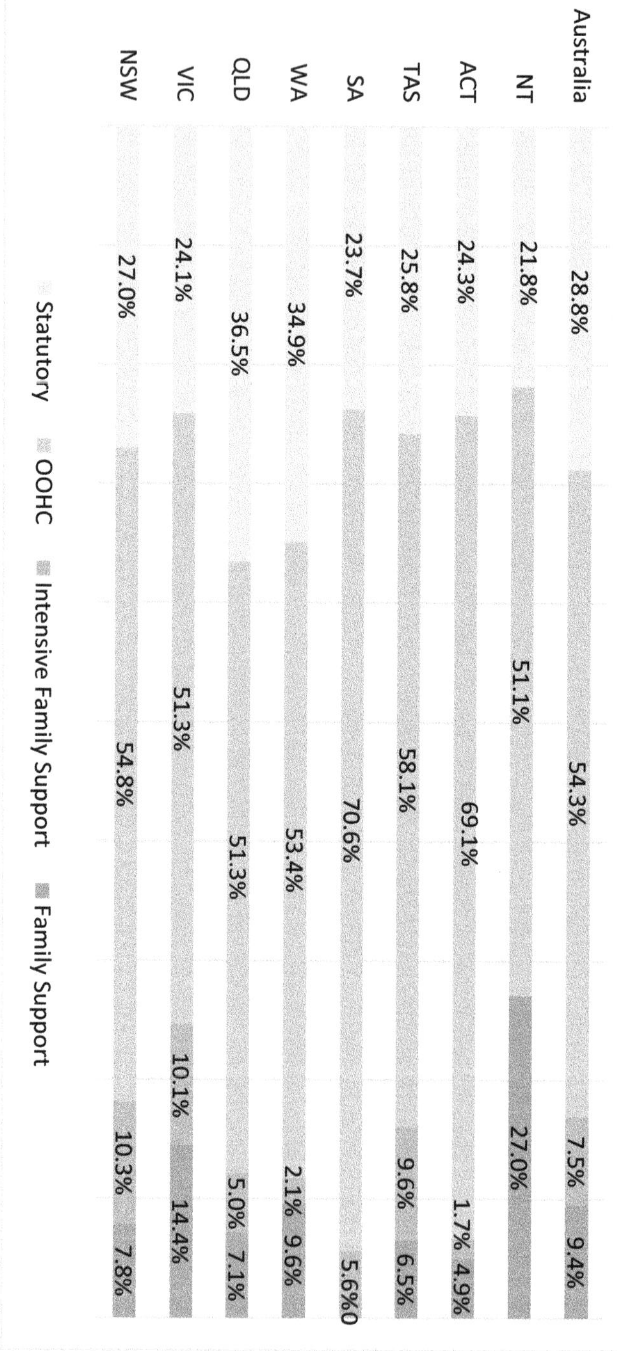

	Statutory	OOHC	Intensive Family Support	Family Support
NSW	27.0%	54.8%	10.3%	7.8%
VIC	24.1%	51.3%	10.1%	14.4%
QLD	36.5%	51.3%	5.0%	7.1%
WA	34.9%	53.4%	2.1%	9.6%
SA	23.7%	70.6%		5.6%
TAS	25.8%	58.1%	9.6%	6.5%
ACT	24.3%	69.1%	1.7%	4.9%
NT	21.8%	51.1%	27.0%	
Australia	28.8%	54.3%	7.5%	9.4%

Why Adoption Will Rescue Australia's Underclass Children 251

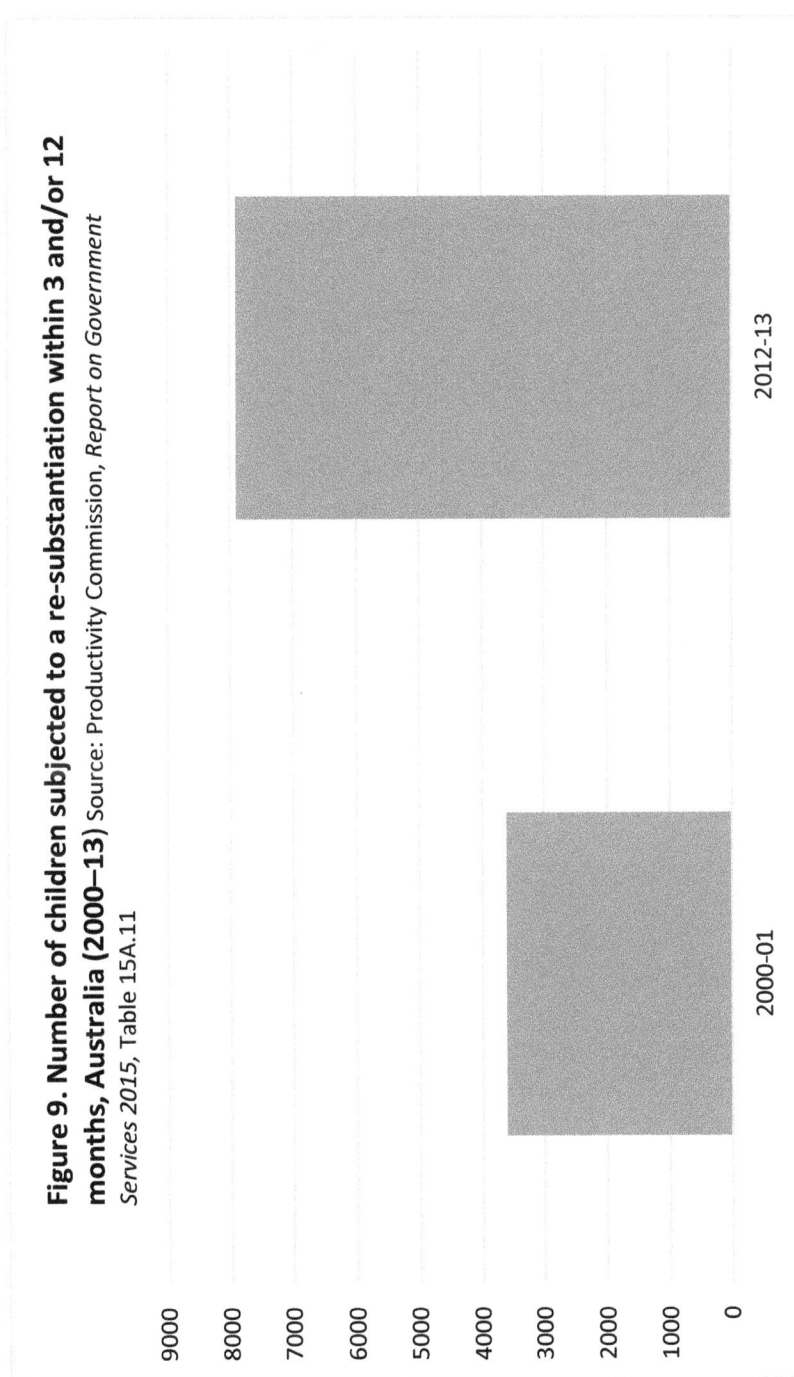

Figure 9. Number of children subjected to a re-substantiation within 3 and/or 12 months, Australia (2000–13) Source: Productivity Commission, *Report on Government Services 2015*, Table 15A.11

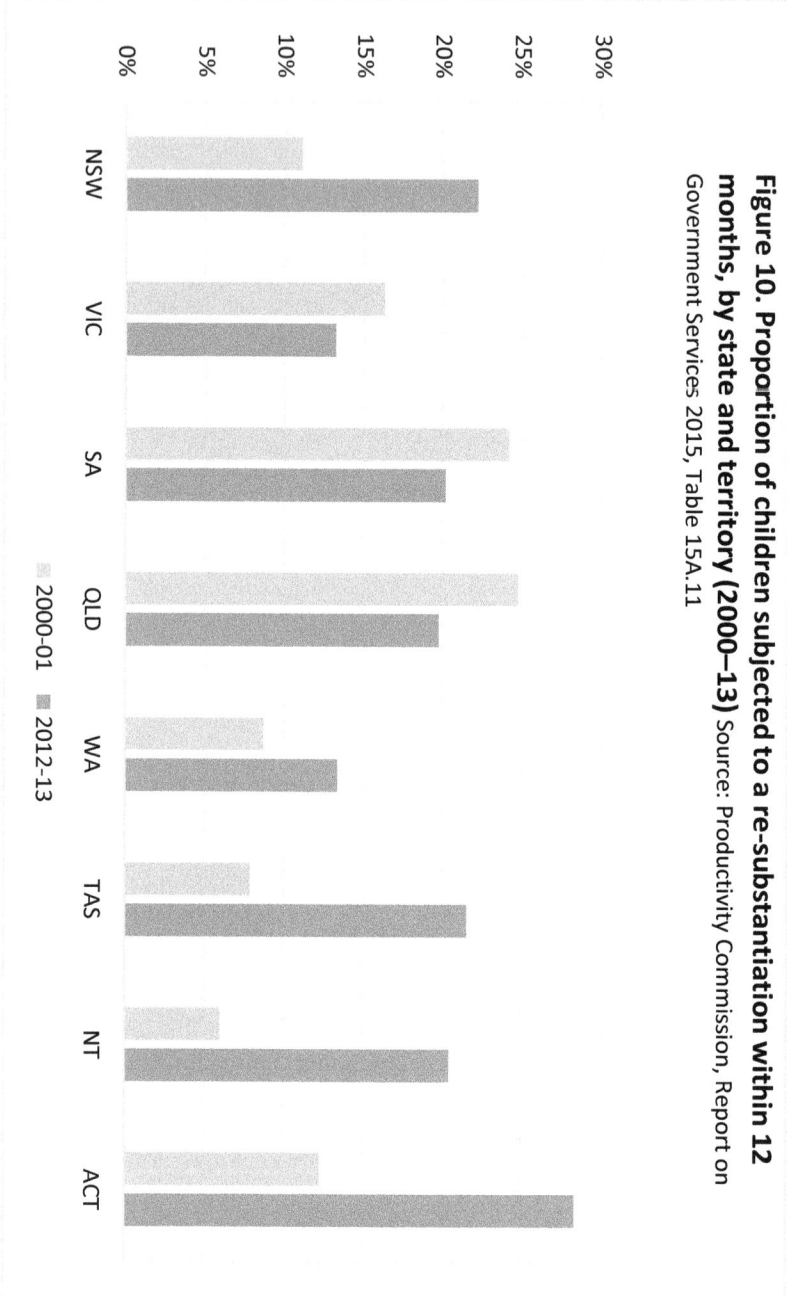

Figure 10. Proportion of children subjected to a re-substantiation within 12 months, by state and territory (2000–13) Source: Productivity Commission, Report on Government Services 2015, Table 15A.11

Why Adoption Will Rescue Australia's Underclass Children 253

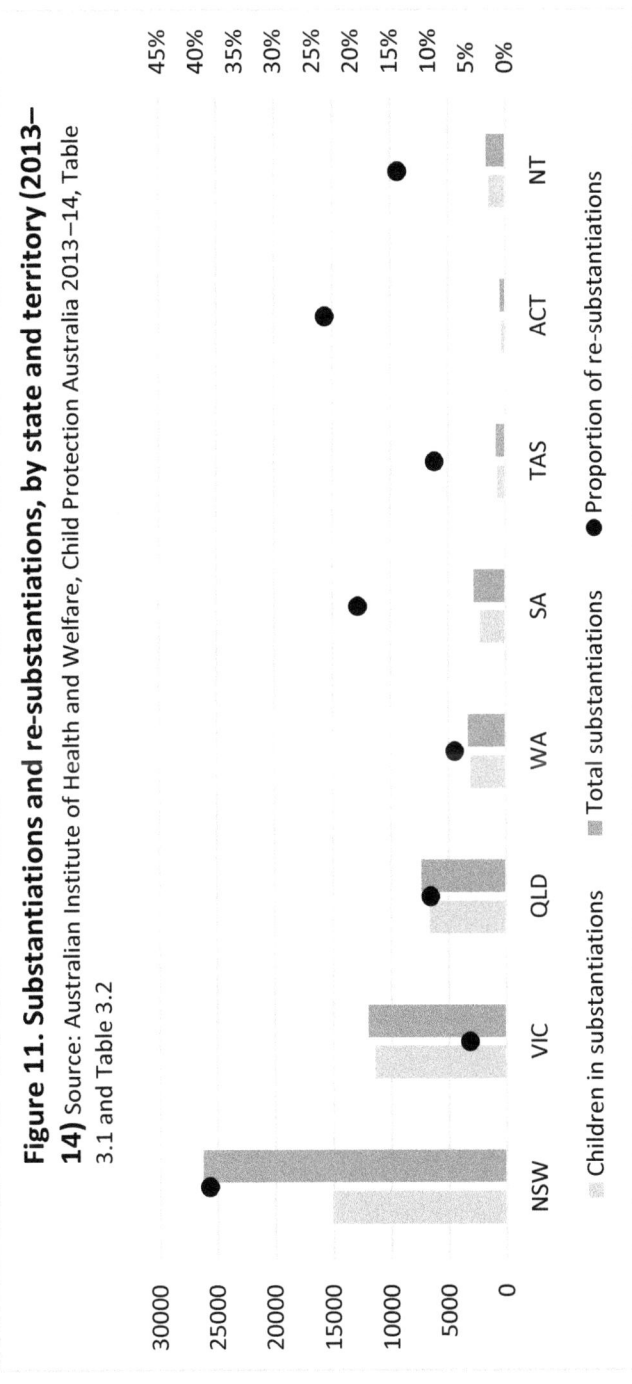

Figure 11. Substantiations and re-substantiations, by state and territory (2013–14) Source: Australian Institute of Health and Welfare, Child Protection Australia 2013–14, Table 3.1 and Table 3.2

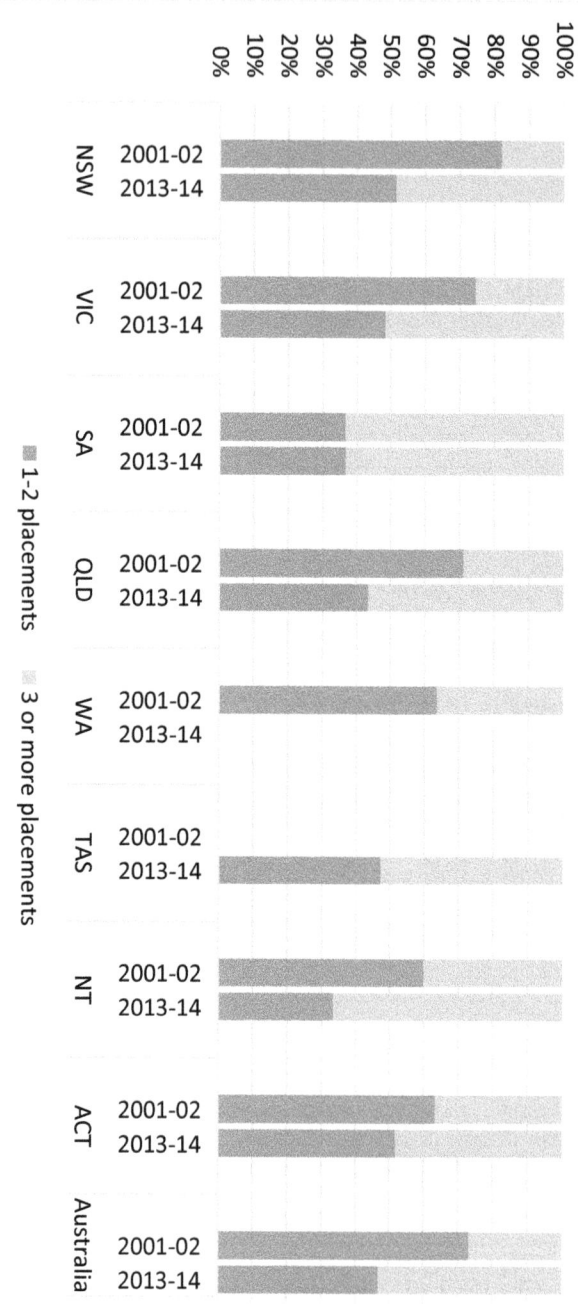

Figure 12. Percentage of children on care and protection order and exiting out-of-home care during the year, after 12 months or more in care, by number of placements, Australia (2001–14) Source: Productivity Commission, Report on Government Services 2015,

Why Adoption Will Rescue Australia's Underclass Children   255

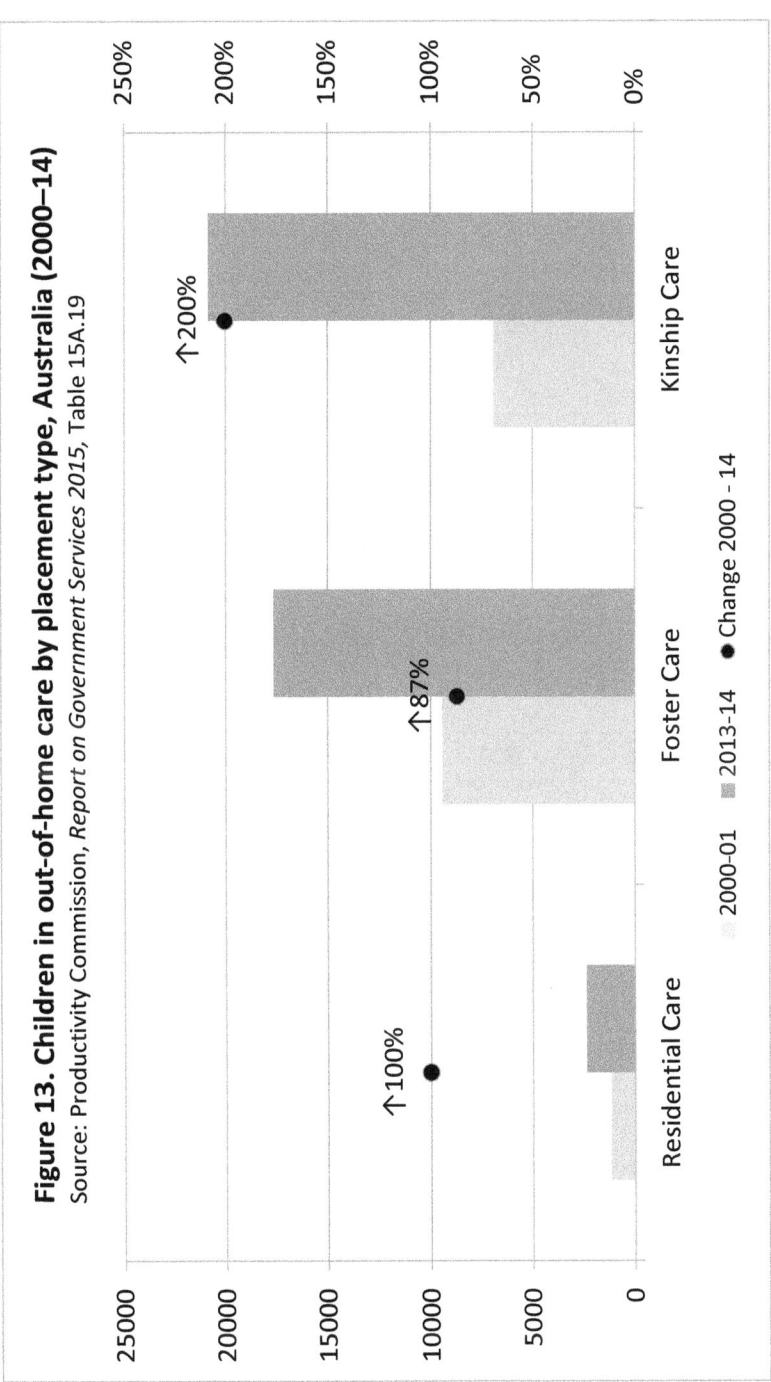

Figure 13. Children in out-of-home care by placement type, Australia (2000–14)
Source: Productivity Commission, *Report on Government Services 2015*, Table 15A.19

256 The Madness of Australian Child Protection

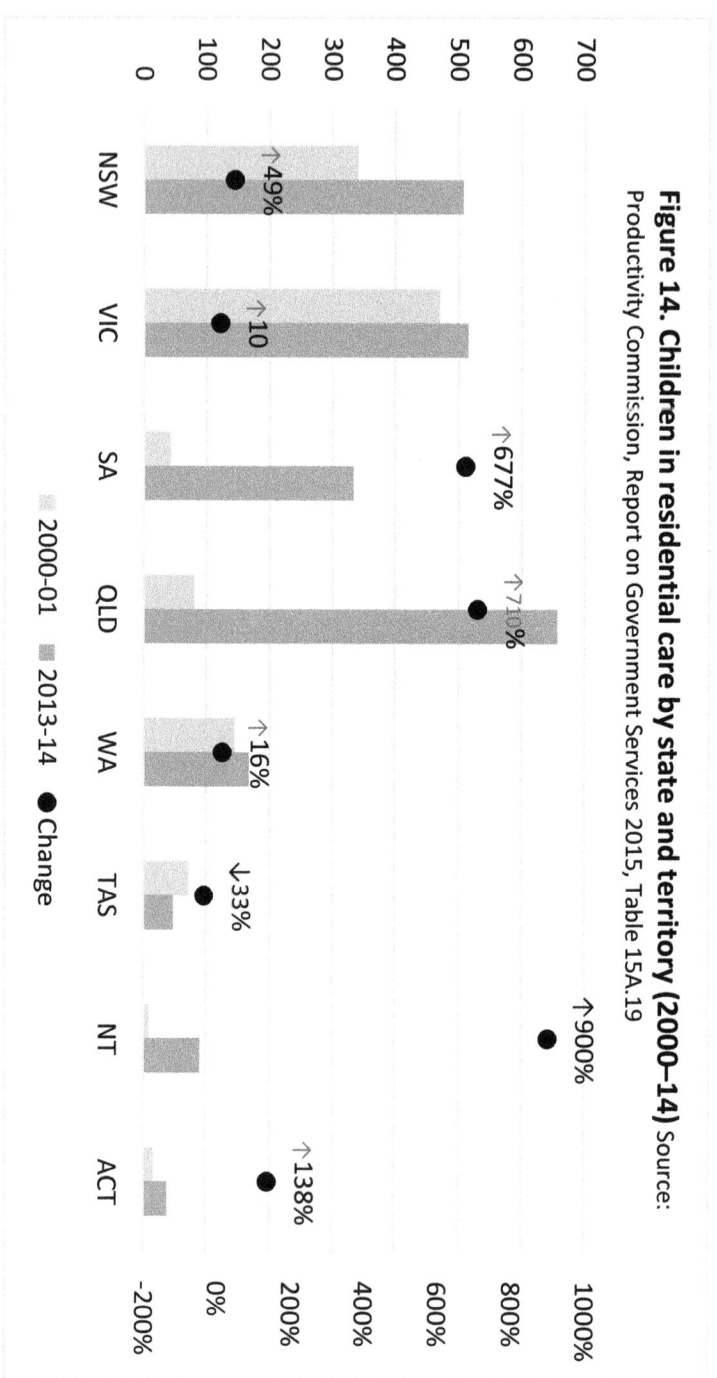

Figure 14. Children in residential care by state and territory (2000–14) Source: Productivity Commission, Report on Government Services 2015, Table 15A.19

Figure 15. Real (adjusted for inflation) recurrent out-of-home care expenditure per child, Australia (2000–14) Source: Productivity Commission, Report on Government Services 2015, Table 15A.3 * Data not available for the Northern Territory for 2000–01

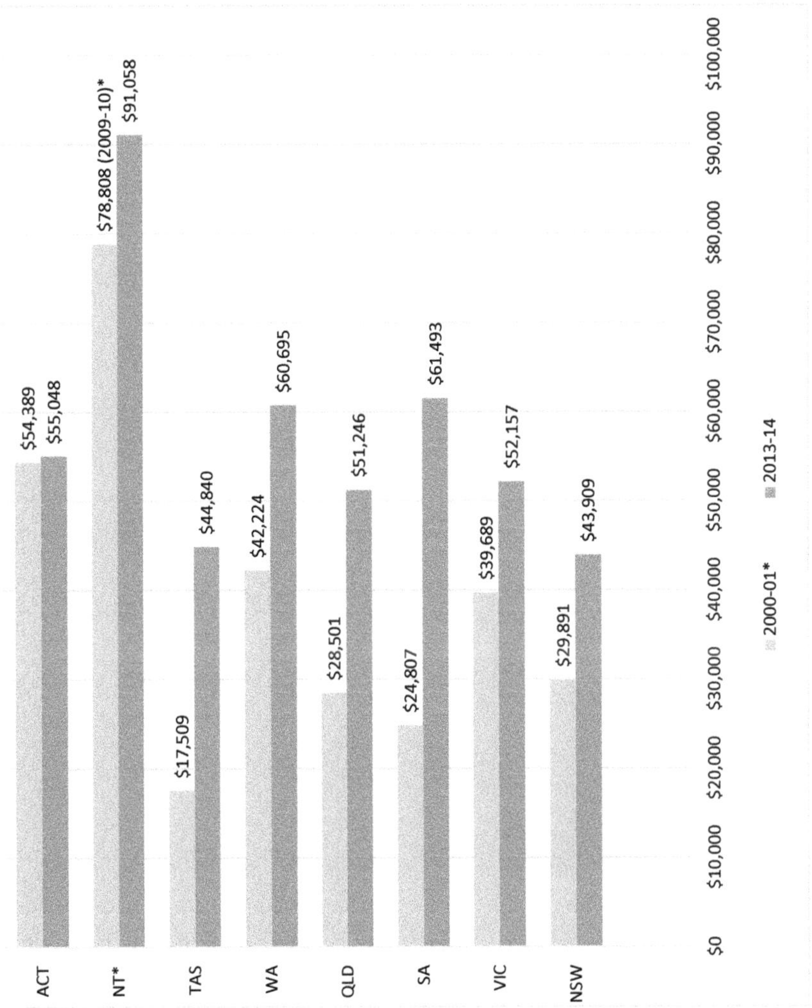

State	2000-01*	2013-14
ACT	$54,389	$55,048
NT*	$78,808 (2009-10)*	$91,058
TAS	$17,509	$44,840
WA	$42,224	$60,695
QLD	$28,501	$51,246
SA	$24,807	$61,493
VIC	$39,689	$52,157
NSW	$29,891	$43,909

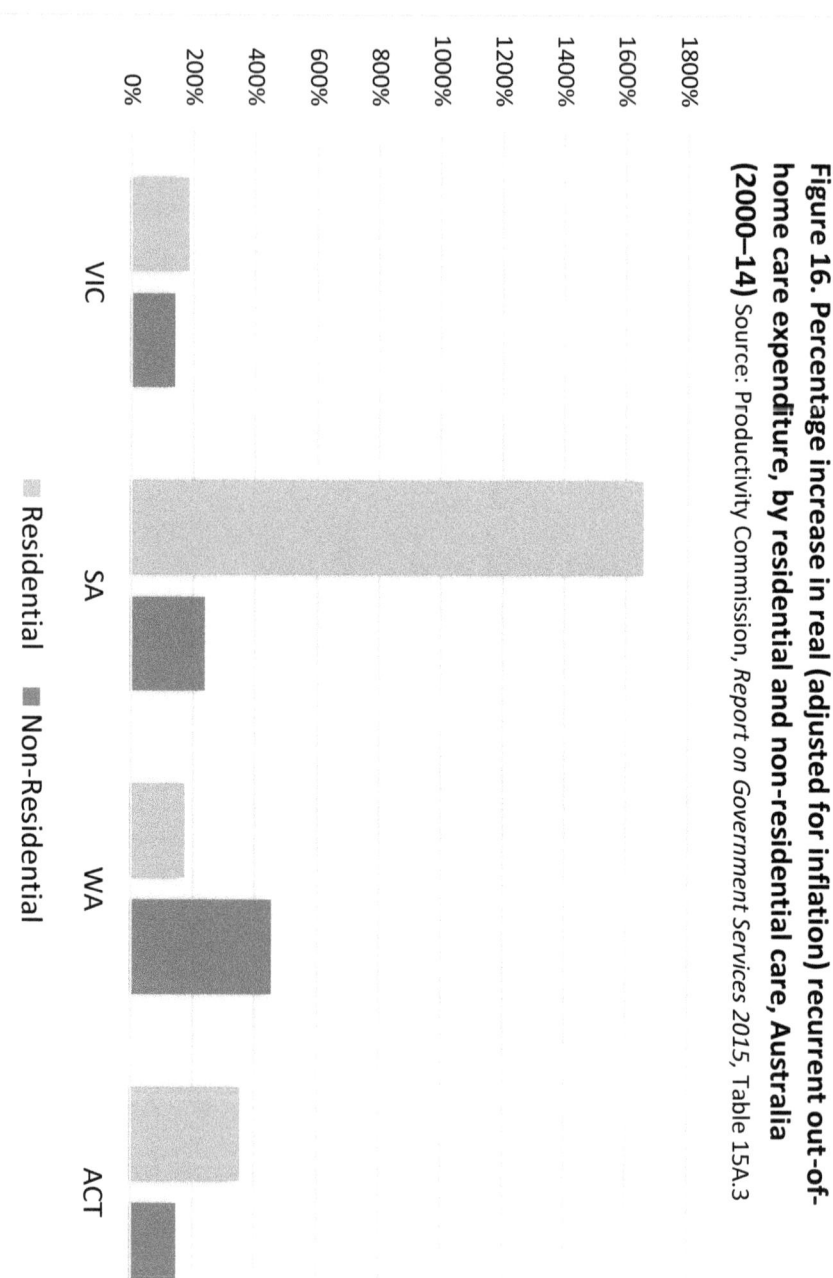

Figure 16. Percentage increase in real (adjusted for inflation) recurrent out-of-home care expenditure, by residential and non-residential care, Australia (2000–14) Source: Productivity Commission, *Report on Government Services 2015*, Table 15A.3

Why Adoption Will Rescue Australia's Underclass Children 259

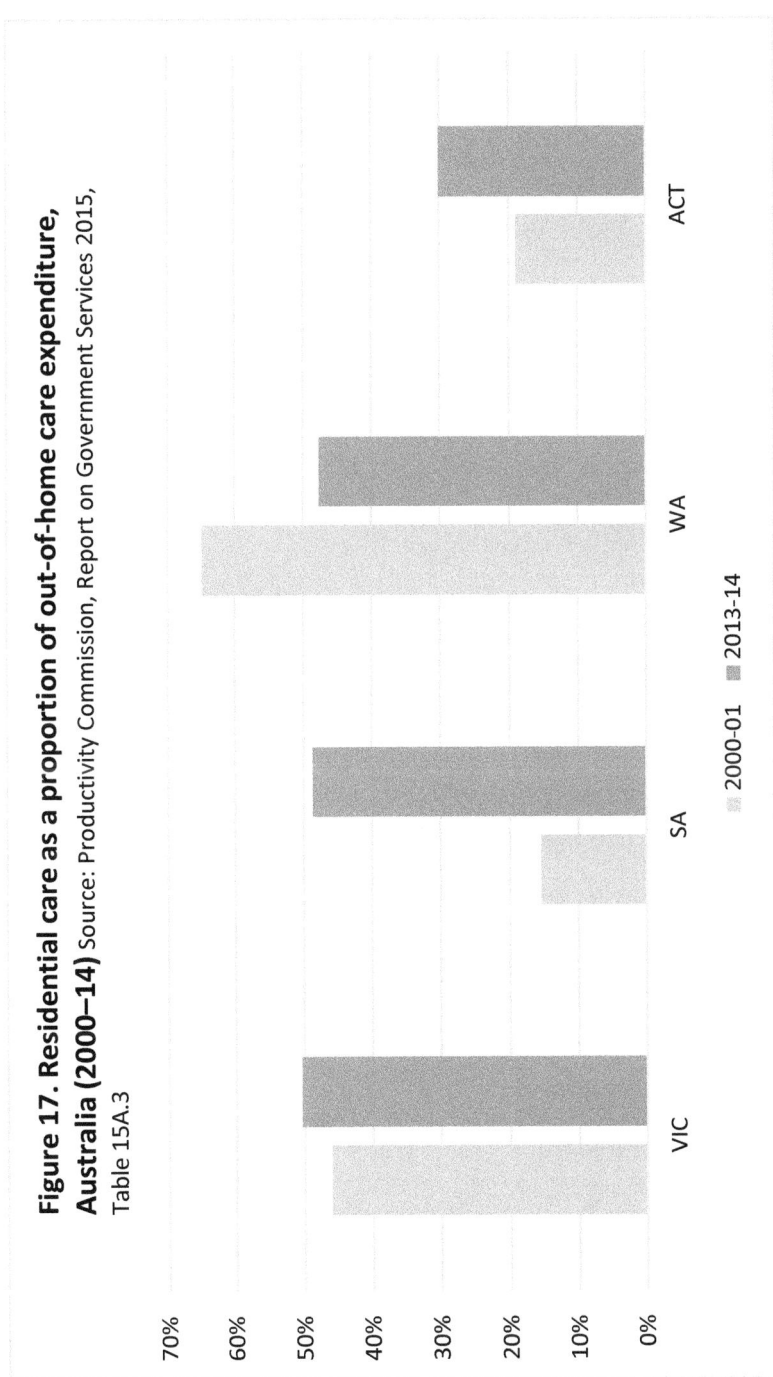

Figure 17. Residential care as a proportion of out-of-home care expenditure, Australia (2000–14) Source: Productivity Commission, Report on Government Services 2015, Table 15A.3

Figure 18. Average real (adjusted for inflation) expenditure per child for residential and non-residential placements, by state or territory (2000–14)
Source: Productivity Commission, Report on Government Services 2015, Table 15A.3

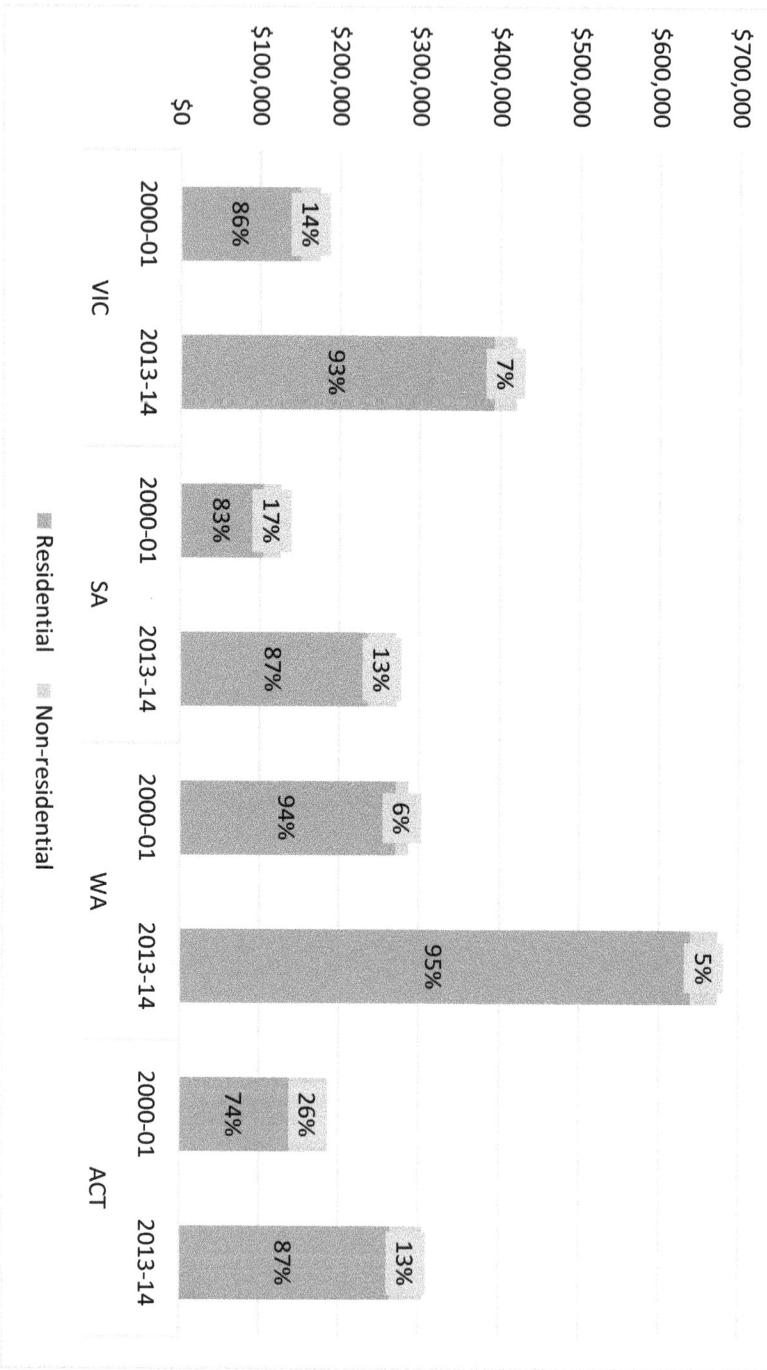

State	Year	Non-residential	Residential
VIC	2000-01	14%	86%
VIC	2013-14	7%	93%
SA	2000-01	17%	83%
SA	2013-14	13%	87%
WA	2000-01	6%	94%
WA	2013-14	5%	95%
ACT	2000-01	26%	74%
ACT	2013-14	13%	87%

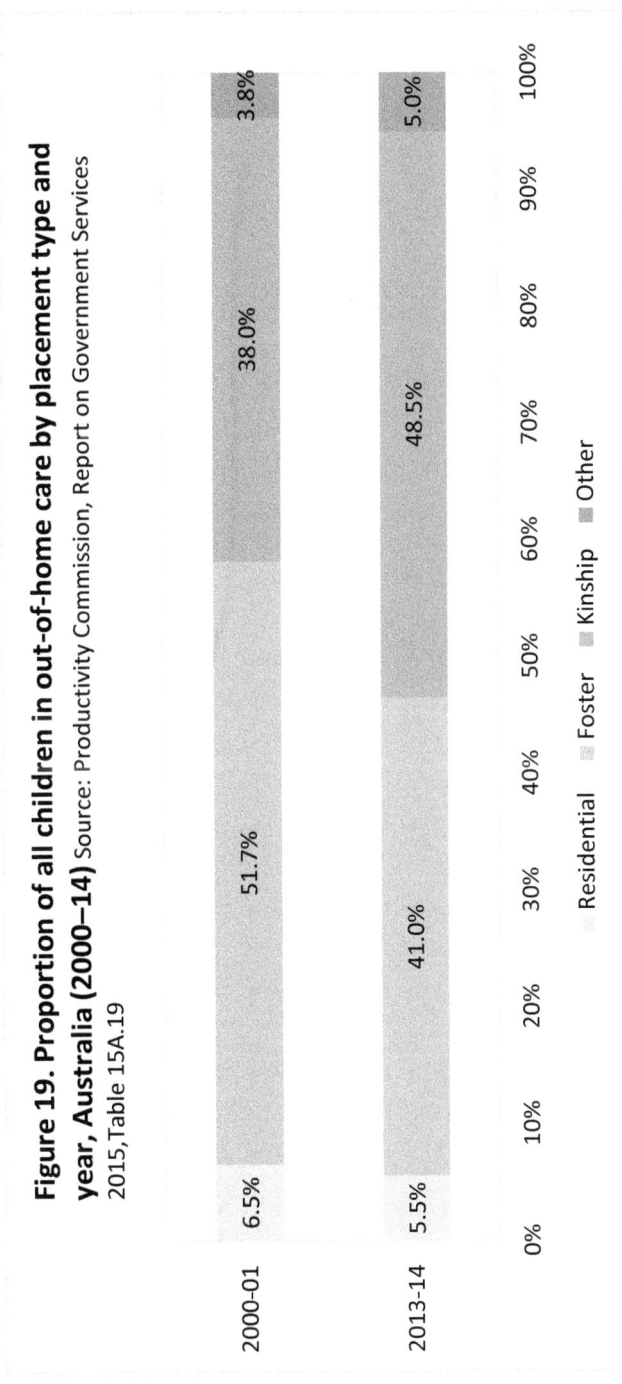

Figure 19. Proportion of all children in out-of-home care by placement type and year, Australia (2000–14) Source: Productivity Commission, Report on Government Services 2015, Table 15A.19

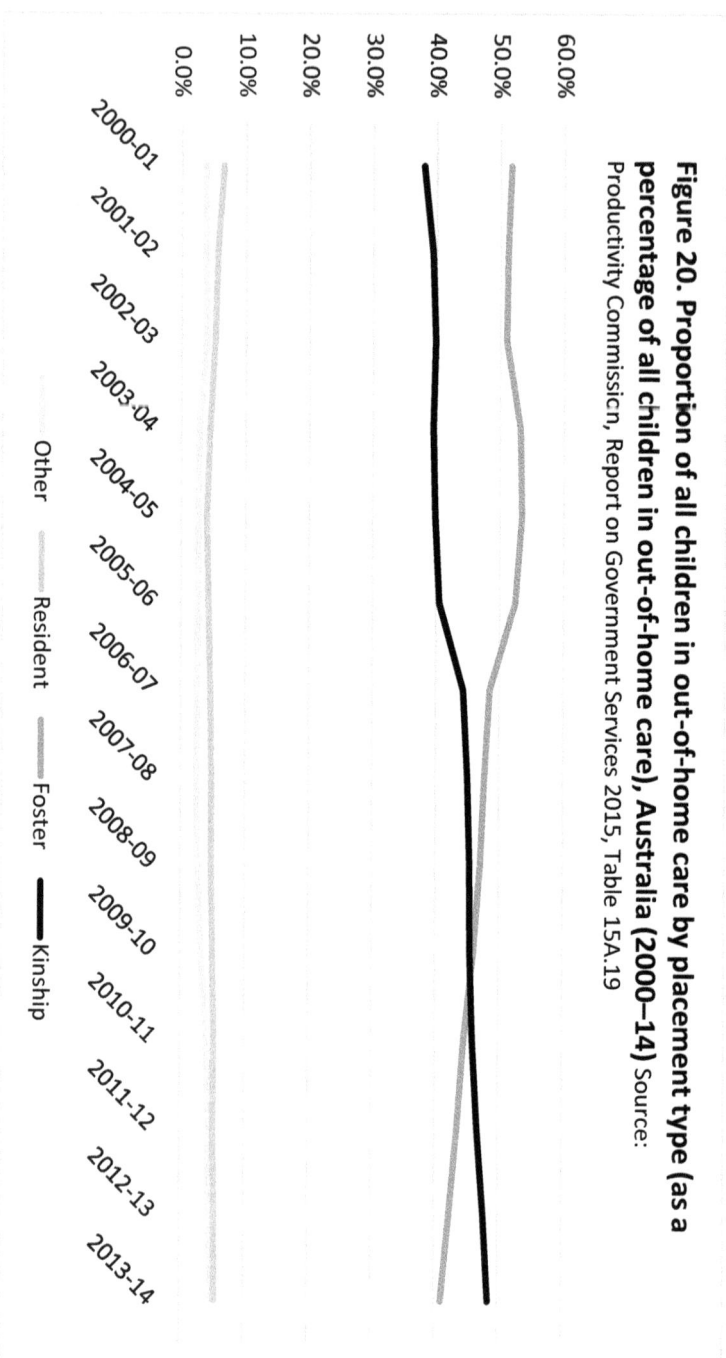

Figure 20. Proportion of all children in out-of-home care by placement type (as a percentage of all children in out-of-home care), Australia (2000–14) Source: Productivity Commission, Report on Government Services 2015, Table 15A.19

Why Adoption Will Rescue Australia's Underclass Children   263

Figure 21. Proportion of all children in out-of-home care, by placement type and state and territory (2000–14) Source: Productivity Commission, Report on Government Services 2015, Table 15A.19

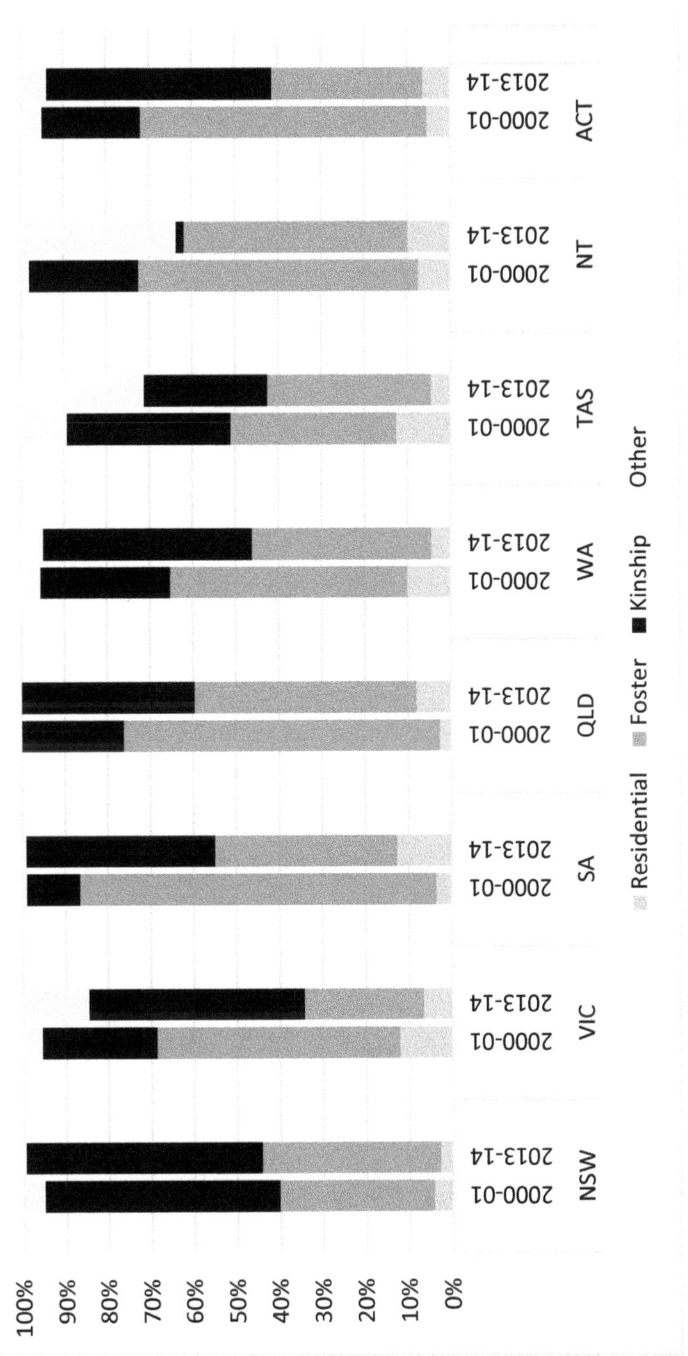

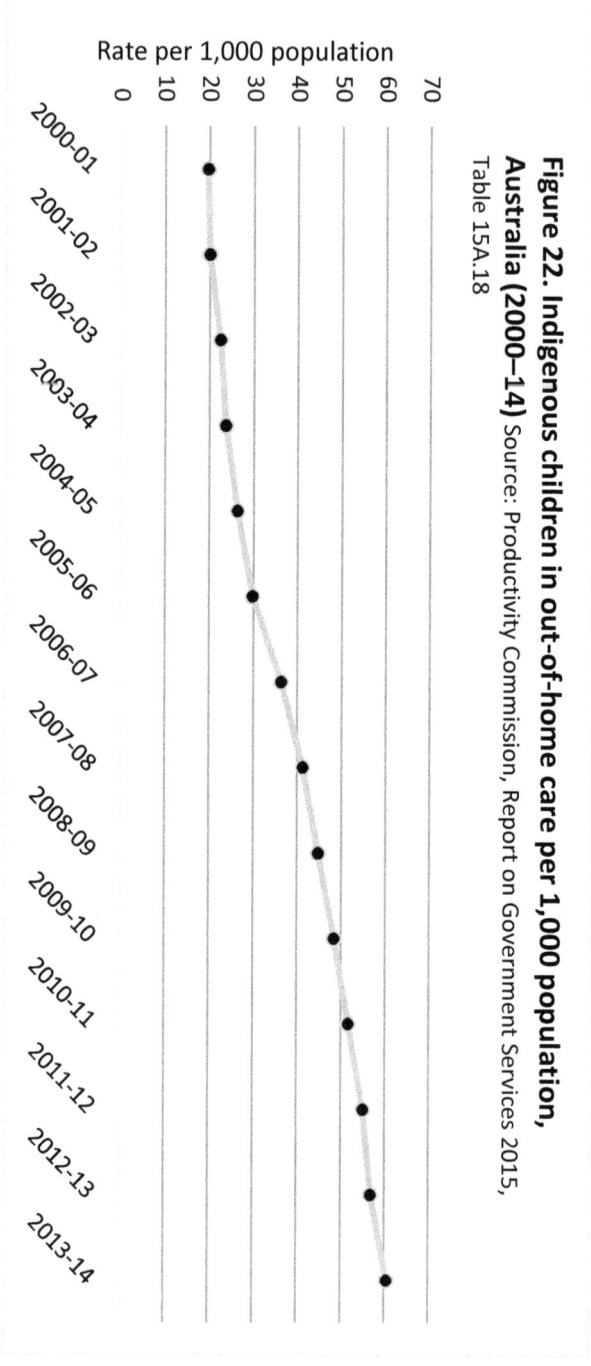

Figure 22. Indigenous children in out-of-home care per 1,000 population, Australia (2000–14) Source: Productivity Commission, Report on Government Services 2015, Table 15A.18

Why Adoption Will Rescue Australia's Underclass Children 265

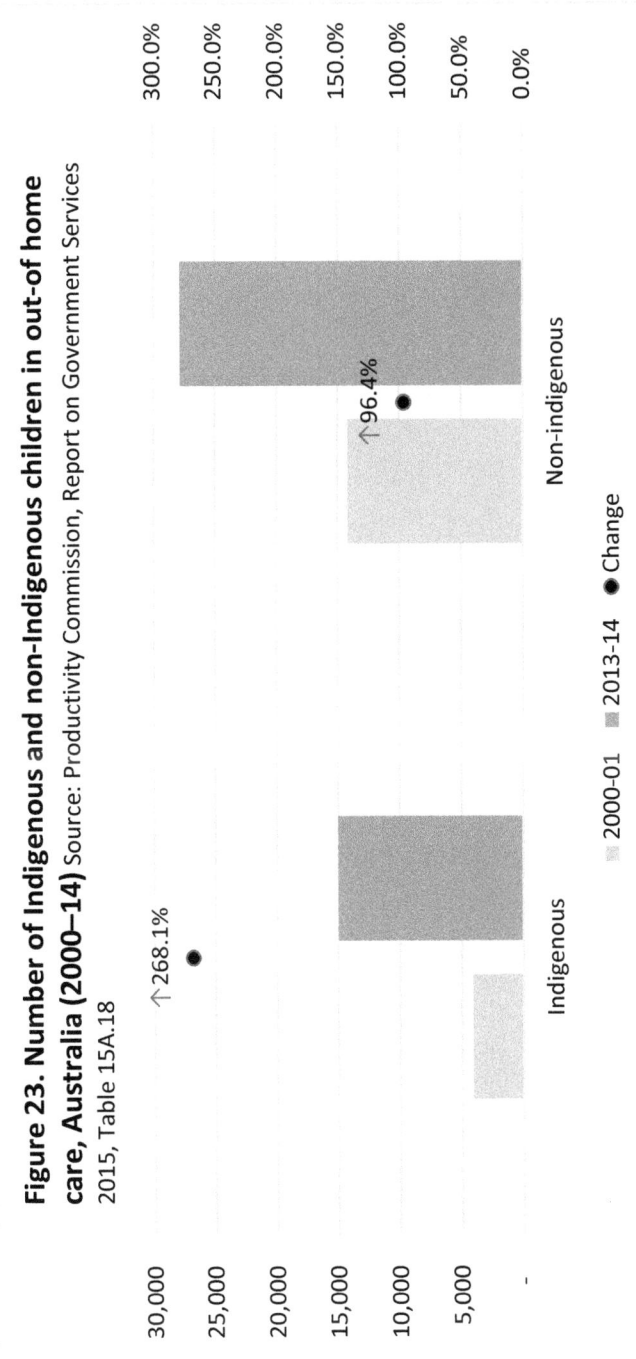

Figure 23. Number of Indigenous and non-Indigenous children in out-of home care, Australia (2000–14) Source: Productivity Commission, Report on Government Services 2015, Table 15A.18

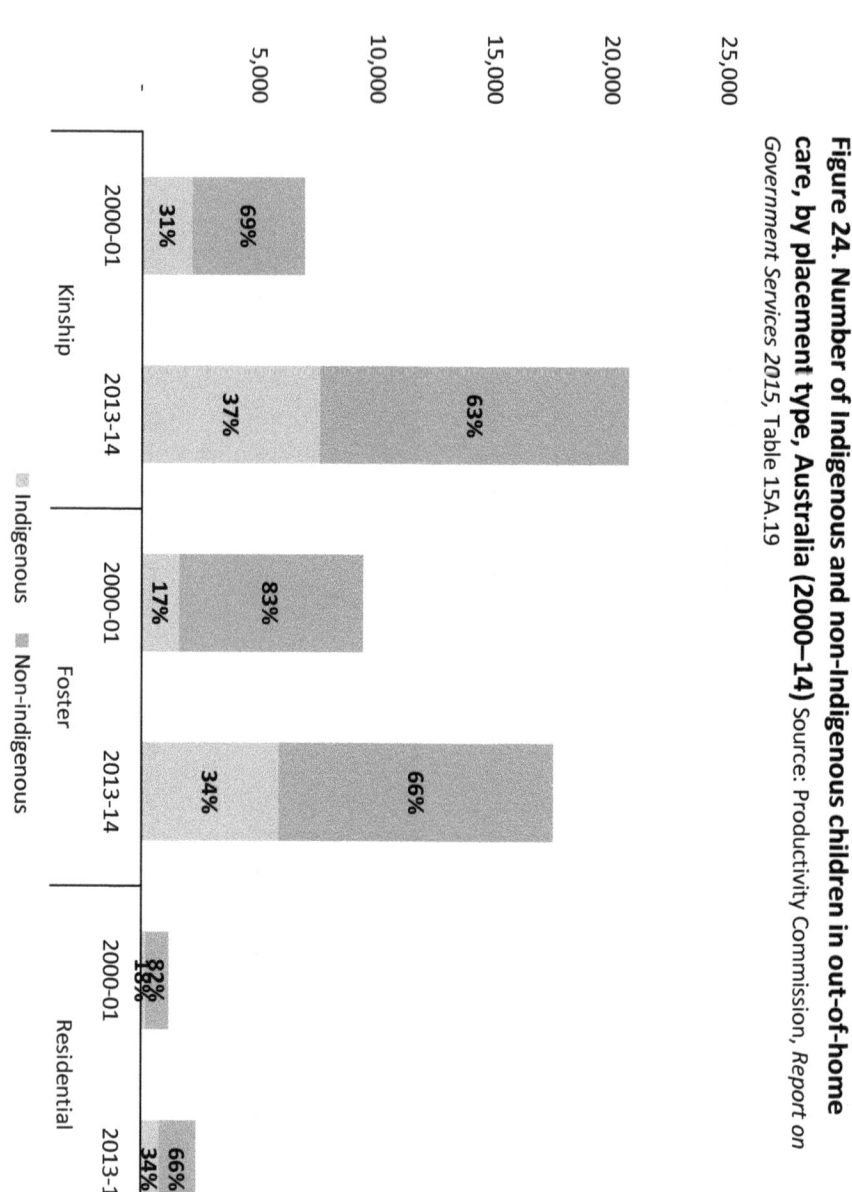

Figure 24. Number of Indigenous and non-Indigenous children in out-of-home care, by placement type, Australia (2000–14) Source: Productivity Commission, *Report on Government Services 2015*, Table 15A.19

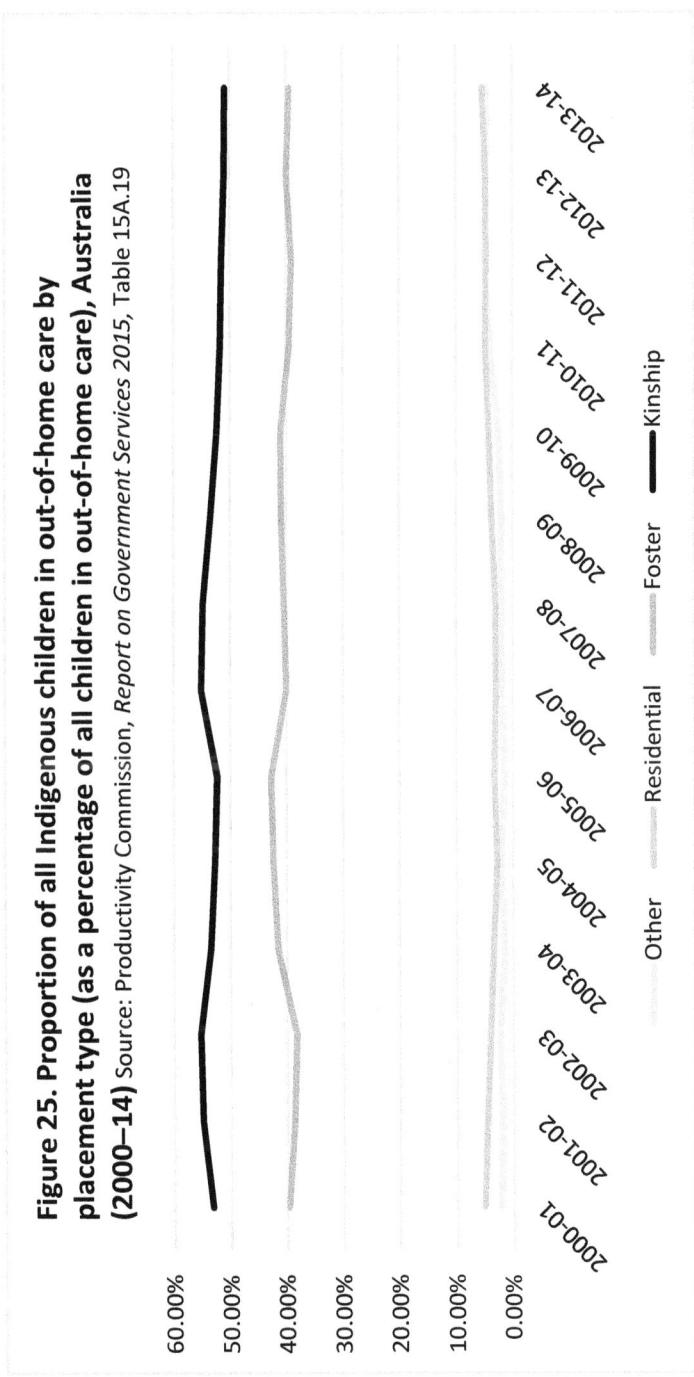

Figure 25. Proportion of all Indigenous children in out-of-home care by placement type (as a percentage of all children in out-of-home care), Australia (2000–14) Source: Productivity Commission, *Report on Government Services 2015*, Table 15A.19

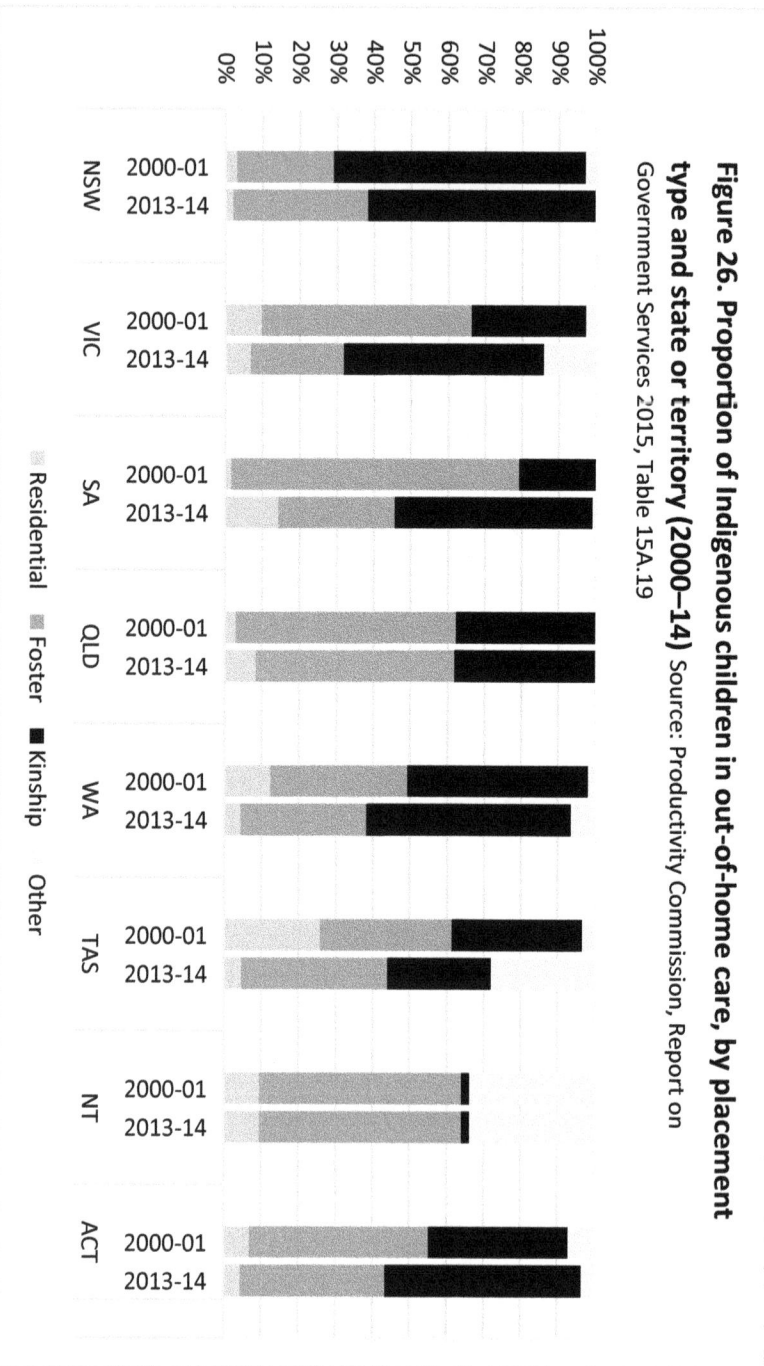

Figure 26. Proportion of Indigenous children in out-of-home care, by placement type and state or territory (2000–14) Source: Productivity Commission, Report on Government Services 2015, Table 15A.19

Why Adoption Will Rescue Australia's Underclass Children 269

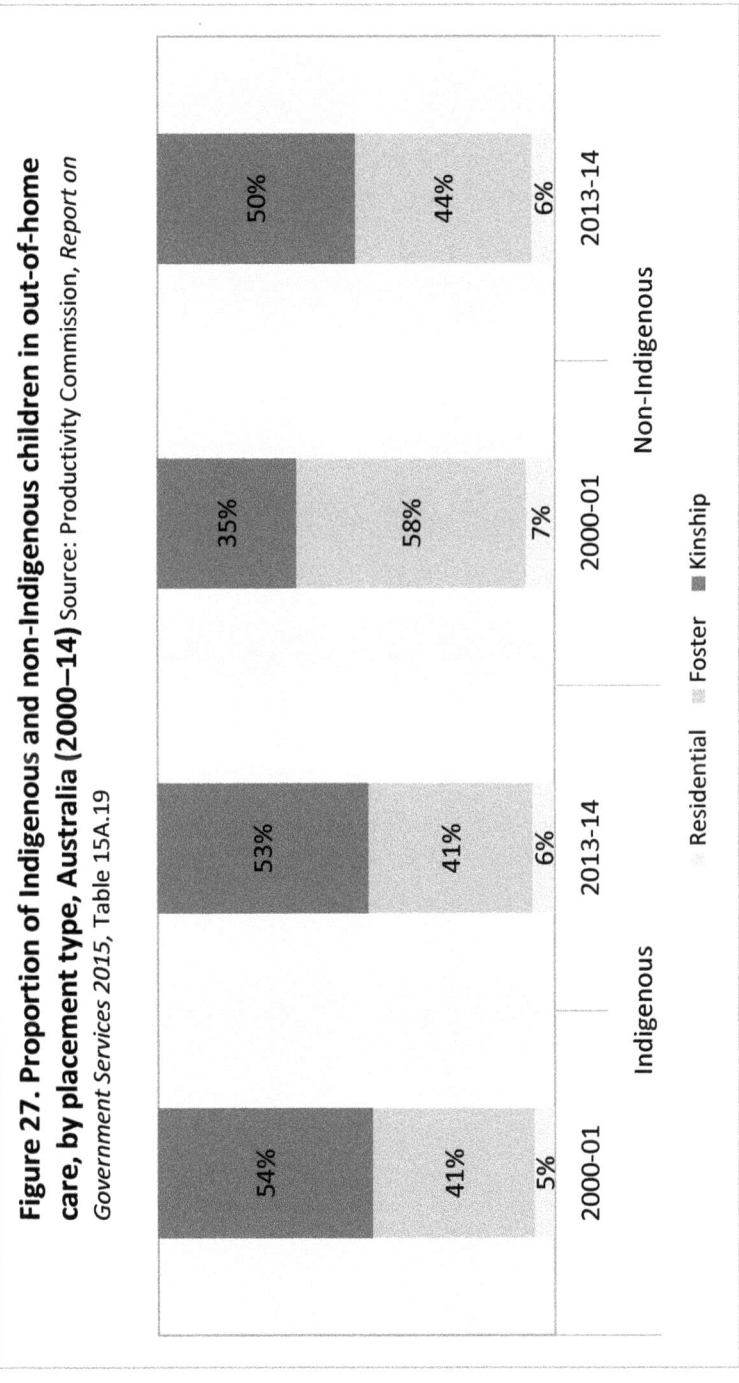

Figure 27. Proportion of Indigenous and non-Indigenous children in out-of-home care, by placement type, Australia (2000–14) Source: Productivity Commission, *Report on Government Services 2015*, Table 15A.19

Selected Bibliography

This bibliography includes the reports, books, and journal articles consulted in researching and writing this book. Articles from websites and newspapers have been omitted, though citations to them appear in footnotes to the main text.

Ainsworth, Frank, and Patricia Hansen. "A Dream Come True: No More Residential Care. A Corrective Note." *International Journal of Social Welfare* 14 (2005): 195–199.

Allen Consulting Group and Australian Research Alliance for Children and Youth. *Inverting the Pyramid: Enhancing Systems for Protecting Children*. Melbourne: Allen Consulting Group, 2009.

Amato, Paul R. "Research on Divorce: Continuing Trends and New Developments." *Journal of Marriage and Family* 72 (2010): 650–666.

Australian Bureau of Statistics (ABS). *Population Distribution, Aboriginal and Torres Strait Islander Australians*. Cat. No. 4705.0. Canberra: ABS, 2006.

— *Census of Population and Housing: Characteristics of Aboriginal and Torres Strait Islander Australians, 2011*. Cat. No. 2076.0. Canberra: ABS, 2012.

— *Australian Social Trends, March Quarter 2012*. Cat. No. 4102.0. Canberra: ABS, 2012.

Australian Early Development Index (AEDI). *Summary of the 2012 AEDI Results*. Factsheet, 2013.

Australian Government Productivity Commission. *Report on Government Services 2003*. Canberra: Commonwealth of Australia, 2003.

— *Report on Government Services 2009*. Canberra: Commonwealth of Australia, 2009.

— *Report on Government Services 2014*. Canberra: Commonwealth of Australia, 2014.

— *Report on Government Services 2015*. Canberra: Commonwealth of Australia, 2015.

Australian Institute of Family Studies (AIFS), "Family Facts and Figures: Births." www3.aifs.gov.au/institute/info/charts/births/index.html#number

Australian Institute of Family Studies (AIFS), and Child Family Community Australia (CFCA). *Child Protection and Aboriginal and Torres Strait Islander Children.* Factsheet, 2013.

Australian Institute of Health and Welfare (AIHW). *Adoptions Australia 1990–91.* Child Welfare Series No. 1. Canberra: AIHW, 1993.

— *Child Protection Australia 2008–09.* Canberra: AIHW, 2009.

— *Child Protection Australia 2009–10.* Canberra: AIHW, 2010.

— *Child Protection Australia 2010–11.* Canberra: AIHW, 2012.

— *Child Protection Australia 2011–12.* Canberra: AIHW, 2013.

— *Child Protection Australia 2012–13.* Canberra: AIHW, 2014.

— *Adoptions Australia 2013–14.* Canberra: AIHW, 2014.

— *Child Protection Australia 2013–14.* Canberra: AIHW, 2015.

Bamblett, M., Howard Bath, and Rob Roseby. *Growing them Strong, Together: Promoting the Safety and Wellbeing of the Northern Territory's Children* (Bath Report). Report of the Board of Inquiry into the Child Protection System in the Northern Territory. Darwin: Department of the Chief Minister, 2010.

Barber, James G., and Paul H. Delfabbro. "Placement Stability and the Psychological Well-being of Children in Foster Care." *Research on Social Work Practice* 13 (2003): 415–431.

— *Children in Foster Care.* London: Taylor and Francis, 2004.

Behlmer, George. *Child Abuse and Moral Reform in England, 1870–1908.* Palo Alto: Stanford University Press, 1982.

Bell, Terri, and Terri Libesman. *Aboriginal and Torres Strait Islander Child Protection Outcomes Project Report, From Aboriginal Child Welfare to Aboriginal Children's Wellbeing.* Commissioned by Secretariat of National Aboriginal and Islander Child Care and the Department of Human Services Victoria, 2005. Unpublished.

Berlyn, Claire, Leah Bromfield, and Alister Lamont. *Child Protection and Aboriginal and Torres Strait Islander Children.* National Child Protection Clearinghouse Resource Sheet. Melbourne: AIFS, 2011.

Bloom, Allan. *The Closing of the American Mind: How Higher Education has Failed Democracy and Impoverished the Souls of Today's Students.* New York: Simon & Schuster, 1987.

Boetto, Heather. "Kinship Care: A Review of Issues." *Family Matters* 85 (2010): 60–67.

Brennan, Deborah, and Bettina Cass. "Grandparents as Primary Carers of Their Grandchildren: Policy and Practice Insights from Research." In *Families, Policy and the Law: Selected Essays on Contemporary Issues for Australia*, edited by Alan Hayes and Darrell Higgins, 109–118. Melbourne: AIFS, 2014.

Briggs, Freda, and Donna Broadhurst. "The Abuse of Foster Carers in Australia." *Journal of Home Economics Institute of Australia* 12 (2005): 25–35.

Broadley, Karen, Chris Goddard, and Joe Tucci. *They Count for Nothing: Poor Child Protection Statistics Are a Barrier to a Child-centred National Framework*. Melbourne: Australian Childhood Foundation and Child Abuse Prevention Research Australia, 2014.

Bromfield, Leah, Daryl Higgins, Alexandra Osborn, Stacey Panozzo, and Nicholas Richardson. *Out-of-home Care in Australia: Messages from Research*. Melbourne: AIFS, 2005.

Bromfield, Leah, and Prue Holzer. *A National Approach for Child Protection: Project Report – A Report to the Community and Disability Services Minister's Advisory Council*. Melbourne: AIFS, 2008.

Brown, Susan L. "Marriage and Child Well-being: Research and Policy Perspectives." *Journal of Marriage and Family* 72 (2010): 1059–1077.

Buckingham, Jennifer, John Fleming, Jean Illingworth, and Chris Goddard. *Educating the Disadvantaged*. Issue Analysis 116. Sydney: Centre for Independent Studies, 2009.

Cashmore, Judy. "Kinship Care: A Differentiated and Sensitive Approach." *Developing Practice* 1 (2001): 5–8.

Cashmore, Judy, Dorothy Scott, and Gillian Calvert. *Think Child, Think Family, Think Community: From a Child Protection System to a System for Protecting Children*. Submission to the Special Commission of Inquiry into Child Protection Services in NSW, 2008. Sydney: NSW Commission for Children and Young People, 2008.

Cassells, Rebecca, Natasha Cortis, Alan Duncan, Christine Eastman, Grace Gao, Gianfranco Giuntoli, Ilan Katz, Marcia Keegan, Michelle Macvean, Astghik Mavisakalyan, Aron Shlonsky, Jen Skattebol, Ciara Smyth, and Kylie Valentine. *Keep Them Safe Outcomes Evaluation Final Report*. Sydney: NSW Department of Premier and Cabinet, 2014.

Commission for Children and Young People and Child Guardian (CCYPCG). *Views of Children and Young People in Foster Care, Queensland*. Brisbane: CCYPCG, 2010.

Council of Australian Governments (COAG). *Protecting Children is Everyone's Business: National Framework for Protecting Australia's Children, 2009–2020*. Canberra: Commonwealth of Australia, 2009.

Cummins, Philip, Dorothy Scott, and Bills Scales. *Protecting Victoria's Vulnerable Children Inquiry* (Cummins Report). Melbourne: Department of Premier and Cabinet, 2012.

Cuthbert, Denise, and Marian Quartly. " 'Forced Adoption' in the Australian Story of National Regret and Apology," *Australian Journal of Politics and History* 58 (2012): 82–96.

Dalrymple, Theodore. *In Praise of Prejudice: The Necessity of Preconceived Ideas*. New York: Encounter Books, 2007.

Davies, Carolyn, and Harriett Ward. *Safeguarding Children Across Services: Messages from Research*. London: Jessica Kingsley Publishers, 2012.

Delfabbro, Paul H., and James G. Barber. "The Micro-economics of Foster Care in South Australia." *Children Australia* 27 (2002): 29–34.

Delfabbro, Paul H., James G. Barber, and Lesley Cooper. "Placement Disruption and Dislocation in South Australian Substitute Care." *Children Australia* 25 (2000): 16–20.

— "Children Entering Out-of-home Care in South Australia: Baseline Analyses for a 3-year Longitudinal Study." *Children and Youth Services Review* 24 (2002): 917–932.

Delfabbro, Paul, Helen Jeffreys, Nancy Rogers, Ros Wilson, and Mignon Borgas. *Certainty for Children in Care: A Study into the Placement History and Social Background of Infants Placed into South Australian Out-of-home Care 2000–2005*. Research Bulletin. Adelaide: Department for Families and Communities, 2007.

Delfabbro, Paul H., Alexanda Osborn, and James G. Barber. "Beyond the Continuum: New Perspectives on the Future of Out of Home Care in Australia." *Children Australia* 30 (2005): 11–18.

Department for Communities and Local Government. *The Fiscal Case for Working with Troubled Families: Analysis and Evidence on the Costs of Troubled Families to Government*. London: Department of Communities and Local Government, 2013.

Department for Education. *Children Looked After in England (Including Adoption and Care Leavers) Year Ending 31 March 2014*. London: Department for Education, 2014.

Department of Communities, Child Safety, and Disability Services. *Child Safety Services Grant Funding Information Paper 2009–10, Placement Services, Residential Care*. Brisbane: Queensland Government, 2009.

— *Invitation to Offer Com-01117 for the Provision of a Child Safety Practice Framework*. Brisbane: Queensland Government, 2013.

Department of Families, Housing, Community Services and Indigenous Affairs (FaHCSIA). *An Outline of National Standards for Out-of-home Care*. Canberra: Commonwealth of Australia, 2011.

Department of Human Services (DHS). *Protecting Children: Ten priorities for Children's Wellbeing and Safety in Victoria*. Melbourne: DHS, 2004.

— *Directions for Out of Home Care*. Melbourne: DHS, 2009.

— *Stability Planning and Permanent Care Project Final Report*. Melbourne: DHS, 2014.

Department of Social Services. *Income Support Customers: A Statistical Overview 2013*. Statistical Paper No. 12. Canberra: Commonwealth of Australia, 2014.

— *A New System for Better Employment and Social Outcomes: Report of the Reference Group on Welfare Reform to the Minister for Social Services*. Canberra: Commonwealth of Australia, 2015.

de Vaus, David. *Diversity and Change in Australian Families: Statistical Profiles*. Melbourne: AIFS, 2004.

de Vaus, David, and Matthew Gray. "The Changing Living Arrangements of Children, 1946–2001." *Journal of Family Studies* 10 (2004): 9–19.

Dillon, Anthony, and Nigel Parbury, eds. *In Black & White: Australians All at the Crossroads*. Ballan: Connor Court, 2013.

Donzelot, Jacques. *The Policing of Families*. New York: Pantheon, 1979.

Fagan, Patrick F., and Aaron Churchill. *The Effects of Divorce on Children*. Washington, DC: Family Research Council, 2012.

Fahlberg, Vera. *Attachment and Separation*. London: British Agencies for Adoption & Fostering (BAAF), 1982.

Frederick, John, and Chris Goddard. "Exploring the Relationship Between Poverty, Childhood Adversity and Child Abuse from the Perspective of Adulthood." *Child Abuse Review* 16 (2007): 323–341.

Gardiner-Garden, John. *The Definition of Aboriginality: Research Note 18, 2000–01*. Canberra: Parliament of Australia, 2000.

Gauthier, Yvon, Gilles Fortin, and Gloria Jéliu. "Clinical Application of Attachment Theory in Permanency Planning for Children in Foster Care: The Importance of Continuity of Care." *Infant Mental Health Journal* 25 (2004): 379–396.

Goddard, Chris. Introduction to *Fatally Flawed: The Child Protection Crisis in Australia*, Policy Monograph No. 97, by Jeremy Sammut and Toby O'Brien. Sydney: Centre for Independent Studies, 2009.

Goddard, Chris. "The State of Victoria's Child Protection." *Children Australia* 35 (2010): 4–5.

Goddard, Chris, and Joe Tucci, Joe. *Responding to Child Abuse and Neglect in Australia*. Melbourne: Child Abuse Prevention Research Australia and Australian Childhood Foundation, 2008.

Gordon, Sue, Kay Hallahan, and Darrell Henry. *Putting the Picture Together: Inquiry into Response by Government Agencies to Complaints of Family Violence and Child Abuse in Aboriginal Communities*. Perth: Department of Premier and Cabinet, Western Australia, 2002.

Hansen, Patricia, and Frank Ainsworth. "Viewpoints: Australian Child Protection Services: A Game without End." *International Journal of Child Welfare* 22 (2013): 104–110.

Healy, Karen. "Critical Questions about the Quest for Clarity in Child Protection Regimes." *Communities, Children and Families Australia* 4 (2009): 52–58.

Heard, Genevieve, Siew-Ean Khoo, and Bob Birrell. *Intermarriage in Australia: Patterns by Birthplace, Ancestry, Religion and Indigenous Status. A Report Using Data from the 2006 Census*. Clayton: Monash University Centre for Population and Urban Research, 2009.

Heneghan, Amy M., Sarah M. Horwitz, and John M. Leventhal. "Evaluating Intensive Family Preservation Programs: A Methodological Review." *Pediatrics* 97 (1996): 535–542.

Higgins, Darly, and Ilan Katz. "Enhancing Service Systems for Protecting Children: Promoting Child Wellbeing and Child Protection Reform in Australia." *Family Matters* 80 (2008): 43–50.

Holzer, Prue, Jenny Higgins, Leah Bromfield, and Daryl Higgins. *The Effectiveness of Parent Education and Home Visiting Child Maltreatment Prevention Programs*. Melbourne: AIFS, 2006.

House of Representatives Standing Committee on Family and Human Services. *Overseas Adoption in Australia.* Canberra: Commonwealth of Australia, 2005.

—— *The Winnable War on Drugs: The Impact of Illicit Drug Use on Families* Canberra: Commonwealth of Australia, 2007.

Hudson, Sara. "Politics of Difference," in *In Black & White: Australians All at the Crossroads*, edited by Rhonda Craven, Anthony Dillon, and Nigel Parbury. Ballan: Connor Court, 2013.

Hughes, Helen. *Lands of Shame: Aboriginal and Torres Strait Islander 'Homelands' in Transition.* Sydney: Centre for Independent Studies, 2007.

—— "Strangers in Their Own Country: A Diary of Hope." *Quadrant* 52 (2008).

Hughes, Helen, and Mark Hughes. "The Undercover Guide to Indigenous Statistics." In *In Black & White: Australians All at the Crossroads*, edited by Rhonda Craven, Anthony Dillon, and Nigel Parbury. Ballan: Connor Court, 2013.

Human Rights and Equal Opportunity Commission. *Bringing them home: Report of the National Inquiry into the Separation of Aboriginal and Torres Strait Islander Children from Their Families.* Canberra: Commonwealth of Australia, 1997.

Human Services Community Services. *Working with Parental Substance Misuse.* Sydney: NSW Government, 2010.

Humphreys, Cathy, Maria Harries, Karen Healy, Robert Lonne, Philip Mendes, Marilyn McHugh, and Rosemary Sheehan. "Shifting the Child Protection Juggernaut to Earlier Intervention." *Children Australia* 34 (2009): 5–8.

Hunter, Cathryn, and Rhys Price-Robertson. *Family Structure and Child Maltreatment.* Child Family Community Australia Paper No.10. Melbourne: AIFS, 2012.

Hunter, James Davison. *Culture Wars: The Struggle to Define America.* New York: Basic Books, 1991.

Hymowitz, Kay S. "American Caste." *City Journal* 22 (2012): 44–49.

Inglis, Kate. *Living Mistakes: Mothers Who Consented to Adoption.* North Sydney: Allen & Unwin, 1984.

Inquest into the Death of Chloe Lee Valentine. Conducted by Mark Johns, State Coroner, South Australia. August 2014–April 2015.

Izmir, Gul. Presentation at the Australasian Conference on Child Abuse and Neglect. See *Breaking Down the Barriers between Prevention, Early Intervention and Child Protection* (31 October 2007 to 2 November 2007), www.ccm.com.au/

accan/content/papers/Wed_Rm5-RanahanSTARTBarnardosFarinolaJackson.pdf

Johns, Gary. *Aboriginal Self-determination: The Whiteman's Dream*. Ballan: Connor Court, 2011.

Kenny, Pauline, Daryl Higgins, Carol Soloff, and Reem Sweid. *Past Adoption Experiences: National Research Study on the Service Response to Past Adoption Practices*, Research Report No. 21. Melbourne: AIFS, 2012.

Kiraly, Meredith, and Cathy Humphreys. *'It's the Story of All of Us': Learning from Aboriginal Communities about Supporting Family Connection*. Melbourne: Child Safety Commissioner, 2011.

Kinship Care: Benefits and Challenges, 22 October 2013. aifs.gov.au/cfca/2013/10/22/kinship-care-benefits-and-challenges

Lamont, Alister. *Effects of Child Abuse and Neglect for Adult Survivors*. National Child Protection Clearinghouse Resource Sheet. Melbourne: AIFS, 2010.

Lane, Joe, and Marie Lane. "Hard Grind: The Making of an Urban Indigenous Population." In *Proceedings of the Bennelong Society Conference 2008: The NT Emergency Response – Appraisal and Future*. pandora.nla.gov.au/pan/38309/20091109-0945/conference2008.html

Lohoar, Shaun, Nick Butera, and Edita Kennedy. *Strengths of Australian Aboriginal Cultural Practices in Family Life and Child Rearing*. Child Family Community Australia Paper No.25. Melbourne: CFCA, 2014.

Maley, Barry. *Family and Marriage in Australia*. Sydney: Centre for Independent Studies, 2001.

Manne, Robert. "In Denial: The Stolen Generations and the Right." *Quarterly Essay* 1 (2001).

Marshall, Audrey, and Margaret McDonald. *The Many-sided Triangle: Adoption in Australia*. Melbourne: Melbourne University Press, 2001.

Matthews, Ben, and Donald C. Boss. "Mandated Reporting is Still Policy with Reason: Empirical Evidence and Philosophical Grounds." *Child Abuse and Neglect* 32 (2008): 511–516.

McCallum, Andrew. "Child Protection and Wood: Will We Rise to the Challenge?" *Developing Practice* 23 (2009): 4–6.

McDowall, Joseph J. *Transitioning from Care: Tracking Progress*. CREATE Report Card 2009. Sydney: CREATE Foundation, 2009.

McHugh, Marilyn. "A Further Perspective on Kinship Care: Indigenous Foster Care." *Developing Practice* 8 (2003): 21–22.

— "An Exploratory Study of Risks to Stability in Foster and Kinship Care in NSW: Final Report." Social Policy Research Centre Report Series. Sydney: UNSW, 2013.

— "Should Australian Foster Carers Be Entitled to Receive a Fee/Salary Wage for Caring?" Paper presented to the Australian Community Workers Association Conference, Sydney, 2008.

McHugh, Marilyn, Justin McNab, Ciara Smyth, Jenny Chalmers, Peter Siminski, and Peter Saunders. *The Availability of Foster Carers*. Sydney: Social Policy Research Centre, University of New South Wales, 2004.

McHugh, Marilyn, and Anita Pell. *Reforming the Foster Care System in Australia: A New Model of Support, Education and Payment for Foster Parents*. Sydney: Berry Street, UNSW, 2013.

McHugh, Marilyn, and Kylie Valentine. "Financial and Non-financial Support to Formal and Informal Out of Home Carers." Occasional Paper No. 38. Canberra: FaHCSIA, 2011.

Mead, Lawrence. *Beyond Entitlement: The Social Obligations of Citizenship*. New York: The Free Press, 1986.

Mendes, Philip. *Inside the Welfare Lobby: A History of the Australian Council of Social Services – The Role of Interest Groups in Australian Social Policy*. Eastbourne: Sussex Academic Press, 2006.

— "The Historical and Political Context of Mandatory Reporting and its Impact on Child Protection Practice in Victoria." *Australian Social Work* 12 (1996): 25–32.

Messing, Jill. "From the Child's Perspective: A Qualitative Analysis of Kinship Care Placements." *Children and Youth Services Review* 28 (2006): 1415–1434.

Mill, John Stuart. *On Liberty*. Cambridge: Cambridge University Press, 1989.

Morgan, Patricia. *Adoption and the Care of Children: The British and American Experience*. London: IEA Health and Welfare Unit, 1998.

Murphy, Kate, Marian Quartly, and Denise Cuthbert. " 'In the Best Interests of the Child': Mapping the (Re)-emergence of Pro-adoption Politics in Contemporary Australia." *Australian Journal of Politics and History* 55 (2009), 201–218.

Murray, Charles, *Coming Apart: The State of White America, 1960–2010*. New York: Crown Forum, 2012.

National Child Protection Clearing House. "Child Abuse Prevention: What Works?" AIFS PowerPoint presentation, 2006. aifs.gov.au/nch/pubs/presentations/bromfield8.ppt.

Newton, Rae R., Alan J. Litrownik, and John A. Landsverk. "Children and Youth in Foster Care: Disentangling the Relationship between Problem Behaviours and Number of Placements." *Child Abuse and Neglect* 24 (2000): 1363–1374.

Nock, Steven L. "Marriage as a Public Issue." *The Future of Children* 15 (2005): 13–34.

NSW Department of Families and Community Services. "A Safe Home for Life: Report on the Outcomes of Public Consultation on the Child Protection Legislative Reforms Discussion Paper 2012." Sydney: NSW Government, 2013.

NSW Government, *Keep Them Safe: A Shared Approach to Child Wellbeing*. Sydney: Department of Premier and Cabinet, 2009.

NSW Ombudsman, *Report of Reviewable Deaths in 2006: Volume 2 – Child Deaths*. Annual Report, 2007.

— *Review of a Group of Children Aged 10 to 14 in Out-of-home Care and Under the Parental Responsibility of the Minister for Community Services*. Sydney: NSW Ombudsman, 2009.

— *Review of the NSW Child Protection System: Are Things Improving?* Sydney: NSW Ombudsman, 2014.

— *Special Commission of Inquiry into Child Protection in NSW: Submission of NSW Ombudsman, Part 4 – Mandatory Reporting*. Sydney: NSW Ombudsman, 2008.

— *Special Commission of Inquiry into Child Protection in NSW: Submission of NSW Ombudsman, Part 6 – Assessment and Early Intervention and Prevention*. Sydney: NSW Ombudsman, 2008.

— *The Death of Ebony: The Need for an Effective Interagency Response to Children At-risk*. Sydney: NSW Ombudsman, 2009.

— *The Death of Dean Shillingsworth: Critical Challenges in the Context of Reforms to the Child Protection System*. Sydney: NSW Ombudsman, 2009.

Ombudsman Victoria. *Own Motion Investigation into the Department of Human Services Child Protection Program*. Report tabled November, 2009. (Melbourne: Ombudsman Victoria, 2009).

— *Own Motion Investigation into Child Protection: Out of Home Care*. Report tabled May 2010. (Melbourne: Ombudsman Victoria, 2010).

Osborn, Alexandra, and Leah Bromfield. *Residential and Specialised Models of Care*. Research Brief No. 9. Melbourne: National Child Protection Clearinghouse, 2007.

Osborn, Alexandra, and Paul H. Delfabbro. *National Comparative Study of Children and Young People with High Support Needs in Australian Out of Home Care*. Final Report. Adelaide: University of Adelaide, 2006.

Parbury, Nigel. *Survival: A History of Aboriginal Life in New South Wales*. Sydney: NSW Department of Aboriginal Affairs, 1986.

Parkinson, Patrick. *For Kids' Sake: Repairing the Social Environment for Australian Children and Young People*. Sydney: University of Sydney, 2011.

Paxman, Marina. "Outcomes for Children and Young People in Kinship Care." An issues paper. Ashfield: Centre for Parenting & Research, 2006.

Pearson, Noel. *Up from the Mission: Selected Writings*. Melbourne: Black Ink, 2009.

Phillips, Janet. "Child Abuse and Protection in Australia." Background Note. Canberra: Parliamentary Library, 2009.

Picton, Cliff, and Peter Boss. *Child Welfare in Australia: An Introduction*. Sydney: Harcourt Brace Jovanovich, 1981.

Porter, Christian. "Adoption and Child Protection." *Australian Polity* 5, no. 1 (2015), 15–25.

Price, David, and Bess Price, "Good Culture, Bad Culture: Where Do We Go From Here?" In *In Black & White: Australians All at the Crossroads*, edited by Rhonda Craven, Anthony Dillon, and Nigel Parbury. Ballan: Connor Court, 2013.

Pyne, Christopher. "*My School* Updated with Improved School Attendance Data." Media Release, 17 December 2014.

Qu, Lixia, and Ruth Weston. *Parental Marital Status and Children's Wellbeing*. Occasional Paper No. 46. Canberra: FaHCSIA, 2012.

Queensland Child Protection Commission of Inquiry. *Queensland Child Protection Commission of Inquiry: Options for Reform*. Brisbane: 2012.

— *Queensland Child Protection Commission of Inquiry Final Report. Taking Responsibility: A Roadmap for Queensland Child Protection* (Carmody Report). Brisbane: 2013.

Queensland Crime and Misconduct Commission. *Protecting Children: An Inquiry into Abuse of Children in Foster Care.* Brisbane: Queensland Crime and Misconduct Commission, 2004.

Read, Peter. *The Stolen Generations: The Removal of Aboriginal Children in New South Wales 1883 to 1969.* Sydney: NSW Department of Aboriginal Affairs, 1981.

Reynolds, Arthur, Lindsay Mathieson, and James Topitzes. "Do Early Childhood Interventions Prevent Child Maltreatment? A Review of Research." *Child Maltreatment* 14 (2009): 182–206.

Richardson, Nick, Daryl Higgins, and Leah Bromfield. "Making the 'Right' Choices about Child Protection Programs and Services." Presentation at National Conference of the Association for the Welfare of Child Health, *Healthy Solutions for Children: Making the Right Choice*, Sydney, April 2005.

Sammut, Jeremy. *Fatally Flawed: The Child Protection Crisis in Australia.* Policy Monograph No. 97. Sydney: Centre for Independent Studies, 2009.

— "Still Damaging and Disturbing: Australian Child Protection Data and the Need for National Adoption Targets." Issue Analysis 145. Sydney: Centre for Independent Studies, 2014.

Saunders, Peter, and Martin Stewart-Weeks, eds. *Supping with the Devil.* Policy Forum No. 16. Sydney: Centre for Independent Studies, 2009.

Sawyer, Michael G., Josephine A. Carbone, Amelia K. Searle, and Philip Robinson. "The Mental Health and Wellbeing of Children and Adolescents in Home-based Foster Care." *Medical Journal of Australia* 186 (2007): 181–184.

Scott, Dorothy, and Shurlee Swain. *Confronting Cruelty: Historical Perspectives on Child Protection in Australia.* Melbourne: Melbourne University Press, 2002.

Senate Community Affairs References Committee. *Forgotten Australians: A Report on Australians who Experienced Institutional or Out-of-home Care as Children.* Canberra: Senate Printing Unit, 2004.

— *Protecting Vulnerable Children: A National Challenge.* Canberra: Senate Printing Unit, 2005.

— *Commonwealth Contribution to Former Forced Adoption Policies and Practices.* Submission No. 70 by Family Inclusion Network of New South Wales, January 2011.

— *Commonwealth Contribution to Former Forced Adoption Policies and Practices.* Canberra: Senate Printing Unit, 2012.

—— *Grandparents who Take Primary Responsibility for Raising Grandchildren*. Canberra: Senate Printing Unit, 2014.

—— *Out of Home Care*. Canberra: Senate Printing Unit, 2015.

Shonkoff, Jack P. and Deborah A. Phillips eds. *From Neurons to Neighbourhoods: The Science of Early Childhood Development*. Washington, DC: National Academy Press, 2000.

Smyth, Ciara, and Tony Eardley. *Out of Home Care for Children in Australia: A Review of Literature and Policy*. Sydney: Social Policy Research Centre, 2008.

Earl, Catherine. *South Australian Council of Social Service Submission to the Child Protection Systems Royal Commission*. Unley: SACOSS, 2015.

Spark, Ceridwen, and Denise Cuthbert, eds. *Other People's Children: Adoption in Australia*. Melbourne: Australian Scholarly Publishing, 2009.

Statutory Child Protection in NSW: Issues and Options for Reform. Sydney: NSW Department of Community Services (DoCS), 2006.

Success Works. *Evaluation of the TRACK Program*. Melbourne: DHS, 2005.

Sullivan, Lucy. *Behavioural Poverty*. Policy Monograph No. 45. Sydney: Centre for Independent Studies, 2000.

Sutton, Peter. *The Politics of Suffering*. Melbourne: Melbourne University Press, 2009.

Swain, Shurlee, and Renate Howe. *Single Mothers and Their Children: Disposal, Punishment and Survival in Australia*. Cambridge: Cambridge University Press, 1995.

Taren-Sweeney, Michael J. and Philip Hazell. "Mental Health of Children in Foster and Kinship Care in NSW, Australia." *Journal of Paediatrics and Child Health* 42 (2006): 89–97.

Taylor, Penny, Peter Moore, Lynne Pezzullo, Joe Tucci, Chris Goddard, and Lillian De Bortoli. *The Cost of Child Abuse in Australia*. Melbourne: Australian Childhood Foundation, and Child Abuse Prevention Research Australia, 2008.

Thomas, Adam, and Isabel Sawhill. "For Love or Money? The Impact of Family Structure on Family Income." *Future Child* 15 (2005): 57–74.

Thomas, Shane. *The Victorian Family Support Innovation Projects: Final Evaluation Overview Report*. Melbourne: Department of Human Services, Victoria and Monash University, 2007.

Triseliotis, John. "Long-term Foster Care or Adoption? The Evidence Examined." *Child and Family Social Work* 7 (2002): 23–33.

US Department of Health and Human Services. *The AFCARS Report: Preliminary FY 2013 Estimates as of July 2014*. www.acf.hhs.gov/sites/default/files/cb/afcarsreport21.pdf

Victorian Auditor-General. *Early Intervention Services for Vulnerable Children and Families*. Victorian Auditor-General's Report. Melbourne: Victorian Government Printer, 2015.

Victorian Child Death Review Committee. *Annual Report of Inquiries into the Deaths of Children Known to Child Protection 2010*. Melbourne: Office of the Child Safety Commissioner, 2010.

Victorian Department of Human Services. *An Integrated Strategy for Child Protection and Placement Services*. Melbourne: Community Care Division, Victoria Department of Human Services, 2002.

— *A Strategic Framework for Family Services*. Melbourne: Office for Children, DHS, 2007.

Watson, Johanna. *Child Neglect: Literature Review*. Research Report. Ashfield: Centre for Parenting & Research, 2005.

Wise, Sarah, and Samuel Egger. *Looking After Children Outcomes Data Project Final Report*. Melbourne: AIFS, 2009.

Wise, Sarah, Sarah Pollock, Gaye Mitchell, Cathy Argus, and Peta Farquhar. *Care-system Impacts on Academic Outcomes*. Melbourne: Anglicare Victoria and Wesley Mission Victoria, 2010.

Windschuttle, Keith. *The Stolen Generations 1881–2008*. Vol. 3 of *The Fabrication of Aboriginal History*. Sydney: Macleay Press, 2009.

Wood, James. *Report of the Special Commission of Inquiry into Child Protection Services in NSW* (Wood Report). Sydney: State of NSW, 2008.

Zhou, Albert. *Estimate of NSW Children Involved in the Child Welfare System*. Sydney: Department of Community Services, 2010.

ENDNOTES

1 Courts suppressed her real name to protect her siblings' identity.
2 "Starving Girl Could Have Lived: Watchdog," *Sydney Morning Herald*, 7 October 2009.
3 NSW Ombudsman, *The Death of Ebony: The Need for an Effective Interagency Response to Children at Risk* (Sydney: NSW Ombudsman, 2009); "Starved Girl's Death of 'Torture'," *The Australian*, 22 November 2007; "Starved Girl's Sister Was Taken From Her Family," *Sydney Morning Herald*, 8 November 2007; "Girl Prisoner's 'Torturous Death'," *Sydney Morning Herald*, 22 November 2007; "Starved Girl Died 'Slow, Torturous Death'," *The Australian*, 21 November 2007.
4 NSW Ombudsman, *The Death of Dean Shillingsworth: Critical Challenges in the Context of Reforms to the Child Protection System* (Sydney: NSW Ombudsman, 2009).
5 Judy Cashmore, Dorothy Scott, and Gillian Calvert, *Think Child, Think Family, Think Community: From a Child Protection System to a System for Protecting Children*. Submission to the Special Commission of Inquiry into Child Protection Services in NSW, NSW Commission for Children and Young People (March 2008), 14.
6 Council of Australian Governments, *Protecting Children is Everyone's Business: National Framework for Protecting Australia's Children, 2009–2020* (Canberra: Australian Government, 2009).
7 Australian Institute of Health and Welfare (AIHW), *Child Protection Australia 2008–09* (Canberra: AIHW, 2009), 36.
8 AIHW, *Child Protection Australia 2011–12* (Canberra: AIHW, 2013), 3.
9 Ben Matthews and Donald C. Boss, "Mandated Reporting is Still Policy with Reason: Empirical Evidence and Philosophical Grounds," *Child Abuse and Neglect* 32 (2008): 511–516.
10 "On the Road with the DoCS Crisis Response Team," *Daily Telegraph*, 10 June 2011.
11 Jeremy Sammut, *Fatally Flawed: The Child Protection Crisis in Australia*, Policy Monograph 97 (Sydney: The Centre for Independent Studies, 2009).
12 On the role that welfare plays as cause of the personal and social pathologies that lead to child harm, see the great insights on this point in the Noel

Pearson collection *Up From the Mission: Selected Writings* (Melbourne: Black Inc., 2009).

13 Lawrence Mead, *Beyond Entitlement: The Social Obligations of Citizenship* (New York: The Free Press, 1986).

14 Australian Early Development Index (AEDI), *Summary of the 2012 AEDI Results, Factsheet* (March 2013).

15 Christopher Pyne, "My School Updated with Improved School Attendance Data," media release, 17 December 2014.

16 Jennifer Buckingham et al., *Educating the Disadvantaged*, Issue Analysis 116 (Sydney: The Centre for Independent Studies 2009).

17 Chris Goddard, "Introduction," in Jeremy Sammut, *Fatally Flawed*.

18 State of Victoria, *Protecting Victoria's Vulnerable Children* Inquiry (Cummins Report) (Melbourne: State of Victoria, 2012), xxviii.

19 Ombudsman Victoria, *Own Motion Investigation into the Department of Human Services Child Protection Program* (Melbourne: Ombudsman Victoria, 2009), 24.

20 Leah Bromfield et al., *Out-of-Home Care in Australia: Messages from Research* (Melbourne: Australian Institute of Family Studies, Commonwealth of Australia, 2005), 3.

21 Patricia Hansen and Frank Ainsworth, "Viewpoints: Australian Child Protection Services: A Game without End," *International Journal of Child Welfare* 22 (2013), 104–110.

22 Chris Goddard and Joe Tucci, *Responding to Child Abuse and Neglect in Australia* (Melbourne: Child Abuse Prevention Research Australia and Australian Childhood Foundation, 2008), 12.

23 Kate Legge, "Adoption: Why is it So Hard?" *Weekend Australian Magazine*, 30 May 2015

24 AIHW, *Adoption Australia 2013–14* (Canberra: AIHW, 2014).

25 AIHW, *Child Protection Australia 2013–14* (Canberra: AIHW, 2014), 49, table 5.2.

26 "Faster NSW Adoption May Not Be Best for Children, Warns Former Judge Nahum Mushin," *Sun-Herald*, 13 June 2015.

27 Royal Australian and New Zealand College of Psychiatrists, "RANZCP Submission: Senate Standing Committees on Community Affairs Inquiry into Out of Home Care" (October 2014), aph.gov.au/DocumentStore.ashx?id=4292ed53-61cb-4496-a157-eb44314b3066&subId=301231.

28 Jeremy Sammut, *Still Damaging and Disturbing: Australian Child Protection Data and the Need for National Adoption Targets*, Issue Analysis 145 (Sydney: The Centre for Independent Studies, 2014).

29 Marilyn McHugh and Kylie Valentine, *Financial and Non-Financial Support to Formal and Informal Out of Home Carers*, Final Report for FaHCSIA (Department of Families, Housing, Community Services and Indigenous Affairs) (Sydney: Social Policy Research Centre, University of New South Wales, 2010), 96–97.

30 "Child Welfare 'Stuck in the 1960s'," *The Australian*, 18 August 2014.

31 "South Australia Risks Creating Another Stolen Generation," *The Advertiser*, 10 September 2014.

32 "Finding Better Ways to Defend the Defenceless," *The Advertiser*, 9 November 2014.

33 "Alcohol or Drug Abuse Not a Trigger for Removal of Children: Families SA," *ABC News*, 30 September 2014.

34 "Welfare System Central to Toddler Chloe's Death," *Herald Sun*, 28 September 2014; "SA Coroner Mark Johns Continues Inquest into Sad Life of Chloe Valentine, Who Died Despite 21 Child Abuse Reports to Families SA," *The Advertiser*, 26 September 2014.

35 "Chloe Valentine: How Families SA Failed Her," *The Australian*, 4 April 2015.

36 "SA Coroner Mark Johns Continues Inquest into Sad Life of Chloe Valentine, Who Died Despite 21 Child Abuse Reports to Families SA," *The Advertiser*, 26 September 2014.

37 *Inquest into the Death of Chloe Lee Valentine*, conducted by Mark Johns, State Coroner, South Australia (August 2014–April 2015), www.courts.sa.gov.au/CoronersFindings/Lists/Coroners%20Findings/Attachments/613/VALENTINE%20Chloe%20Lee.pdf, 9–11, 24–28, 86.

38 "SA Coroner Mark Johns Continues Inquest into Sad Life of Chloe Valentine."

39 *Inquest into the Death of Chloe Lee Valentine*, 146–7.

40 Ibid., 11.

41 "Adelaide Couple Face Court Accused of Starving Son in 'House of Horror' Neglect Case," *The Advertiser*, 28 October 2014.

42 Mick Gooda, "Discussions on Indigenous Matters Don't Fall Foul of Racial Discrimination Act," *The Australian*, 26 January 2015.

43 This section is based on Leah Bromfield and Prue Holzer, *A National Approach for Child Protection: Project Report – A Report to the Community and Disability Services Minister's Advisory Council*, National Child Protection Clearinghouse, Australian Institute of Family Studies (2008), 12–14.

44 Denise Cuthbert and Marian Quartly, " 'Forced Adoption' in the Australian Story of National Regret and Apology," *Australian Journal of Politics and History* 58: 1 (2012): 82–96. See also Philip Mendes, *Inside the Welfare Lobby: A History of the Australian Council of Social Services: The Role of Interest Groups in Australian Social Policy* (Eastbourne, Sussex Academic Press: 2006), Chapter 2.

45 Bromfield and Holzer, *A National Approach for Child Protection*, 18.

46 Victorian Department of Human Services, *A Strategic Framework for Family Services*, (Melbourne: Office for Children, Victorian Department of Human Services, 2007), 21–22.

47 For the "welfare paradigm" and critique, see John Frederick and Chris Goddard, "Exploring the Relationship between Poverty, Childhood Adversity and Child Abuse from the Perspective of Adulthood," *Child Abuse Review* 16, no. 5 (2007), 323–341.

48 Leah Bromfield, "Abuse and Neglect: Australia's Child Protection 'Crisis'," *The Conversation*, 23 October 2014, theconversation.com/abuse-and-neglect-australias-child-protection-crisis-32664.

49 James Wood, *Report of the Special Commission of Inquiry into Child Protection Services in NSW* (Wood Report) (Sydney: State of NSW, 2008), i–ii.

50 Chris Goddard and Joe Tucci, "Secretive System Doesn't Bear Scrutiny," *The Australian*, 28 November 2008.

51 What follows is based on the joint submission to the Wood Commission prepared by Judy Cashmore, Professor Dorothy Scott, and Commissioner Gillian Calvert, *Think Child, Think Family, Think Community: From a Child Protection System to a System for Protecting Children. Submission to the Special Commission of Inquiry into Child Protection Services in NSW*, NSW Commission for Children and Young People (March 2008).

52 Cashmore, Scott, and Calvert, *Think Child*, 21.

53 Ibid., 2.

54 Ibid., 21–22.

55 Ibid., 21.

56 Allen Consulting Group and Australian Research Alliance for Children and Youth, *Inverting the Pyramid: Enhancing Systems for Protecting Children* (Melbourne: Allen Consulting Group, 2009), 3

57 Productivity Commission, *Report on Government Services 2009* (Canberra: Commonwealth of Australia 2009), 15.4.

58 Cashmore, Scott, and Calvert, *Think Child*, 21.

59 Ibid., 21.

60 Ibid., 36.

61 Ibid., 21–22.

62 Wood Report, ii–iii.

63 NSW Ombudsman, *Report of Reviewable Deaths in 2006: Volume 2 – Child Deaths* (Sydney: NSW Ombudsman, 2007), iv–v.

64 NSW Ombudsman, *Special Commission of Inquiry into Child Protection in NSW: Submission of NSW Ombudsman, Part 6: Assessment and Early Intervention and Prevention* (Sydney: NSW Ombudsman, 2008), 6.

65 Cashmore, Scott, and Calvert, *Think Child*, 21.

66 Ibid., 28.

67 Ibid., 27, 39.

68 Ibid., 27.

69 Ibid., 20.

70 AIHW, *Child Protection Australia 2013–14*.

71 Darly Higgins and Ilan Katz, "Enhancing Service Systems for Protecting Children: Promoting Child Wellbeing and Child Protection Reform in Australia," AIFS *Family Matters*, 80 (2008), 47–48.

72 On the gaps and other deficiencies in Australian child protection data, including the differences in definitions by the states and territories that make comparisons problematic, see Karen Broadley, Chris Goddard, and Joe Tucci, "They Count for Nothing: Poor Child Protection Statistics Are a Barrier to a Child-Centred National Framework" (Melbourne: Australian Childhood Foundation and Monash University, Child Abuse Prevention Research Australia, 2014).

73 Council of Australian Governments, *Protecting Children is Everyone's Business: National Framework for Protecting Australia's Children 2009–2020*, 7–8, emphasis in original.

74 See the Wood Report, 245; NSW Ombudsman, *Special Commission of Inquiry into Child Protection in NSW: Submission of NSW Ombudsman, Part 6*, 14.

75 Cashmore, Scott, and Calvert, *Think Child*, 6.

76 Wood Report, vi–viii.

77 Victorian Department of Human Services, *A Strategic Framework for Family Services*, 21–22

78 Wood Report, v.

79 Ibid., 369.

80 Ibid., vii.

81 Ibid., viii.

82 Allen Consulting Group, *Inverting the Pyramid*, 48.

83 NSW Government, *Keep Them Safe: A Shared Approach to Child Wellbeing* (Sydney: Department of Premier and Cabinet, 2009), 10.

84 NSW Ombudsman, *The Death of Ebony*, 51.

85 NSW Government, *Keep Them Safe*, 1.

86 Cashmore, Scott, and Calvert, *Think Child*, 20.

87 Wood Report, 183.

88 NSW Ombudsman, *Special Commission of Inquiry into Child Protection in NSW: Submission of NSW Ombudsman. Part 4: Mandatory Reporting* (Sydney: NSW Ombudsman, 2008), 2.

89 Wood Report, 137

90 Shane Thomas, *The Victorian Family Support Innovation Projects: Final Evaluation Overview Report* (Melbourne: Department of Human Services, Victoria and Monash University, 2007), 10; Victorian Department of Human Services, *An Integrated Strategy for Child Protection and Placement Services* (Melbourne: Community Care Division, Victoria Department of Human Services, 2002).

91 NSW Government, *Keep Them Safe*, 14. See NSW Ombudsman, *Special Commission of Inquiry into Child Protection in NSW: Submission of NSW Ombudsman, Part 6*, 11. This data was originally reported in a presentation by then DoCS deputy director Dr Gul Izmir, at the Australasian Conference on Child Abuse

and Neglect. See *Breaking Down the Barriers between Prevention, Early Intervention and Child Protection* (31 October 2007–2 November 2007), ccm.com.au/accan/content/papers/Wed_Rm5-RanahanSTARTBarnardosFarinolaJackson.pdf

92 Wood Report, 135

93 Ibid., 171.

94 Ibid., 1025.

95 Albert Zhou, *Estimate of NSW Children Involved in the Child Welfare System*, Department of Community Services (Sydney: NSW Department of Human Services, 2010), 2–3

96 Wood Report, 127.

97 Ibid., 192.

98 NSW Government, *Keep Them Safe: A Shared Approach to Child Wellbeing* (Sydney: 2009), 14; *Growing them Strong, Together: Promoting the Safety and Wellbeing of the Northern Territory's Children*, Report of the Board of Inquiry into the Child Protection System in the Northern Territory (Darwin: 2010), 157; See also Cummins Report, xxviii.

99 See Judge John Fogarty, quoted to this effect concerning the situation in Victoria in Carol Nader, "Children Overload," *The Age*, 12 August 2009.

100 AIHW, *Child Protection Australia 2013–14*, Table A5.

101 AIHW, *Child Protection Australia 2013–14*, 13–14.

102 Bromfield and Holzer, *A National Approach for Child Protection*, 54.

103 Bromfield and Holzer, *A National Approach for Child Protection*, 62.

104 Nick Richardson, Daryl Higgins, and Leah Bromfield, "Making the 'Right' Choices about Child Protection Programs and Services," Healthy Solutions for Children: Making the Right Choice, 10th National Conference of the Association for the Welfare of Child Health (Sydney, April 2005).

105 For this light on the evidence, see National Child Protection Clearing House, "Child Abuse Prevention: What Works?" (AIFS: Australian Government, 2006), aifs.gov.au/nch/pubs/presentations/bromfield8.ppt.

106 Prue Holzer et al., *The Effectiveness of Parent Education and Home Visiting Child Maltreatment Prevention Programs*, Child Abuse Prevention Issues No. 24 (Melbourne: Australian Institute of Family Studies, 2006), 8, 10, 14–15.

107 Ibid., 18, 20.

108 Richardson, Higgins, and Bromfield, "Making the 'Right' Choices."

109 Arthur Reynolds, Lindsay Mathieson, and James Topitzes, "Do Early Childhood Interventions Prevent Child Maltreatment? A Review of Research," *Child Maltreatment* 14, no. 2 (2009), 200.

110 Amy M. Heneghan, Sarah M. Horwitz, and John M. Leventhal, "Evaluating Intensive Family Preservation Programs: A Methodological Review," *Pediatrics* 97, no. 4 (1 April 1996), 535–542.

111 Holzer et al., *The Effectiveness of Parent Education*, 11–12.

112 Cashmore, Scott, and Calvert, *Think Child*, 25.

113 For an account of "behavioural poverty," see Lucy Sullivan, *Behavioural Poverty*, Policy Monograph No. 45 (Sydney: CIS, 2000).

114 See Council of Australian Governments, *Protecting Children is Everyone's Business*, 7–8.

115 Department of Communities, Child Safety, and Disability Services, *Invitation to Offer Com-01117 for the Provision of a Child Safety Practice Framework* (Queensland Government, Brisbane, 2013), 8.

116 Cummins Report, xxviii.

117 Victorian Auditor-General, *Early Intervention Services for Vulnerable Children and Families*, (Melbourne: 2015).

118 Victorian Auditor-General, *Early Intervention Services for Vulnerable Children and Families*, xi–xii.

119 UNSW Social Policy Research Centre, *Keep Them Safe Outcomes Evaluation Final Report*, (NSW Department of Premier and Cabinet: Sydney, 2014), 6.

120 Ibid., 8.

121 NSW Ombudsman, *Review of the NSW Child Protection System: Are Things Improving?* (Sydney: NSW Ombudsman, 2014), 1

122 Wood Report, 376.

123 NSW Ombudsman, *Review of a Group of Children Aged 10 to 14 in Out-of-home Care and Under the Parental Responsibility of the Minister for Community Services* (Sydney: NSW Ombudsman, 2009), 5–6.

124 Peter Saunders and Martin Stewart-Weeks (eds), *Supping with the Devil*, CIS Policy Forum No. 16 (Sydney: The Centre for Independent Studies, 2009).

125 Henry Ergas, "Maggie Showed Keating the Way," *The Australian*, 12 January 2010.

126 Andrew McCallum, "Child Protection and Wood: Will We Rise to the Challenge?" *Developing Practice* 23 (Autumn/Winter 2009): 4–6.

127 NSW Ombudsman, *The Death of Ebony*, 51.

128 "DoCS Child Protection Role to be Reduced," *Sydney Morning Herald*, 3 March 2009.

129 Council of Australian Governments, *Protecting Children is Everyone's Business*, xiv.

130 Ombudsman Victoria, *Own Motion Investigation into the Department of Human Services Child Protection Program* (Melbourne: Ombudsman Victoria, 2009).

131 Ibid., 10–11, 24–25.

132 Ibid., 13

133 Ibid., 9.

134 Ibid., 8

135 Ibid., 10.

136 Ibid., 14.

137 NSW Ombudsman, *Report of Reviewable Deaths in 2006, Volume 2*, iv–v.

138 "Children at Risk Left to Fend for Themselves," *The Age*, 7 June 2009.

139 "Urgent Call to Help Families in Crisis," *The Age* (26 November 2009).

140 "Children's Overload," *The Age* (12 August 2009).

141 Chris Goddard, "The State of Victoria's Child Protection," *Children Australia*, 35, no. 1 (2010): 4–5.

142 Janet Phillips, *Child Abuse and Protection in Australia, Background Note* (Canberra: Parliamentary Library, 2009),

143 Karen Healy, "Critical Questions about the Quest for Clarity in Child Protection Regimes," *Communities, Children and Families Australia* 4, no. 1 (October 2009): 52–58.

144 Chris Goddard and Joe Tucci, "Sins of Omission," *The Australian*, 15 July 2008.

145 Wood Report, 212.

146 Cummins Report, xxviii.

147 AIHW, *Child Protection Australia 2013-14*, 19-20.

148 "Open Adoptions to Undergo Barnados' Microscope," *Sydney Morning Herald*, 11 July 2014.

149 House of Representatives Standing Committee on Human and Family Services, *Overseas Adoption in Australia* (Canberra: Commonwealth of Australia, 2005), ix, 126.
150 "Take Children from Addicts, Inquiry Urges," *The Age*, 14 September 2007.
151 "Children of Addicts 'Should be Removed'," *Sydney Morning Herald*, 23 July 2007.
152 Ibid.
153 "Take Children from Addicts, Inquiry Urges," *The Age*, 14 September 2007.
154 Kate Murphy, Marian Quartly, and Denise Cuthbert, " 'In the Best Interests of the Child': Mapping the (Re) emergence of Pro-adoption Politics in Contemporary Australia," *Australian Journal of Politics and History* 55, no. 2 (2009), 201–218.
155 House of Representatives Standing Committee on Family and Human Services, *The Winnable War on Drugs: The Impact of Illicit Drug Use on Families* (Canberra: Commonwealth of Australia, 2007), Chapter 3, "Protecting Children."
156 Jacques Donzelot, *The Policing of Families* (New York: Pantheon, 1979).
157 "Newborn Left with Drug Addict Mum," *The Advertiser*, 10 February 2008.
158 See, for instance, Human Services Community Services, *Working with Parental Substance Misuse*, Research to Practice Note (Sydney: NSW Government, February 2010), www.community.nsw.gov.au/docswr/_assets/main/documents/researchnotes_parental_misuse.pdf.
159 Alister Lamont, *Effects of Child Abuse and Neglect for Adult Survivors*, National Child Protection Clearinghouse Resource Sheet (Australian Institute of Family Studies: Melbourne 2010).
160 Senate Community Affairs Committee, *Protecting Vulnerable Children: A National Challenge* (Canberra: Commonwealth of Australia, 17 March 2005), 22.
161 Penny Taylor, Peter Moore, Lynne Pezzullo, Joe Tucci, Chris Goddard, and Lillian De Bortoli, *The Cost of Child Abuse in Australia* (Melbourne: Access Economics, Australian Childhood Foundation, and Child Abuse Prevention Research Australia, 2008).

162 *The Fiscal Case for Working with Troubled Families: Analysis and Evidence on the Costs of Troubled Families to Government* (London: Department of Communities and Local Government, 2013).

163 "500,000 Troubled Families Cost Taxpayers $30 Billion a Year," *Daily Mail*, 18 August 2014.

164 *A New System for Better Employment and Social Outcomes: Report of the Reference Group on Welfare Reform to the Minister for Social Services* (Canberra: Commonwealth of Australia, 2015).

165 Philip Mendes, "Conservative Zealotry and the Child Protection Debate," *ABC Religion and Ethics*, 24 November 2014.

166 John Stuart Mill, *On Liberty* (Cambridge: Cambridge University Press, 1989), 105.

167 John Stuart Mill, *On Liberty*, 105.

168 George Behlmer, *Child Abuse and Moral Reform in England, 1870–1908* (Palo Alto: Stanford University Press, 1982).

169 Cliff Picton and Peter Boss, *Child Welfare in Australia: An Introduction* (Sydney: Harcourt Brace Jovanovich, 1981), 21.

170 For this history, see Dorothy Scott and Shurlee Swain, *Confronting Cruelty: Historical Perspectives on Child Protection in Australia* (Melbourne: Melbourne University Press, 2002).

171 South Australian Council of Social Services, *SACOSS Submission to the Child Protection Systems Royal Commission* (January 2015).

172 Ciara Smyth and Tony Eardley, *Out of Home Care for Children in Australia: A Review of Literature and Policy* (Social Policy Research Centre, University of New South Wales: Sydney, 2008), ix.

173 Paul H. Delfabbro and James G. Barber, "The Micro-economics of Foster Care in South Australia," *Children Australia* 27, no. 2 (2002): 29.

174 See Jay Weatherill, quoted again to this effect in "An Infant Dead, a System at Fault," *The Australian*, 19 April 2008.

175 Ombudsman Victoria, *Own Motion Investigation into Child Protection: Out of Home Care*, 66.

176 Department of Health and Human Services, *Stability Planning and Permanent Care Project Final Report* (Melbourne: 2014), 2.

177 AIHW, *Child Protection Australia 2013–14*, 45, Table 5.1

178 Productivity Commission, *Report on Government Services 2015* (Canberra: Commonwealth of Australia 2015), Table 15A.19.

179 "Parents Demand Answers after Toddler Drowned in Foster Carer's Pool," *Sydney Morning Herald*, 22 May 2015.

180 "Kids Lose Out in Foster Care Cash In," *The Australian*, 8 November 2008.

181 AIHW, *Child Protection Australia 2013–14*, 58, Figure 6.1.

182 Marilyn McHugh and Kylie Valentine, *Financial and Non-Financial Support to Formal and Informal Out of Home Carers,* final report for FaHCSIA (Department of Families, Housing, Community Services and Indigenous Affairs) (Social Policy Research Centre, University of New South Wales: Sydney, 2010), viii.

183 Senate Community Affairs Committee, *Protecting Vulnerable Children: A National Challenge.*

184 Alexandra Osborn and Leah Bromfield, *Residential and Specialised Models of Care*, Research Brief No. 9 (Melbourne: National Child Protection Clearinghouse, 2007), 8.

185 Alexandra Osborn and Paul H. Delfabbro, *National Comparative Study of Children and Young People with High Support Needs in Australian Out of Home Care*, final report (University of Adelaide: 2006), 36.

186 Osborn and Delfabbro, *National Comparative Study*, 32, 92.

187 Ibid., 83.

188 Ibid., 32, 92.

189 Ibid., 34.

190 Ibid., 14–17.

191 Ibid., 92, 94.

192 Bromfield, et al., *Out-of-Home Care in Australia*, 3.

193 Osborn and Delfabbro, *National Comparative Study*, 86–87, 96.

194 Smyth and Eardley, *Out of Home Care for Children in Australia*, v.

195 Senate Community Affairs Committee, *Protecting Vulnerable Children*, 103.

196 Paul Delfabbro et al., *Certainty for Children in Care: A Study into the Placement History and Social Background of Infants Placed into South Australian Out-of-home Care 2000–2005*, Research Bulletin (Adelaide: Department for Families and Communities, 2007), 6.

197 Smyth and Eardley, *Out of Home Care for Children in Australia*, 1.

198 Vera Fahlberg, *Attachment and Separation* (London: British Agencies for Adoption & Fostering [BAAF], 1982); Jack P. Shonkoff and Deborah A. Phillips (eds), *From Neurons to Neighbourhoods: The Science of Early Childhood Development* (Washington, DC: National Academy Press, 2000).

199 Yvon Gauthier, Gilles Fortin, and Gloria Jeliu, "Clinical Application Of Attachment Theory in Permanency Planning for Children in Foster Care: The Importance of Continuity of Care," *Infant Mental Health Journal* 25, no. 4 (2004): 379–396.

200 M. Bamblett, Howard Bath, and Rob Roseby, *Growing them Strong, Together: Promoting the Safety and Wellbeing of the Northern Territory's Children* (Bath Report), Report of the Board of Inquiry into the Child Protection System in the Northern Territory (Darwin: Department of the Chief Minister, 2010), "Summary Report," 35.

201 Ombudsman Victoria, *Own Motion Investigation into Child Protection*, 101.

202 *An Outline of National Standards for Out of Home Care* (Canberra: Commonwealth of Australia, 2011), 3.

203 Wood Report, 614.

204 Ombudsman Victoria, *Own Motion Investigation into Child Protection*, 101.

205 Department of Health and Human Services, *Stability Planning and Permanent Care Project Final Report*, 5.

206 House of Representatives Standing Committee on Human and Family Services, *Overseas Adoption in Australia*, 127–128.

207 James G. Barber and Paul H. Delfabbro, "Placement Stability and the Psychological Well-Being of Children in Foster Care," *Research on Social Work Practice* 13, no. 4 (July 2003): 416.

208 Joe Tucci and Chris Goddard, "Kept in Dark on Child Protection," *The Age*, 3 November 2010.

209 Marilyn McHugh and Kylie Valentine, *Financial and Non-Financial Support*, 4.

210 "Kin vs Foster Care Dilemma," *Daily Telegraph*, 15 October 2009.

211 Paul H. Delfabbro, James G. Barber, and Lesley Cooper, "Placement Disruption and Dislocation in South Australian Substitute Care," *Children Australia* 25, no. 2 (2000), 16–20.

212 Cited in Senate Community Affairs Committee, *Protecting Vulnerable Children* (see endnote 27), 99.

213 *Protecting Children: An Inquiry into Abuse of Children in Foster Care* (Brisbane: Queensland Crime and Misconduct Commission, 2004).

214 *Statutory Child Protection in NSW: Issues and Options for Reform* (Sydney: NSW DoCS [Department of Community Services], 2006), 14.

215 Wood Report, 600–602, 608, 638.

216 Sarah Wise and Samuel Egger, *Looking After Children Outcomes Data Project Final Report* (Melbourne: Victorian Department of Human Services: 2009), 97.

217 Bath Report, "Summary Report," 45.

218 Cummins Report, 229.

219 Queensland Child Protection Commission of Inquiry, *Taking Responsibility: A Roadmap for Queensland Child Protection*, (Brisbane: State of Queensland, 2013), 222.

220 *Successworks. Evaluation of the TRACK Program* (Victoria: Department of Human Services, 2005).

221 Paul H. Delfabbro, Alexandra Osborn, and James G. Barber, "Beyond the Continuum: New Perspectives on the Future of Out of Home Care in Australia," *Children Australia* 30, no. 2 (2005): 12.

222 Commission for Children and Young People and Child Guardian (CCYPCG), *Views of Children and Young People in Foster Care, Queensland* (Brisbane: CCYPCG, 2010), 22.

223 Michael J. Taren-Sweeney and Philip Hazell, "Mental Health of Children in Foster and Kinship Care in NSW, Australia," *Journal of Paediatrics and Child Health* 42 (2006): 89–97; Michael G. Sawyer et al., "The Mental Health and Wellbeing of Children and Adolescents in Home-based Foster Care," *Medical Journal of Australia* 186, no. 4 (2007): 181–184.

224 Sarah Wise et al., *Care-system Impacts on Academic Outcomes* (Melbourne: Anglicare Victoria and Wesley Mission Victoria, 2010).

225 James G. Barber and Paul H. Delfabbro, *Children in Foster Care* (Taylor and Francis: London, 2004).

226 Rae R. Newton, Alan J. Litrownik, and John A. Landsverk, "Children and Youth in Foster Care: Disentangling the Relationship between Problem Be-

haviours and Number of Placements," *Child Abuse and Neglect* 24, no. 10 (2000): 1363–1374.

227 Paul H. Delfabbro, James G. Barber, and Lesley Cooper, "Children Entering Out-of-home Care in South Australia: Baseline Analyses for a 3-year Longitudinal Study," *Children and Youth Services Review* 24, no. 12 (2002): 917–932.

228 Victorian Child Death Review Committee, *Annual Report* (2010), xiv, 51.

229 Freda Briggs and Donna Broadhurst, 'The Abuse of Foster Carers in Australia," *Journal of Home Economics Institute of Australia* 12, no. 1 (2005): 25–35.

230 Productivity Commission, *Report on Government Services 2015*, Table 15A.19.

231 Heather Boetto, "Kinship Care: A Review of Issues," *Family Matters* 85 (2010): 64.

232 Ibid., 61.

233 Jill T. Messing, "From the Child's Perspective: A Qualitative Analysis of Kinship Care Placements," *Children and Youth Services Review* 28 (2006), 1415–1434.

234 Boetto, "Kinship Care," 61.

235 Marilyn McHugh, *An Exploratory Study of Risks to Stability in Foster and Kinship Care in NSW: Final Report* (Social Policy Research Centre, UNSW: Sydney, 2013); Wood Report, 632.

236 Meredith Kiraly and Cathy Humphreys, "Kinship Care: Benefits and Challenges," 22 October 2013, aifs.gov.au/cfca/2013/10/22/kinship-care-benefits-and-challenges.

237 Wood Report, 631.

238 Boetto, "Kinship Care," 67.

239 Bath Report, 357.

240 Department of Community Services, *Outcomes for Children and Young People in Kinship Care: An Issues Paper* (December 2006). See also Wood Report, 630-1.f.

241 Meredith Kiraly and Cathy Humphreys, *'It's the Story of All of Us": Learning from Aboriginal Communities about Supporting Family Connection* (Melbourne: Child Safety Commissioner, 2011), 8.

242 Smyth and Eardley, *Out of Home Care for Children in Australia*, vi–vii; Boetto, "Kinship care," 62–3; Marilyn McHugh, "A Further Perspective on Kinship

Care: Indigenous Foster care," *Developing Practice: The Child, Youth and Family Work Journal* (Summer 2003): 21–22.

243 Senate Standing Committee on Community Affairs, *Grandparents Who Take Primary Responsibility for Raising Grandchildren* (Canberra: Australian Government, 2014).

244 Deborah Brennan and Bettina Cass, "Grandparents as Primary Carers of Their Grandchildren: Policy and Practice Insights from Research," in Alan Hayes and Darrell Higgins (eds) *Families, Policy and the Law: Selected Essays on Contemporary Issues for Australia* (Melbourne: Australian Institute of Family Studies, 2014), 109–118.

245 Bath Report, 357; Judy Cashmore, "Kinship Care: A Differentiated and Sensitive Approach," *Developing Practice* 1 (2001), 5–8.

246 "Children of Addicts 'Should be Removed'," *Sydney Morning Herald* (23 July 2007).

247 Cashmore, et al., *Think Child*, 13.

248 Karen Healy, "Critical Questions about the Quest for Clarity in Child Protection Regimes," *Communities, Children and Families Australia* 4, no. 1 (October 2009), 52–58.

249 Cathy Humphreys, Maria Harries, Karen Healy, Robert Lonne, Philip Mendes, Marilyn McHugh, and Rosemary Sheehan, "Shifting the Child Protection Juggernaut to Earlier Intervention," *Children Australia* 34, no. 3 (2009), 5–8.

250 McHugh and Valentine, *Financial and Non-Financial Support*, 4.

251 Smyth and Eardley, *Out of Home Care for Children in Australia*, 4.

252 Bromfield, et al., *Out of Home Care in Australia*, 8.

253 Osborn and Delfabbro, *National Comparative Study*, 15–18.

254 Frank Ainsworth and Patricia Hansen, "A Dream Come True – No More Residential Care. A Corrective Note," *International Journal of Social Welfare* 14, no. 3 (2005), 195–199.

255 Smyth and Eardley, *Out of Home Care for Children in Australia*, 18.

256 Marilyn McHugh et al., *The Availability of Foster Carers* (Sydney: Social Policy Research Centre, University of New South Wales, 2004)

257 Smyth and Eardley, *Out of Home Care for Children in Australia*, vii.

258 Marilyn McHugh, "Should Australian Foster Carers Be Entitled to Receive

a Fee/Salary Wage for Caring?" (paper presented at the ACWA08 – Strong, Safe and Sustainable: Responding to Children, Young Persons and Families in a Civil Society conference, Sydney, August 2008).

259 Osborn and Delfabbro, *National Comparative Study*, 95.

260 Senate Community Affairs Committee, *Protecting Vulnerable Children* (see endnote 27), 108–109.

261 ACIL Allen Consulting, *Professional Foster Care: Barriers, Opportunities, and Options*, (Melbourne: 2013).

262 Ibid., v, 34–35.

263 COAG, *Protecting Children is Everyone's Business*, 58, 31.

264 Smyth and Eardley, *Out of Home Care for Children in Australia*, 25–48; and *Report on Government Services 2011*, 90–97. See also Department of Human Services, *Directions for Out of Home Care* (DHS: Melbourne, 2009); Department of Communities, *Child Safety Services Grant Funding Information Paper 2009–10, Placement Services, Residential Care* (Brisbane: Queensland Government, 2009); Wood Report, 597; Bromfield, et al., *Out of Home Care in Australia,* as above, vi.; ACIL Allen Consulting, *Professional Foster Care*, 12–13.

265 Ombudsman Victoria, *Own Motion Investigation into Child Protection*, 115.

266 Only half of children in care are estimated to be receiving treatment for all problems. Wise and Egger, *Looking After Children Outcomes Data*, 17. See also Marilyn McHugh and Kylie Valentine, *Financial and Non-Financial Support*, 72.

267 Smyth and Eardley, *Out of Home Care for Children in Australia*, 14.

268 Osborn and Bromfield, *Residential and Specialised Models of Care*, 5, 11.

269 Ainsworth and Hansen, "A Dream Come True," 198.

270 NSW Ombudsman, *Review of a group of children Aged 10 to 14 in Out of Home Care*, 5–6.

271 Joseph J. McDowall, CREATE Report Card 2009. *Transitioning From Care: Tracking Progress* (Sydney: CREATE Foundation, 2009).

272 Senate Standing Committee on Community Affairs, *Forgotten Australians: A Report on Australians Who Experienced Institutional or Out-of-home Care as Children* (Canberra: Government of Australia, 2004).

273 Bromfield, et al., *Out of Home Care in Australia*, 47.

274 "Royal Commission: Department Admits Child Still Being Abused in Care," *Sydney Morning Herald*, 3 March 2014.

275 "Paedophile Gangs Targeting Children in State Care in Victoria for Sexual Abuse," *ABC News Online*, 11 March 2014.

276 "Child Sexual Abuse: Royal Commission to Look at Foster Care," *Sydney Morning Herald*, 6 February 2015.

277 House of Representatives Standing Committee on Human and Family Services, *Overseas Adoption in Australia*, ix, 126.

278 Patricia Morgan, *Adoption and the Care of Children: The British and American Experience* (London: IEA Health and Welfare Unit, 1998).

279 Carolyn Davies and Harriet Ward, *Safeguarding Children Across Services: Messages from Research*, (London: Jessica Kingsley Publishers, 2012), 9.

280 Davies and Ward, *Safeguarding Children Across Services*, 146.

281 Davies and Ward, *Safeguarding Children Across Services*, 92.

282 Davies and Ward, *Safeguarding Children Across Services*, 147.

283 John Triseliotis, "Long-term Foster Care or Adoption? The Evidence Examined," *Child and Family Social Work*, 7, no. 1 (2002): 23–33,.

284 Ibid., 31.

285 AIHW, *Child Protection Australia 2013–14*, 49, Table 5.2.

286 ACIL Allen Consulting, *Professional Foster Care*, 8–9.

287 AIHW, *Adoptions Australia 2013–14*, 22–26.

288 AIHW, *Child Protection Australia 2009–10*, (Canberra: 2011), 12, 29.

289 Ceridwen Spark and Denise Cuthbert, " 'Society Moves to Make its Own Solutions': Re-thinking the Relationship between Intercountry and Domestic Adoption in Australia," in Ceridwen H. Spark and Denise M. Cuthbert (eds), *Other People's Children: Adoption in Australia* (Melbourne: Australian Scholarly Publishing, 2009), 59.

290 Audrey Marshall and Margaret McDonald, The Many-sided Triangle: Adoption in Australia (Melbourne: Melbourne University Press, 2001), 171–182.

291 Ibid., 171–182.

292 AIHW, *Adoptions Australia 1990–91*, Child Welfare Series No. 1. (Canberra: AIHW, 1993).

293 AIHW, *Adoptions Australia 2013–14*, 18–19.

294 Department for Education, *Children Looked After in England (Including Adoption and Care Leavers) Year Ending 31 March 2014* (London: Department for education, 2014).

295 U.S. Department of Health and Human Services, "Trends in Foster Care and Adoption: FFY 2002–FFY 2013," accessed 25 August 2015, acf.hhs.gov/sites/default/files/cb/trends_fostercare_adoption2013.pdf.

296 US Department of Health and Human Services, *The AFCARS Report: Preliminary FY 2013 Estimates as of July 2014.*'

297 Pauline Kenny et al., "Past Adoption Experiences: National Research Study on the Service Response to Past Adoption Practices," Research Report No. 21 (Melbourne: Australian Institute of Family Studies, 2012), 8.

298 Marshall and McDonald, *The Many-sided Triangle*, 254.

299 AIHW, *Child Protection Australia 2010–11*, (Canberra: AIHW, 2012), 98.

300 AIHW, *Child Protection Australia 2013–14*, 84.

301 Alexandra Smith, 'Foster Care Risks a New 'Stolen' Generation,' *Sydney Morning Herald*, 14 July 2011.

302 Audrey Marshall and Margaret McDonald, *The Many-sided Triangle*, 15.

303 Senate Community Affairs References Committee, *Commonwealth Contribution to Former Forced Adoption Policies and Practices* (Canberra: Commonwealth of Australia, 2012), 8.

304 Ibid., 208.

305 "Government to Apologise for Forced Adoptions," *Sydney Morning Herald*, 23 June 2012.

306 Senate Community Affairs References Committee, *Commonwealth Contribution to Former Forced Adoption Policies and Practices*, 12.

307 Ibid., 209.

308 Ibid., Chapter 2, "Attitudes Towards Adoption." For the full history and background, see Kate Inglis, *Living Mistakes: Mothers Who Consented to Adoption* (North Sydney: Allen & Unwin, 1984).

309 Hence, the Senate inquiry specifically recommended that official apologies should "not be qualified by reference to values or professional practice during the period in question." Senate Community Affairs References Committee, *Commonwealth Contribution to Former Forced Adoption Policies and Practices*, ix.

310 Ibid., 19.

311 See ibid., Chapter 5, "Commonwealth Role: Social Security and Benefits System."

312 Ibid., 97.

313 Ibid., 180–181.

314 On changing social attitudes to the family, see Barry Maley, *Family and Marriage in Australia* (Sydney: The Centre for Independent Studies, 2001).

315 AIFS (Australian Institute of Family Studies), "Family Facts and Figures: Births." www3.aifs.gov.au/institute/info/charts/births/index.html#number

316 ABS (Australian Bureau of Statistics), *Australian Social Trends, March Quarter 2012*, Cat. No. 4102.0 (Canberra: ABS, 2012), 14.

317 David de Vaus and Matthew Gray, "The Changing Living Arrangements of Children, 1946–2001," *Journal of Family Studies* 10, no. 1 (2004): 12.

318 Shurlee Swain with Renate Howe, *Single Mothers and Their Children: Disposal, Punishment and Survival in Australia* (Cambridge: Cambridge University Press, 1995), 197–201.

319 Senate Community Affairs References Committee, *Commonwealth Contribution to Former Forced Adoption Policies and Practices*, 180.

320 Murphy, Quartly, and Cuthbert, "'In the Best Interests of the Child."

321 Senate Community Affairs References Committee, *Commonwealth Contribution to Former Forced Adoption Policies and Practices*, 182–187.

322 Ibid., Chapter 2, "Attitudes Towards Adoption," especially 39–42.

323 Swain, *Single Mothers and Their Children*, 206.

324 Isabel Sawhill, "20 Years Later, It Turns Out Dan Quayle Was Right about Murphy Brown and Unmarried Moms," *Washington Post*, 25 May 2012. On the link between single motherhood and family poverty in the United States, see Adam Thomas and Isabel Sawhill, "For Love or Money? The Impact of Family Structure on Family Income," *Future Child* 15, no. 2 (Fall 2005), 57–74.

325 Patrick Parkinson, *For Kids' Sake: Repairing the Social Environment for Australian Children and Young People* (Sydney: University of Sydney, 2011), 57–58.

326 Productivity Commission, *Report on Government Services 2009*, 15.4.

327 ABS, *4442.0 – Family Characteristics, Australia, 2009–10*.

328 AIHW, *Child Protection Australia, 2013–14*, Table A10.

329 The evidence has been exhaustively compiled and comprehensively reviewed in Patrick F. Fagan and Aaron Churchill, *The Effects of Divorce on Children* (Washington, DC: Marriage & religion Research Council, 2012).

330 Susan L. Brown, "Marriage and Child Well-being: Research and Policy Perspectives," *Journal of Marriage and Family* 72, no. 5 (October 2010), 1062.

331 Barry Maley, *Family and Marriage in Australia* (Sydney: Centre for Independent Studies, 2001), 9.

332 Charles Murray, *Coming Apart: The State of White America, 1960–2010* (New York: Crown Forum, 2012), 158.

333 Kay S. Hymowitz, "American Caste," *City Journal* (Spring 2012), 44–49.

334 Lixia Qu and Ruth Weston, *Parental Marital Status and Children's Wellbeing*, Occasional Paper No. 46, (Canberra: Department of Families, Housing, Community Services and Indigenous Affairs [FaHCSIA], 2012), vi.

335 Qu and Weston, *Parental Marital Status and Children's Wellbeing*, 5.

336 Paul R. Amato, "Research on Divorce: Continuing Trends and New Developments," *Journal of Marriage and Family* 72, no. 3 (June 2010): 650–666.

337 Susan L. Brown, "Marriage and Child Well-being: Research and Policy Perspectives," 1061.

338 Steven L. Nock, "Marriage as a Public Issue," *The Future of Children* 15, no. 2 (Fall 2005), 13–32.

339 ABS, *Family Characteristics, Australia, 2009–10*, Cat. No. 4442.0,

340 Maley, *Family and Marriage in Australia*, 133.

341 David de Vaus, *Diversity and Change in Australian Families: Statistical Profiles* (Melbourne: Australian Institute of Family Studies, 2004), 43.

342 DSS (Department of Social Services), *Income Support Customers: A Statistical Overview 2013*, Statistical Paper No. 12 (Canberra: Commonwealth of Australia, 2014).

343 Jane Stanley in "Letters to the Editor," *The Australian*, 7 September 2011.

344 Murray, *Coming Apart*, 158.

345 For an account of the cultural impact of "the Sixties," see Allan Bloom, *The Closing of the American Mind: How Higher Education has Failed Democracy and*

Impoverished the Souls of Today's Students (New York: Simon & Schuster, 1987). For the role of politically correct elites in shaping the culture, see James Davison Hunter, *Culture Wars: The Struggle to Define America* (New York: Basic Books, 1991).

346 John Hirst, "The Re-moralising of Australian Politics," *The Age*, 5 February 2004.

347 For an eloquent explanation of the causes and consequences of the triumph of non-judgemental attitudes concerning the family, see Theodore Dalrymple, *In Praise of Prejudice: The Necessity of Preconceived Ideas* (New York: Encounter Books, 2007).

348 Qu and Weston, *Parental Marital Status and Children's Wellbeing*, vi.

349 Bettina Arndt, "The Distorted Social World of the ABC," *Counterpoint*, ABC Radio National, 8 January 2007.

350 Cathryn Hunter and Rhys Price-Robertson, *Family Structure and Child Maltreatment: Do Some Family Types Place Children at Greater Risk?*, Child Family Community Australia Paper No. 10 (Melbourne: AIFS, 2012).

351 Hunter and Price-Robertson, *Family Structure and Child Maltreatment*.

352 NSW Department of Community Services, *Child Neglect: Literature Review* (Sydney: Centre for Parenting & Research 2005), 19.

353 On social workers' attitudes to adoption and parents' "rights", see Denise Cuthbert and Marian Quartly, "'Forced Adoption" in *The Australian Story of National Regret and Apology*, 89–92.

354 Patricia Fronek and Denise Cuthbert, "An Apology to Forced Adoption Birth Mothers: It's About Time," *The Conversation* (25 June 2012).

355 Senate Community Affairs References Committee, *Commonwealth Contribution to Former Forced Adoption Policies and Practices*, Submission No. 70 by Family Inclusion Network of New South Wales (January 2011), 9.

356 Esther Han, "Secrets and Lies in the Histories of Overseas Babies," *Sydney Morning Herald*, 26 November 2012.

357 Cited in Senate Community Affairs References Committee, *Commonwealth Contribution to Former Forced Adoption Policies and Practices*, 196.

358 Shurlee Swain, "Lessons from the Past: Adoption Isn't the Answer to Child Protection," *The Conversation*, 6 March 2012.

359 Senate Community Affairs References Committee, *Commonwealth Contribution to Former Forced Adoption Policies and Practices*, 283.

360 Senate Community Affairs References Committee, *Commonwealth Contribution to Former Forced Adoption Policies and Practices*, 281–83.

361 Western Australian Hansard, 19 October 2010, 7856b–7858a.

362 Victorian Hansard, 25 October 2012, 4772.

363 Pru Goward, NSW Hansard, 20 September 2012, 15540.

364 Tasmanian Hansard, 18 October 2012, 6–7.

365 Ibid., 16–17.

366 Pru Goward, NSW Hansard, 5542.

367 Parliament of Australia, "National Apology for Forced Adoptions 21 March 2013," ag.gov.au/About/ForcedAdoptionsApology/Documents/Nationalapologyforforcedadoptions.PDF

368 "National Apology for Forced Adoptions," video, 21 March 2013, parlview.aph.gov.au/mediaPlayer.php?videoID=190367#/3

369 Ibid.

370 "Abbott Heckled for Offensive Terms at Forced Adoption Apology," *The Australian* (21 March 2013).

371 *Queensland Child Protection Commission of Inquiry: Options for Reform* (Brisbane: 2012), 28.

372 *Queensland Child Protection Commission of Inquiry: Options for Reform*, 29.

373 Senate Community Affairs References Committee, *Commonwealth Contribution to Former Forced Adoption Policies and Practices*, 214.

374 Even the Senate inquiry report concedes that supporters of forced adoption "were genuinely concerned about the welfare of children." Senate Community Affairs References Committee, *Commonwealth Contribution to Former Forced Adoption Policies and Practices*, 154.

375 "Choose Adoption Instead of Having an Abortion, Teen Mothers Told," *Daily Mail*, 6 July 2011.

376 Nigel Parbury, *Survival: A History of Aboriginal Life in New South Wales* (Sydney: NSW Department of Aboriginal Affairs 1986), 104–110.

377 Council of Australian Governments, "Closing the Gap in Aboriginal Disadvantage," accessed 12 August 2015, coag.gov.au/closing_the_gap_in_indigenous_disadvantage.

378 Australian Institute of Family Studies (AIFS) and Child Family Community Australia (CFCA), *Child Protection and Aboriginal and Torres Strait Islander Children*, Factsheet (June 2013).

379 Productivity Commission, *Report on Government Services 2015*, 15.37–15.38.

380 Bath Report, 327.

381 Productivity Commission, *Report on Government Services 2015*, Table 15A.19.

382 Queensland Child Protection Commission of Inquiry, *Taking Responsibility* (Carmody Report), 258.

383 Cummins Report, 295.

384 Cummins Report, Figure 12.3.

385 Cummins Report, 295. See C. Berlyn, L. Bromfield, and A. Lamont, *Child Protection and Aboriginal and Torres Strait Islander Children* (Melbourne: National Child Protection Clearinghouse, Australian Institute of Family Studies, Melbourne, 2011), 5.

386 Cummins Report, 310.

387 Carmody Report, 258.

388 Bath Report, 133–34, 357–360.

389 Cummins Report, 305; Carmody Report, 349.

390 Wood Report, 632.

391 Cummins Report, 294.

392 Carmody Report, 260.

393 Gary Johns, *Aboriginal Self-Determination: The Whiteman's Dream* (Ballarat: Connor Court, 2011), 202–3.

394 "Australia in the Grip of a 'New Stolen Generation,' Indigenous Children Forcibly Removed from Homes," *News.com.au*, 2 August 2014.

395 "Scheme to Avoid 'Second Stolen Generation' Criticised for Paternalism," *Guardian Australia*, 30 October 2014.

396 Nyunggai Warren Mundine, "Protection of Children Must be Colourblind," *The Australian*, 27 August 2014; Ngiare Brown, "Stop Blaming Aboriginal Culture, Just Combat Child Abuse at Every Level," *The Australian*, 16 September 2014.

397 Anthony Dillon, "Culture Can Be Deadly for Kids," *The Australian*, 23 July 2013.

398 Helen Hughes, *Lands of Shame: Aboriginal and Torres Strait Islander 'Homelands' In Transition* (Sydney: The Centre for Independent Studies, 2007), 32.

399 Cited in *Putting the Picture Together: Inquiry into Response by Government Agencies to Complaints of Family Violence and Child Abuse in Aboriginal Communities* (Perth: Department of Premier and Cabinet, Western Australia, 2002), 82.

400 *Putting the Picture Together*, 152.

401 Johns, *Aboriginal Self-Determination*, 166, 172–4, 177.

402 Ibid., 18–9

403 Ibid., 48.

404 Ibid., 32–3, 153, 173.

405 "Fear of Racism Puts Aboriginal Kids at Risk," *The Australian*, 10 February 2010.

406 As the literature suggests. Marina Paxman, *Outcomes for Children and Young People in Kinship Care, An Issues Paper* (Sydney: NSW Department of Community Services, 2006), 4.

407 Human Rights and Equal Opportunity Commission, *Bringing Them Home: Report of the National Inquiry into the Separation of Aboriginal and Torres Strait Islander Children from Their Families* (Canberra: Commonwealth of Australia, 1997).

408 Wood Report, 397–8.

409 Hughes, *Lands of Shame*, 11–13.

410 Johns, *Aboriginal Self-Determination*, 44.

411 Hughes, *Lands of Shame*, 9–10

412 Ibid., 4, 12–3.

413 Wood Report, 630

414 Ibid., 737

415 Peter Read, *The Stolen Generations: The Removal of Aboriginal Children in New South Wales 1883 to 1969* (Sydney: NSW Department of Aboriginal Affairs, 1981).

416 Wood Report, 398–9; Cummins Report, 278.

417 Wood Report, 739.

418 For the controversy over the racist rationale for Aboriginal child removal, see Robert Manne, "In Denial: The Stolen Generations and the Right,"

Quarterly Essay 1 (April 2001); Keith Windschuttle, *The Fabrication of Aboriginal History, Vol 3: The Stolen Generations 1881–2008* (Sydney: Macleay Press 2009).

419 *Bringing Them Home*, 400.

420 Ibid., 392–3, 401.

421 Ironically, the report blamed "systemic inequalities" and "cultural distortion" for having led to "Aboriginal children remaining in abusive situations which non-Aboriginal children would not be left in." *Bringing Them Home*, 396.

422 AIFS and CFCA, *Child Protection*.

423 *Bringing Them Home*, 400.

424 Wood Report, 777.

425 Department of Human Services, *Protecting Children: Ten Priorities for Children's Wellbeing and Safety in Victoria*," (Melbourne: Victorian Government, 2004).

426 Terri Bell and Terri Libesman, *Aboriginal and Torres Strait Islander Child Protection Outcomes Project Report, From Aboriginal Child Welfare to Aboriginal Children's Well-being*, unpublished paper commissioned by Secretariat of National Aboriginal and Islander Child Care and the Department of Human Services Victoria (2005), 18.

427 Johns, *Aboriginal Self-Determination*, 152–3.

428 I am indebted to Kerryn Pholi for this explanation.

429 John Pilger, "Another Stolen Generation: How Australia Still Wrecks Aboriginal Families," *The Guardian*, 22 March 2014.

430 "Australia in the Grip of a 'New Stolen Generation,' Indigenous Children Forcibly Removed from Homes," *News.com.au*, 2 August 2014.

431 Paddy Gibson, "Stolen Futures," *Overland* (Spring 2013).

432 Ibid.

433 Johns, *Aboriginal Self-Determination*, 203.

434 Hughes, *Lands of Shame*, 29.

435 Cummins Report, Chapter 12, "Meeting the Needs of Aboriginal Children and Young People," 271.

436 Ibid., 273.

437 Ibid., 272.id.

438 Ibid., 272.
439 Ibid., 305.
440 Carmody Report, 349.
441 Ibid., 351
442 Ibid., 361.
443 Ibid., 364, 369.
444 Ibid., 366–7.
445 Ibid., 368.
446 Ibid., 368.
447 Peter Sutton, *The Politics of Suffering* (Melbourne: Melbourne University Press, 2009).
448 Sutton, *The Politics of Suffering*, 10–11, 17, 36.
449 Sutton, *The Politics of Suffering*, 55
450 Sutton, *The Politics of Suffering*, 61, 75–6, 112–113
451 Sutton, *The Politics of Suffering*, 139, 141.
452 Sutton, *The Politics of Suffering*, 108
453 Sutton, *The Politics of Suffering*, 218.
454 Shaun Lohoar, Nick Butera, and Edita Kennedy, "Strengths of Australian Aboriginal Cultural Practices in Family Life and Child Rearing," CFCA Paper No. 25 (Melbourne: Child and Family Community Australia, 2014), 2.
455 Hughes, *Lands of Shame*, 181.
456 *Taking Responsibility* (Carmody Report), 222–229.
457 Cummins Report, xxxvii.
458 "Judges Call for Adoption Overhaul," *The Australian*, 28 August 2014.
459 "Record number of children in care," *The Australian*, 25 July 2014.
460 Brendan Trembath "National Children's Commissioner 'Very Concerned' by Figures Showing Hundreds of Kids in Foster Care Abused," *The World Today*, 28 January 2015, abc.net.au/news/2015-01-28/hundreds-of-children-in-foster-care-abused-last-year-report-find/6052006.
461 *Inquest into the Death of Chloe Lee Valentine*, 44.
462 Ibid., 147.
463 Ibid., 142.

464 Ibid., 142.

465 Ibid., 117.

466 Ibid., 85, 114–117.

467 Ibid., 117.

468 "Early Intervention Key to Child Welfare Overhaul," *The Australian*, 4 March 2009.

469 "Children to Get Families, Not Foster Care," *Sydney Morning Herald*, 22 November 2012.

470 NSW Department of Families and Communities, *A Safe Home for Life: Report on the Outcomes of Public Consultation on the Child Protection Legislative Reforms Discussion Paper 2012* (Sydney: NSW Government, 2013), 30.

471 "Adoption Changes Could Create New Stolen Generation Say Community Groups', *Sydney Morning Herald*, 11 November 2013.

472 Department of Human Services, "Changes to Child Protection Law," last updated 15 January 2015, www.dhs.vic.gov.au/about-the-department/documents-and-resources/policies,-guidelines-and-legislation/changes-to-child-protection-law

473 "Government Announces Streamlining of Adoption Process," *ABC World Today*, 19 December 2013.

474 "Abbott's Plan to Overhaul Adoption Laws," *Daily Telegraph*, 25 January 2015.

475 Jeremy Sammut, "Still Damaging and Disturbing: Australian Child Protection Data and the Need for National Adoption Targets," Issue Analysis 145 (Sydney: Centre for Independent Studies, 2014).

476 Carrie Craft, "What is the Adoption and Safe Families Act?" *About Parenting*, accessed 13 August 2015, about.com/od/legalfinancial/f/What-Is-The-Adoption-And-Safe-Families-Act.htm.

477 "States Must Set Adoption Targets, Barnardos Australia Says," *Sydney Morning Herald*, 10 November 2014.

478 "Freer Foreign Adoptions Risks Past 'Travesties', Warns Senior Judge," *The Australian*, 17 November 2014.

479 Christian Porter, "Adoption and Child Protection," *Australian Polity* 5, no. 1 (2015), 15–25.

480 Kate Legge, "Adoption: Why is it So Hard?" *Weekend Australian Magazine*, 30 May 2015.

481 Andrew McCallum, "Abandoned Babies Highlight Need for Good Foster Carers," *Sydney Morning Herald*, 1 December 2014.

482 "Adoptions Up 60% in Just Four Years as Gove Shake-up Cuts the Red-tape," *Daily Mail*, 1 October 2014.

483 "Michael Gove Calls for Hundreds More Vulnerable Children a Year to be Taken into Care, and for an End to 'Preoccupation with Rights of Biological Parents'," *The Independent*, 16 November 2012.

484 Michael Gove, speech on adoption, 23 February 2012. https://www.gov.uk/government/speeches/michael-gove-speech-on-adoption

485 Michael Gove, "Saved by the Love of Strangers: Michael Gove Describes How Adoption Transformed His Life," *Daily Mail*, 5 November 2011.

486 "Michael Gove Relaunches Adoption Rules with Attack on 'Ridiculous Bureaucracy'," *The Guardian*, 23 February 2011.

487 Michael Gove, speech on adoption, 23 February 2012.

488 Ibid.

489 Michael Gove, "Saved by the Love of Strangers."

490 David Cameron, speech on families, 18 August 2014. https://www.gov.uk/government/speeches/david-cameron-on-families

491 Senate Community Affairs References Committee, *Out of Home Care* (Canberra: Senate Printing Unit, 2015), 293–298.

492 *A Safe Home for Life*, 2.

493 AbSec website, accessed 18 August 2015, www.absec.org.au.

494 "Aboriginal Child Placement Principle Not Broken, Says Linda Burney," *The Australian*, 10 December 2010.

495 "Indigenous Ransom Threat: Pay Up or Don't See Kids," *The Australian*, 1 July 2015.

496 Ibid.

497 ABS, *4705.0 – Population Distribution, Aboriginal and Torres Strait Islander Australians, 2006*; *2076.0 – Census of Population and Housing: Characteristics of Aboriginal and Torres Strait Islander Australians, 2011*.

498 Helen Hughes and Mark Hughes, "The Undercover Guide to Indigenous

Statistics," in Rhonda Craven, Anthony Dillon, and Nigel Parbury (eds), *In Black & White: Australians All at the Crossroads* (Ballarat: Connor Court, 2013), 4.

499 Johns, *Aboriginal Self-Determination*, 22; Australian Bureau of Statistics, *3238.0.55.001 – Estimates of Aboriginal and Torres Strait Islander Australians, June 2011*, 30 August 2013, abs.gov.au/ausstats/abs@.nsf/mf/3238.0.55.001.

500 Australian Bureau of Statistics, *3238.0.55.001 - Experimental Estimates of Aboriginal and Torres Strait Islander Australians, June 2006;* Australian Bureau of Statistics, *3238.0.55.001 – Estimates of Aboriginal and Torres Strait Islander Australians, June 2011*.

501 Sutton, *The Politics of Suffering*, 58, 158–9.

502 Department of Aboriginal Affairs, *Report on a Review of the Administration of the Working Definition of Aboriginal and Torres Strait Islanders* (Canberra: Commonwealth of Australia, 1981) cited in John Gardiner-Garden, *The Definition of Aboriginality: Research Note 18, 2000–01* (Canberra: Parliament of Australia, 2000), 1.

503 Genevieve Heard, Siew-Ean Khoo, and Bob Birrell, *Intermarriage In Australia: Patterns by Birthplace, Ancestry, Religion and Indigenous Status – A Report Using Data From the 2006 Census* (Melbourne: Centre for Population and Urban Research, Monash University, for the Australian Bureau of Statistics Australian Census Analytic Program, 2009), 4–5.

504 Johns, *Aboriginal Self-Determination*, 80.

505 Hughes and Hughes, "Undercover Guide to Indigenous Statistics," 5

506 Ibid. 6.

507 Sutton, *Politics of Suffering*, 159; Hughes and Hughes, "Undercover Guide to Indigenous Statistics," 7.

508 Sutton, *Politics of Suffering*, 158.

509 Sara Hudson, "Politics of Difference," in *In Black & White: Australians All at the Crossroads*, 173–190.

510 Joe Lane and Marie Lane, *Hard Grind: The Making of an Urban Indigenous Population* (Melbourne: Bennelong Society Conference, 2008).

511 See this story, which quoted an Indigenous father in a "mixed" marriage saying "it was important to teach their children about Aboriginal culture and history to ensure that it was not lost": "More Aborigines Enter Mixed

Marriages," *News.com.au*, 6 April 2009, news.com.au/national/more-aborigines-entering-mixed-marriages/story-e6frfkvr-1225696982117

512 Marilyn McHugh and Anita Pell, *Reforming the Foster Care System in Australia: A New Model of Support, Education and Payment for Foster Parents* (Sydney: UNSW Social Policy Research Centre, 2013), 37–8.

513 See Kiraly and Humphreys, 'It's the Story of all of Us', 34.

514 Some have labelled this double standard "hypocritical and profoundly immoral". David Price and Bess Price, "Good Culture, Bad Culture: Where Do We Go From Here?", in *In Black & White: Australians All at the Crossroads*, 207.

515 Helen Hughes, "Strangers in Their Own Country: A Diary of Hope," *Quadrant* 52, no. 3 (March 2008).

INDEX

A

Abbott, Tony, 166–7, 169, 217
Aboriginal and Torres Strait Islander Child Placement Principle, 35–7, 173–4, 177, 178, 181, 183–8, 196–203, 208–9, 230–1, 235, 238–9
Aboriginal and Torres Strait Islander Commission, abolition of, 199
Aboriginal Child, Family and Community Care State Secretariat, 231–2
Aboriginal communities, 178–82, 193–7, 198, 199, 200, 202, 204–5, 238–9
Aboriginal industry, 188–9, 204–5, 237–8
Aboriginal people *see* Indigenous Australians; Indigenous children
Aboriginal self-determination, 34–40, 175, 184, 188–92, 194, 197–201, 202, 204–6, 238
Aboriginal traditional culture as a cause of suffering, 204–7, 236
Adopt Change organisation, 218
adopted children, 138–40, 145–6
adoption, 14–19
 in Australia *see* adoption in Australia
 benefits of, 138–40, 168, 213
 older-age children, 142–3
 open adoption processes, 18, 145–6, 219, 229
 overseas countries, 38, 118–19, 138, 143–4, 222–6
 solution for at-risk children, 14–15, 27, 33–4, 95, 209
Adoption and the Care of Children (Morgan), 138
adoption in Australia, 140–5
 anti-adoption movement, 16–17, 18, 99, 100, 146–7, 159–62, 167–8, 218
 attitudes to, 15–18, 21, 44–5, 142–4, 146–7, 160, 162–9, 215
 cultural change, 228–30
 decline in, 141
 forced *see* forced adoption
 growing official acceptance of role of adoption, 211–17, 219–20
 Indigenous children, 36–40, 209–10, 230, 236–9
 national leadership and targets, 217–21, 226–7, 237
 number of adoptions, 18, 141–2
 at odds with family preservation principle, 16, 144–5
 opportunities for adoption, 18–19, 144
 from overseas countries, 16, 141, 143, 161, 217–18, 237
 state government reforms, 215–17, 220, 221
 under-use of adoption, 97–8
advocacy on behalf of children, absence of, 87

Allen Consulting Group, 58
apologies, 136
  for forced adoption, 137, 146, 147, 148, 161–9
  for past policies, 169–72
  to Stolen Generations, 137, 146, 173
Arndt, Bettina, 158
Association of Children's Welfare Agencies, 79
attachment deprivation, 117–18
Australian and New Zealand College of Psychiatrists, 18
Australian Broadcasting Corporation, 158
Australian Bureau of Statistics Family Characteristics Survey, 153
Australian Childhood Foundation, 15, 88
Australian Community Child Health Nurse home visiting program, 68
Australian Human Rights Commission national commissioner for children, 212–13
Australian Institute of Family Studies, 128, 144
Australian Institute of Health and Welfare, 6, 65, 91
Australian Triple P (Positive Parenting Program), 68

B
Baillieu, Ted, 164
Barnardos Australia, 15, 97, 219
Barnardo's UK, 171
Bath Report, 121, 179
Berry Street family support service, 213
"Big Welfare" lobby, 22, 78–80, 96–7
births in Australia, 151
Bishop, Bronwyn, 98
Board of Inquiry into the Child Protection System in the Northern Territory (Bath Report) *see* Bath Report
Brereton, Paul, 219
Bringing Them Home report 1997, 187, 192–4, 196
Bromfield, Leah et al., 116
Brown, Ngaire, 183
Bryant, Diana, 212
Burney, Linda, 231

C
Calvert, Gillian, 49–53, 56, 60
Cameron government (UK), 222–6
carers
  child abuse by, 137
  kinship carers, 127–30, 178–83, 203, 209
  professionalisation, 130–6
  see also foster care; kinship care
Carmody Report, 72, 122, 202–3, 211–12
Cashmore, Judy, 49–53, 56, 60
charitable organisations *see* NGO family support services
Child Abuse Prevention Research Australia, 88

child and family welfare social services sector *see* "Big Welfare" lobby
child development issues, 9, 15, 18, 102–3
Child Family Community Australia Information Exchange, 159
Child FIRST (Family Information Referral and Support Teams) strategic framework, Victoria, 57, 59, 61–2, 72–3, 80–2
child maltreatment
  abuse by carers, 137
  cost to governments, 103
  definitions, 43–4
  examples, 1–3, 28–32
  Indigenous children *see* Indigenous children
  life-long effects, 12–14, 75–6, 87–8, 102–3
  perceived causes of, 44
  proven cases of (substantiations), 93–6, 251–3
  under-responding to, 7–8, 60, 63–4, 75–6, 81–2, 183
  single-mother households, 153, 160, 172
  South Australia, 26–30
  in UK, 222
  see also high-needs children; removal of children into care
child protection
  cultural change, 226–30
  history, 105–7
  ideology, 21, 22–4, 43–7, 99–108, 167–8
  institutional factors, 21, 25
  politicisation of, 22–4
  reforms, 102–8, 215–17, 220, 221, 230
  see also child protection system; family preservation; out-of-home care; preventive approaches to child protection
Child Protection Australia 2013–14 report, 65
child protection authorities, 43–6
  notifications received, 65
  resistance to adoption, 220–1
  stand-alone agencies, 85–6
  see also Families SA; NSW Department of Community Services; Victorian Department of Human Services
child protection inquiries, 200–3
  continued support for current system, 24–6, 48–9, 71–4
  criticisms of current system, 80–1
  shortcomings of, 66, 71–4
  see also Bath Report; Carmody Report; Cummins Report; Wood Report
child protection legislation, 43–4
  paramount principle of, 32, 46, 98
child protection system
  cultural change, 226–30
  cultural factors, 21–2
  culturally appropriate practices, 34–8, 187–207
  family support *see* family support services

Indigenous Australians *see* Indigenous children

official inquiries *see* child protection inquiries

policy, 4–7, 14, 20–2, 108, 134–6 *see also* family preservation

reporting systems *see* mandatory reporting

statutory intervention, 41–3 *see also* investigations

vested interests, 21, 78–80, 82–5, 88, 96–7

see also "Big Welfare" lobby

child protection system failures, 4, 19–20, 27, 213–15

explanations and policy response, 3–6, 20–1

factors in, 21–2, 42–3, 130–1

official inquiries *see* child protection inquiries

perpetuation of inequality, 33

recommended solutions, 14–15, 33–4

reported, 72–6, 80–2, 91–3

child rescue *see* removal of children into care

Child Welfare Association of Victoria, 82

child well-being

and Aboriginal traditional culture, 204–7, 236

and family structure, 152–9, 160

child-parent bond, 87

children in care *see* kinship care; out-of-home care; residential care

children's rights, 105–7, 171

'best interests of child' principle, 32, 46, 98, 171

see also parental "rights" versus child rights

churn and instability *see* instability

cognitive dissonance, 20, 165

Commonwealth Department of Aboriginal Affairs, 187–8

Coombs, H. C. ("Nugget"), 189

cultural factors, 21–2

cultural politics, 22–4, 99–108, 167–8

cultural relativism, 200, 204–7

culturally appropriate practices in child protection, 34–8, 187–207

see also kinship care

Cummins Report, 72, 122, 182, 200–1

Cuthbert, Denise, 99, 100

D

Davies, Carolyn, 139

Delfabbro, Paul, 115

Dillon, Anthony, 183

Dodson, Mick, 192

drug and alcohol abuse by parents, 8, 28, 31, 32

permissive attitudes towards, 28–9, 98–101, 214

dual-track reporting, 4, 5–6, 53–6, 57–8, 72

dysfunctional parents and families *see* family dysfunction

E

Eardley, Tony, 116

early intervention and family support services model *see* family support services; preventive approaches to child protection

Early Intervention Services for Vulnerable Children and Families, 72–3

Ebony case, 1–3, 32, 48

expenditure on child protection and family preservation, 89–93, 103, 111, 124–5, 246–50, 257–60

F

families in crisis, 51, 57–8

families in need, 51, 57

Families SA, 26–30, 31, 213–14

family breakdown, 152–6

Family Court chief judge comments on adoption, 212

family diversity, 21–2, 100, 147, 152, 156–8, 166–7, 170, 172 *see also* single motherhood

family dysfunction, 8–12, 28–31, 50–1, 54

  non-judgementalism by authorities, 29–32, 46, 98–101, 158–9, 214

  repeat reports *see* re-reporting (problem families)

  support program failure, 69–71

  typical neglecting family, 159

  see also family structure and child well-being; underclass of problem families

family preservation, 6–12, 44–6, 214–15

  commitment to, 17–21, 25–6, 42, 165–6, 217, 221

family reunification, 13–14

  impact on children, 8–10, 12–13, 19, 28–31, 75–6, 115–17

  long-term outcomes, 12–14, 75–6

  at odds with adoption, 16, 144–5

  in South Australia, 26–7

  see also family support services

family structure and child well-being, 152–9, 160 *see also* single motherhood

family support services, 42–3, 45, 47–8, 55, 77–8

  expenditure on, 90–3, 96, 248–50

  failure of, 69–74, 214

  linked to timely achievement of behavioural change, 227–8

  provided by NGOs *see* NGO family support services

  types of support workers, 88

  Wood report recommendations, 56–8, 66

Federal Circuit Court chief judge comments on adoption, 212

forced adoption, 16–17, 21, 136, 146–52

  apologies for, 137, 146, 147, 148, 161–9

  rhetoric of anti-adoption movement, 159–62

  Senate report on, 147–52, 162, 163

  see also Stolen Generations

Forgotten Generations, 136 *see also* forced adoption

foster care, 14, 42, 112–14, 122, 131–2, 134–6, 228

children in (statistics), 126, 255, 266–9
long-term, 139–40, 168
permanent care orders, 144–5, 216–17
placements, 112, 113, 120, 255
shortage of carers, 110, 111, 117
see also kinship care
frequently reported families *see* family dysfunction; re-reporting (problem families); underclass of problem families
Furness, Deborra-lee, 218

G

Gibson, Paddy, 197
Gillard government, 148, 166
Goddard, Chris, 88
Gordon, Sue, 185
Gove, Michael, 222–6
Goward, Pru, 216
group homes, 42, 112, 123–4 *see also* residential care facilities

H

high-needs children, 12–14, 19–20, 75–6, 96, 108–10, 114–18, 122–5, 132–6, 228
Hodgman, Will, 164–5
home visits, 5, 52, 67, 68
House of Representatives Standing Committee on Family and Human Services, 97–8
Howard government, 199

Hudson, Sara, 234
Hughes, Helen, 205, 208, 235
Hughes, Mark, 235
Human Rights and Equal Opportunity Commission, *Bringing Them Home* report, 36, 187, 192–4, 196
Hymowitz, Kay S., 154
hypocrisy, 32–3

I

ideological factors in child protection, 21, 22–4, 43–7, 99–108, 167–8
Indigenous Australians
children *see* Indigenous children
cultural identity, 34, 37–8, 173–4, 210, 232–7
mainstreaming of services for, 36, 37–40, 185–6, 199–200, 207–10, 232, 235–9
politics of suffering, 204–7
self-determination, 34–40, 175, 184, 188–92, 194, 197–201, 202, 204–6, 238
welfare of, 39–40
Indigenous children, 34–40
in child protection system, 34, 112–13, 174–5, 177, 182–5, 196–7, 202–3
current child protection regimes, 35–40
kinship care *see* kinship care
mainstreaming care and adoption, 36, 38–9, 209–10
maltreatment, 176, 184–5, 193–4, 195, 206

out-of-home care, 176–8, 192–3, 201, 230–2, 264–9
separatist child protection regime, 187–210, 232
see also Stolen Generations
Indigenous communities, 178–82, 193–200, 202, 204–5, 238–9
inquiries *see* child protection inquiries
instability
　care placements per child (churn), 119–22, 254
　impact on children, 117–18, 120, 122–3
Institute of Economic Affairs, 138
institutional factors, 21, 25
inter-country adoption, 16, 141, 143, 161, 217–18, 237
Intercountry Adoption Australia, 217
investigations, 41–2, 65, 81

J
Johns, Gary, 184, 205, 235
Johns, Mark, 29, 213–14

K
Keep Them Safe program, 48–9, 59–60, 73–4, 79
kinship care, 35–6, 42, 112–14, 125–30, 173–85, 202–3, 209, 231–2, 238
　children in (statistics), 255, 261–3, 266–9
　reservations about, 200, 201, 231

L
Lands of Shame (Hughes), 208
Left orthodoxy on child protection *see* cultural politics
lobby groups, 21, 22
Looking After Children Outcomes Data Project Final Report, 121

M
madness, definition of, 21
mainstreaming of services for Indigenous Australians, 36, 37–40, 185–6, 199–200, 207–10, 232, 235–9, FLIP??
mandatory reporting, 4–6
　dual-track system *see* dual-track reporting
　identification of the most at-risk children, 10, 62–6
　overloading the system, 3–5, 49–52, 63
　repeat reporting *see* re-reporting (problem families)
　threshold for reporting, 53–6, 81–2
　Wood report recommendations, 56–8
media organisations, 158
Mill, John Stuart, 105–6
Mitchell, Megan, 212–13
Monash University Child Abuse Prevention Research Australia, 15
moral judgements, 47, 99, 149
　non-judgementalism by authorities, 29–32, 46, 98–101, 158–9, 214

shift in values, 46–7, 100, 150, 157
Morgan, Patricia, 138
Mundine, Nyunggai Warren, 183, 239
Murphy, Kate, 99, 100
Murray, Charles, 154, 157
myths of child protection, 86–7, 89, 109, 147

N

Narey, Martin, 171
national apologies *see* apologies
National Child Protection Clearinghouse report, 116
national commissioner for children, comments on adoption, 212–13
National Framework for Protecting Australia's Children, 5, 54, 71, 133
National Standards for Out-of-home Care, 133–4
NGO family support services, 77–8
  in Dean Shillingsworth case, 2
  lobby groups, 22, 79–80
  political influence, 22, 82–7
  role in child protection, 4–5, 7
  vested interests, 21, 78–80, 82–5, 88, 96–7
  Wood report recommendations, 56–8
Northern Territory Emergency Intervention into Homeland Communities, 199
NSW
  child protection inquiries *see* Wood Report

child protection reforms, 215–17, 220, 221, 230
Child Wellbeing Units, 59–60
Keep Them Safe program, 48–9, 59–60, 73–4, 79
lobby groups, 79
see also states and territories
NSW Association of Children's Welfare Agencies, 221
NSW Department of Community Services
  failures to act, 1–3, 51–2, 63–4
  investigations, 5, 51–2, 53–4
  permanency planning, 118–19
  reporting system overload, 3–5, 49–52
  reports received (2007), 4
  re-reports (problem families), 8, 10–12, 60–6
  role, 2, 56–7, 60
NSW Ombudsman, 52, 74–5

O

O'Farrell, Barry, 164, 215
On Liberty (Mill), 105
Osborn, Alexandra, 115
out-of-home care, 12–13, 88–93, 266–9
  children in care (characteristics), 122–5
  children in care (statistics), 18, 19, 89, 92–3, 109–10, 112–13, 124–5, 141, 261–9
  children with high needs, 115–17, 122–5

cost of, 97, 111–14
expenditure on, 89–93, 96, 111, 124–5, 246, 249–50, 257–60
Indigenous children *see* Indigenous children
placement length, 108, 112
placements per child (churn), 119–22, 254
professionalising, 130–6
statutory removal, 42
see also kinship care; removal of children into care; residential care
outsourcing services to NGOs, 4–5, 45, 53, 56–8, 60, 77–8, 112
see also NGO family support services

P

parent education programs, 67–8
parental incapacity *see* family dysfunction
parental "rights" versus child rights, 17, 21, 22–3, 45, 46, 98–101, 165–6, 214 *see also* children's rights; family preservation
parental substance abuse *see* drug and alcohol abuse by parents
parent-child bond, 87
Parenting Payment (single and partnered), 156
parliamentary apologies *see* apologies
Pascoe, John, 212
Pearson, Noel, 205, 239
permanency

importance of, 117–18
planning frameworks, 118–19, 215–17
stable placements (estimation), 122
Petrusma, Jacquie, 165
Pilger, John, 197
placements *see* out-of-home care
policy, 4–7, 14, 20–2, 108, 134–6 *see also* family preservation
political influence of welfare lobby, 22–3, 82–7
politicisation of child protection, 22–4
politics, cultural *see* cultural politics
politics of suffering, 204–7
Porter, Christian, 220
pregnancy out of wedlock, 141, 149
see also forced adoption
preventive approaches to child protection, 25, 26, 47, 58–9
evaluations of, 67–71
home visiting, 5, 52, 67, 68
parent education programs, 67–8
preservation programs, 67, 69–70
see also family preservation; family support services
Price, Bess, 183
Prime Minister's Indigenous Advisory Council, 183
problem families *see* family dysfunction; underclass of problem families
Professional Foster Care: Barriers, Opportunities, Options, 133–4

professionalisation of out-of-home care, 130–6
Protecting Children is Everyone's Business: National Framework for Protecting Australia's Children 2009–2020 see National Framework for Protecting Australia's Children
Protecting Victoria's Vulnerable Children Inquiry 2012 *see* Cummins Report
Protecting Vulnerable Children (Senate Committee report), 103, 114, 133
proven cases of child abuse *see* re-substantiations
Putting the Pictures Together report, 183–4, 185

Q
Qu, Lixia, 155, 158
Quartly, Marian, 99, 100
Queensland Child Protection Commission of Inquiry 2013 *see* Carmody Report
Queensland Child Safety Department, 85–6
Queensland Crime and Misconduct Commission, 85–6, 121, 168
Queensland Department of Communities, 85–6

R
Read, Peter, 190
reconciliation, 231–2
Regional Intake and Referral Services, 56–7
removal of children into care, 42
  attitudes to, 26–7, 44–5
  children of addicts, 98–9
  delay in, 12–13, 110–11
  early removal, 95, 96, 222–3, 228
  Indigenous children, 34–6
  as "last resort", 6–8, 14, 17
  temporary, 13
  timely statutory intervention, 14–15
  see also out-of-home care
re-reporting (problem families), 8, 10–12, 28, 58, 60–6, 72
  states and territories, 65, 243
  see also dual-track reporting; mandatory reporting
residential care
  children in (statistics), 124, 255–6, 261–3, 266–9
  cost of, 125, 135
  expenditure on, 124–5, 258–60
  see also out-of-home care
residential care facilities
  abuses in, 136, 137
  detrimental effects on children, 19, 136, 143
  group homes, 42, 112–13, 123–4
  orphanage closures, 19, 113, 124
  re-opening, 19, 124, 136
re-substantiations, 93–6, 251–3
Review of Australia's Welfare System, 103
Right, role of, in reform *see* cultural politics
rights *see* children's rights; parental "rights" versus child rights

Royal Commission into Institutional Responses to Child Sexual Abuse, 137, 231
Rudd, Kevin, 173

S

Salvation Army case manager, 29
school non-attendance (truancy), 9–10
Scott, Dorothy, 49–53, 56, 60
Secretariat of National Aboriginal and Islander Child Care, 195
Senate Community Affairs References Committee
 Out of Home Care report, 226–7
 report on forced adoption, 147–52, 162, 163
 report on protecting vulnerable children, 103, 114, 133
Shillingsworth, Dean, 2–3, 32, 48
Siewert, Rachel, 17
single motherhood, 22, 100, 141, 150–3, 163–5, 171
 and child well-being, 152–9, 160, 172
Smyth, Ciara, 116
social change, 21–2, 100–1, 141–2, 143, 147, 150–2, 157–8
social values, 47, 99–100, 147, 149–50, 157, 163–6, 170–1
social work (discipline), 21, 25, 44–5, 100–1
South Australia
 child maltreatment examples, 28–32

child protection inquiries, 26–30
 see also states and territories
Special Commission of Inquiry into Child Protection Services in NSW 2008 *see* Wood Report
special-needs children *see* high-needs children
stability *see* permanency
states and territories
 adoptions, 141
 apologies for forced adoption, 162–6
 child protection reforms, 215–17, 220, 221, 230
 children in care (statistics), 89, 124, 254–6
 expenditure on care and family support services, 89–93, 124–5, 246–50, 257–60
 foster care, 126
 Indigenous population, 233
 investigations, 65
 kinship care, 126
 out-of-home care responsibilities, 112
 placements (churn and instability), 120–2
 repeat reports, 65, 243
 re-substantiations, 94–5, 251–3
statutory intervention, 41–3
 NSW Child Wellbeing Units, 59–60
 thresholds, 53–6
statutory investigations *see* investigations

statutory removal, 42 *see also* removal of children into care

statutory services, expenditure on, 90, 91, 93, 95, 247, 249–50

Stolen Generations, 16, 21, 34–40, 146, 173–4, 187

   apology to, 137, 146, 173

   "new Stolen Generation", 84, 182–3, 185, 197–8, 216, 234–5

   politicisation of the issue, 37, 39–40, 175, 187–8, 190–4, 197–8

   see also Indigenous children

Stolen Generations: The Removal of Aboriginal Children in New South Wales 1883 to 1969 (Read), 190

substantiation of child abuse and neglect, 93, 95

   re-substantiations, 93–6, 251–3

Sutton, Peter, 204–6, 235

T

Triseliotis, John, 139–40

truancy, 9–10

Tucci, Joe, 88

U

underclass of problem families, 8–12, 15, 28, 62–4, 70–1, 160

   cost of welfare support, 103

   home conditions, 1, 29, 30–1, 41

   see also family dysfunction

under-responding to reports of child maltreatment, 7–8, 60, 63–4, 75–6, 81–2, 183

United Kingdom

   adoptions, 18, 144, 171, 212, 222–6

   cost of welfare, 103

   maltreated children research, 139–40

United States

   adoption in, 18–19, 119, 143, 144

   adoption incentive payments for states, 218

unmarried mothers *see* pregnancy out of wedlock; single motherhood

V

Valentine, Chloe, 28–30, 32, 213–15

Vanish anti-adoption advocacy group, 161–2

vested interests, 21, 78–80, 82–5, 88, 96–7

Victoria

   Child FIRST strategic framework, 57, 59, 61–2, 72–3, 80–2

   child protection inquiries, 72–3, 80–1

   child protection reforms, 216–17

   investigations, 81

   see also states and territories

Victorian Aboriginal Child Care Agency, 201

Victorian Centre for Excellence in Child and Family Welfare, 82–5

Victorian child safety commissioner, 98

Victorian Department of Human Services, 80–1, 121, 195

Victorian Ombudsman, 80–5

W

war on drugs inquiry, 98
Ward, Harriet, 139
welfare benefits for single mothers, 150, 151–2, 155, 170
  cost of, 156
welfare state, 102–6 *see also* expenditure on child protection and family preservation
Weston, Ruth, 155, 158
Whitlam government, 150, 189
Wood Report, 79
  findings, 60–2, 64, 74, 121, 181, 194–5
  outcomes, 48–9, 59–60, 66
  recommendations, 56–8
  submissions to, 49–53, 56, 60

X

Xamon, Alison, 163–4

www.ingramcontent.com/pod-product-compliance
Ingram Content Group UK Ltd.
Pitfield, Milton Keynes, MK11 3LW, UK
UKHW021301180426
11947UKWH00015B/950